Dawn Songs

Also by Peter Riley (* Shearsman titles)

Poetry
Love-Strife Machine
The Canterbury Experimental Weekend
The Linear Journal
The Musicians, The Instruments
Preparations
Lines on the Liver
Tracks and Mineshafts
Ospita
Noon Province
Sea Watches
Reader
Lecture
Sea Watch Elegies
Royal Signals
Distant Points
Alstonefield *
Between Harbours
Noon Province et autres poèmes
Snow Has Settled ... Bury Me Here *
Author
Passing Measures: A Collection of Poems
The Sea's Continual Code
Aria with Small Lights
Alstonefield (extended edition)
Excavations
A Map of Faring
The Llŷn Writings *
The Day's Final Balance: Uncollected Writings 1965–2006 *
Best at Night Alone
Western States
Twelve Moons
Greek Passages *
The Derbyshire Poems *
The Glacial Stairway
Due North *
Pennine Tales

Prose
Two Essays
Company Week
The Dance at Mociu *

Peter Riley

Dawn Songs

preceded by
Mass Lyric

and followed by
On First Hearing Derek Bailey

Shearsman Books

First published in the United Kingdom in 2017 by
Shearsman Books
50 Westons Hill Drive
Emersons Green
BRISTOL
BS16 7DF

www.shearsman.com

ISBN 978-1-84861-545-8

Copyright © Peter Riley, 2017
The right of Peter Riley to be identified as the author of this work has been asserted by him in accordance with the Copyrights, Designs and Patents Act of 1988. All rights reserved.

ACKNOWLEDGEMENTS
Dawn Songs was first published in a shortened version on the author's website.

Mass Lyric was first published in *Additional Apparitions* edited by David Kennedy and Keith Tuma, The Cherry on the Top Press, 2002, since which it has been revised and extended.

On First Hearing Derek Bailey was first published in *Great Works* no. 2, 1973, and has since been revised.

Contents

Mass Lyric   7

Dawn Songs
    Preface   31
    Dawn Songs   33
    Appendix 1: The Gyimes Laments   73
    Appendix 2: Zorile   82
    Appendix 3: Enter a Peasant, Drunk   88
    Appendix 4: My Mother Cursed me…
       A. The Court   92
       B: The People   97
       C: …that I should Wander the Earth   122
    Additional Notes   123
    The Last Gypsy   166
    List of Writings   178
    List of Recordings   182

On First Hearing Derek Bailey   187

1

Mass Lyric

So mindless were those outpourings!—
  Though I am not aware
That I have gained by subtle thought on things
  Since we stood psalming there.

Hardy, 'Afternoon Service at Mellstock' (c. 1850),
  Moments of Vision.

1

In December 2000 we took part in the third biennial 'Festival of Village Carols' in Cutlers' Hall, Sheffield, which consisted of the congregational singing of some thirty pieces of church music known locally as "carols". These were mostly English parish church pieces on the Nativity, of a kind which flourished in the 18th century and first half of the 19th, with origins in the 17th. Their spread was encouraged in the 18th century as a movement of church music reform, to combat the heterophony of "lining out" congregational singing, which was abhorrent to the educated classes. The music was designed to be sung by voluntary choirs, later assisted by a small group of instruments, as a guidance to the congregation, with the aim of "raising the standard" of congregational singing, though actually to change its nature. It was "west gallery music", as described in Hardy's *Under the Greenwood Tree*.

The pieces written for this movement, mostly by amateurs and music masters, and mostly setting versified psalms, were at first quite simple affairs, but became more sophisticated, with contrapuntal features in some pieces ("fuging tunes")[1] which could be quite extended. The writing is well described as "Handelian" but with "primitive" features such as bare fifths. It did not however derive from Handel, for it already existed before he was in London, but his influence may well have gone into its development during the 18th century, when parish musicians, especially among Lancashire hand-loom weavers, developed a great enthusiasm for Handel and took to performing his works themselves, sometimes entire oratorios. The quite virtuosic chorus "The horse and his rider" from *Israel in Egypt* was a particular favourite. Here and in the general development of west gallery music, the increasing complexity is said to have come to outstrip the capacity of the congregation, which sometimes became merely an audience, and even turned round to face west to listen to the choir and band. But it is also obvious that the music became very popular, and with some musical education or background a greater number of people could participate in it than a small choir, and certainly in some places (again notably Lancashire) the entire congregation joined in.

This music was in turn ejected from the church in mid-19th century reforms, under the dominance of the Oxford Movement. By then the self-same educated classes, ever unable to leave a small parish church to its own devices, were apparently finding the sophistications they introduced a century previously to be rustic, crude and unsuitable for the worship of God. The fuging itself upset them (John Wesley feared it might "confuse God") and as with the reforms of the Council of Trent in the 16th century a specific syllabic clarity of textual projection was demanded of church music: one note to one syllable. The west galleries were dismantled and the music was replaced with a more professional nationally produced music for choir based on concert music, with the Victorian hymn as a separate congregation music, the whole thing anchored on the introduction of the church organ. In small parishes the choir became a children's choir accompanied on the harmonium by the village schoolmistress. But as anyone knows who has read the Hardy novel, the older music was very much taken to heart by the parishioners, whether they took part in it or not, and its redundancy was much resented, especially in the countryside. It was a music specific to its purpose and the capacity of its performers, much of it produced in the local region, though many pieces travelled nation-wide. It occupied the middle-ground between culture-music (choir) and simple music for the people (hymns) into which the 19th-century reforms divided church music. It accepted that local musical talent was not necessarily creamed-off to the conservatoires, but it did necessitate some centralised training which was provided by the ubiquitous music-masters, semi-qualified part-timers who suddenly appeared in great numbers and set themselves up everywhere, even in quite small villages, and who themselves wrote some of the west gallery pieces. But this training probably became less and less necessary as the whole musical climate shifted, and such musical literacy as was required could be passed on locally.

Thousands of these short vocal church pieces were produced all over England, only a proportion of which has survived in printed collections, manuscript, or transferred to Methodist and Salvation Army hymn-books. A significant number of pieces only survive in aural tradition, with no known written version, though they were all written in the first place. Some of them are of high quality by any standards short of the demand for extended complexity. The greatest quantity is preserved in America, where the music flourished and survived better in a Nonconformist context, and extended into more complex forms. Surviving "lining-out" singing from the Western Isles and remote parts of the Southern States shows the full, primitive communistic congregational ensemble which these cultural interventions erased.

As implied, there was a parallel development in the Nonconformist churches which took on many pieces from the established church and added new ones, the work of its own composers, with texts beyond the confines of psalmody. The nonconformists also favoured the use of pre-existing popular tunes supplied with religious texts, many of which were passed on to the parish churches. Among the nonconformists there was no authoritarian reaction against this music, but there was later some resistance to its sophistication and it tends to survive in simplified form.

Most of these pieces are short, twenty to thirty measures without the symphony (a short instrumental interlude between verses, often omitted in modern performance), and follow a fairly fixed procedure: a first section of homophonic chordal writing, rhythmically varied and close to the music of march or slow dance, then a second section with fugal or imitative elements which may be the last part or may be followed by a homophonic refrain, and occasionally a coda. But imitative figures can break in elsewhere. Most people in this country know one of these pieces well, an uncomplicated example with a small amount of two-part imitation, now known as "Ilkley Moor 'baat 'at". This was originally *Cranbrook* by Thomas Clark of Canterbury (1775–1859) setting the words "Grace, 'tis a charming sound…", later widespread as one of the many settings of "While shepherds watched…"; still sung in Padstow (Cornwall) as "Behold the grace appears…" and at some point purloined wholesale into the silly song, which was probably originally a young person's mock version like "While shepherds washed their socks by night…" Such are the adventures of pieces of music which won't go away. But this course of events also demonstrates how "secular" this music was, in keeping with the period in which it was written, without the inbuilt solemnities of either Victorian or Tudor church music, which makes its subsequent fate more understandable. A lot of these anthems "rollick".

When this music was banished from the parish churches, people in many places were not willing to relinquish it entirely. So they took it home, and continued to sing it there alongside secular pieces in much the same manner. The bulk of the repertoire of rural singing families such as the Coppers was of this nature in their earliest documentations. In this context the music was mostly maintained without annotation, passed on aurally or semi-aurally from generation to generation, inevitably undergoing localised re-writing in the process. In fact texts were more stable than music because they were often preserved in manuscript books as an aid to memory. In many places the music merged with the annual outdoor Christmas carolling (or wassailing) tradition and the persistence of that practice preserved it particularly well, if selectively, even to the present time in a few scattered places: the Isle of Man, Padstow in Cornwall, parts of North Yorkshire and Leicestershire – and the moorland villages around Sheffield. Here at some point it ceased to be carted round the houses at Christmas and was taken into the pub for an annual day of carolling, still observed during the Christmas period in the pubs of some dozen villages in South Yorkshire, Derbyshire and Nottinghamshire. In some places it has passed into the hands of the Nonconformist church choir, or is maintained by a special carol choir which only convenes at Christmas and sings from door to door. This tradition is still mainly aural, with the gallery band parts, if they survive, transformed onto piano or electric organ. In Beeston (Notts.) a four-part *a cappella* singing has been maintained aurally to this day. The most authentic sound is maintained by the carol-singers of Padstow, who were present at the 2000 festival, with a tighter-throated singing and less emphatic ensemble, untouched by the brass-band and choral society traditions which inform a lot of the singing in the Sheffield area. There a cult has arisen devoted to preserving and recording this music; it has been collected, transcribed and annotated, gallery band parts recovered from the lofts of farmhouses, etc. (Similar work in preserving west gallery music is going on in Lancashire, the Isle of Man, Dorset and an increasing number of other places.) Several tapes and CDs have been issued of the rather surprising ensemble of the annual Sheffield carolling, in which an 18th-century devotional ethos is projected as, in most places, a fairly raucous pub-singing, long loud and slow, almost reverted at times to the previous heterophony. Bits of Handel-like counterpoint encompassed by pints of beer and packets of crisps.

In Cutlers' Hall there were about six hundred people singing together, normally in four parts, with an accompanying band about 30-strong. This is greatly in excess of any original performing condition, indeed it is a "massification", but the point of the festival was to gather and confirm all concerned. The most authentic sounds were presented by groups from individual villages when they performed separately, especially Padstow. But this essay is about the experience of singing a music such as this, i.e. not commercial, and not traditional, and not dictated by official processes, but a music which has been guarded and preserved purely by local practice, and inhabits a serious and comprehensive textual context. And singing it in such a mass, and participating through that congregation in the devotional ethos of the words, in defiance of belief. The principal assembly room of Cutlers' Hall is big, with a high ceiling, a suitable container for mass acoustics, and in the frieze just below the ceiling a quotation from Ruskin runs round the room painted in black on a blue and gold ground:

> In cutlers' ironwork we have in Sheffield the best of its kind done by English hands unsurpassable when the workman chooses to do all that he knows by that of any living nation.

2

The singing made you belong, to more than one thing – to a series of things, culminating at the highest points in the one thing that mattered. It delivered you from isolation into a company, but achieved revelatory moments which passed the act back to a renovated solitude. The moments were contained in passages, and the passages were contained in structures. The structures were social, the passages were terrestrial, the moments were something else.

Brought into this rally, under the baton of the ring-master, we sang multiple lyrics, all 600 of us, and doing that we belonged to each other and to the occasion and gave our performance into that. We were absolutely cloaked and covered in this belonging. There was no audience to introduce questions of proprietorship, we owned all of it. I, stranger, unknown, ex-Northerner, belonged *while singing / during the lyric* to a northern working class I remember well, and its extensions and its history and its fictions, and the nation from that angle, and to my neighbours to left and right and on all sides resounding into the great hall beribboned in Ruskin's faith. The choral society. The moment the lyric stopped I was alone again. I felt that my neighbours too, much as they belonged in the place and with the music, were gathered for the momentum of a performance, and returned after it to a labyrinthine existence. But there was also that in the lyric which left me not alone, and part of none of that. These were the points at which the voice risked breaking.

At which it became too much. Most of the time the words served to keep the machine going, there was no question any more (in a sense there never had been) of commitment, and I could not but be aware that a proportion of my neighbours had been brought there by their evangelism rather than anything else, or were likely, off-lyric, to manifest an aggressive localism which has spread all over the north since I lived there. But there were points, moments, summits, some of them quite extended, which formed a home above beyond and sometimes in despite of, the occasional home. There were moments, like cracks in an enclosing substance, formed through particular text-music junctions, which opened the mind to a greater prospect. They are why the music continues to exist. And the musicians who wrote these pieces, amateurs most of them, music-teachers, church organists, plasterers, bricklayers, miners… again and again these musicians had intuitively recognised and grasped the potential break-through offered them in the text, and somehow matched it. Their means were limited, and it was usually achieved by striking a strong figuration and making the most of it; and it tended to happen during third lines or refrains. But these points were not just conceived, written and replicated; they were achieved also by the entire history of the music, in which texts were swapped from one piece of music to another, details shifted, pace and emphasis freely revised again and again, including the improvisational present tense. They are the results too of the constructs which enable them, inseparable from that support. Premonitions and echoes of them abound in the pieces where they happen, or they are implicated in the whole cast of the piece, its characteristic figurations. Everyone recognised these moments, the mass singing surged up into them faultlessly.

It is a well-known and elementary principle among professional singers that you must not be too much moved by moments of the song, or your control of the voice will falter. You must keep your distance. For me the summits of the music were precisely the moments at which the singing became most arduous, perhaps because they were all I had; they were not, as they must have been to the original congregations, integral to a continuum: a diurnal and routine involvement extending in its own terms to the sublime, as remains very evident in the American pieces. The epiphanic moments would not then need to break through the occasion, they would revert to it. But for the interloping stranger (as, perhaps, for the modern poet trying to construct lyric stresses in a substance floated out into the unknown) once located, they essentially disband the terms of the occasion. But the lesson of the *mass* lyric is that the enabling structure is of the essence. It gives you the entire vocabulary, and you must in some way return what you gain to it.

What the high points broke through to, was of course, the world, in all its terms. You belonged there, by an elliptical process of exaltation which grasped and surpassed the social middle-ground, and promised a new, totalised solitude beyond and through the fullest participation. Being so sudden and exceptional these high points undermined discourse, and occupied involuntary stops in the voice: sobs, coughs, gasps, in response to sudden glimpses of great reaches of the world. But it was more than the glimpse of extent: it was the movement into it, and by force of momentum, through it. Not elective and not subjective, but quite factual, and ultimately meaning, through image of sky and stone and the vast length of the earth, mass deliverance into / through dying.

So – a great hall full of people belting out anthems for all they're worth, which shoot rockets into the total. Is this the answer to "the limits of lyric humanism"? It is certainly lyric, but is it "the subjective expression of a social antagonism" (Adorno)? Of course it is absolutely nothing of the sort. But more specific instances are needed.

3 Instances

Moments? But it gets increasingly difficult to maintain the distinction – extended moment / tensed passage / epithet of the entire redemptive ethos. First verse line 3: *Bring forth the royal diadem / And crown Him Lord of all* [piece known as *Diadem*, words by Edward Perronet, music by James Ellor (1819–1899) hat-maker of Droylsden, Lancs.] – a sudden simple sequence of descending chords in pastoral metre as if striving has ceased at this glimpse of the night sky, then rolls into a downhill contrapuntal romp with dramatic interjections of *crown him!* like shouts at a football match. Reassertion at fourth verse line 3: *Join in the everlasting song* (which aural transmission in Coal Aston (Notts.) changed to *And shout in universal son***g**). The setting of the same text to the tune *Hecla* [music anonymous, preserved only at Coal Aston] though quite different has the same emphases at this point. "Bring forth…" to a sudden waltz measure then "crown Him…" (several times) sustained over an active bass line. The royal diadem is again the night sky, brought forth by mass pleas.

Triple moment: *Joy love and gratitude combine / The theme the song the joy was new / Though earth and time and life shall fail* [3rd line of each verse of "Mortals awake, with angels join…" known as *Mount Zion* or *Christmas* or *Providence* or *St. Albans* or *Deep Drop* (because it begins with a descending octave leap). Words anon., music attributed to Thomas Clark, shoemaker of Canterbury. A quite steady but gentle march movement in the subdominant progression, again shifting into a serenity by reduced means out of a context of leaps and dotted rhythms, taken in the aural tradition at a very steady pace. The three entities are smoothed over, like taking a walk through them, but with great momentum, for we know perfectly well that they all "fail". We know there's nothing left in the linear continuum beyond its point of reach. Singing this sequence, we are carried into such knowledge with a momentum to thrust us beyond it.

There are also Augustan anti-moments: *O spring to light! th'auspicious Babe be born! / the vocal hills reply, the rocks proclaim th'approaching Deity / He from thick films shall purge the visual ray, and on the sightless eyeball pour the day.* [*Peace o'er the world* or *Bradda Anthem*. Words Pope, ex *Messiah*, tune by Richard Furness of Eyam, 1791–1857] All the materials of transcendence without the ignition. This fancy, static, goulash-soup kind of writing is coped with by almost ignoring it and letting the musical continuum keep control. This self-regarding kind of writing seems to me to deaden any possibility of involvement, but is accepted in the tradition. These people are, or were, notoriously tolerant of interference.

As against the true moment: *Peace on earth and mercy mild* [Piece known as *The Three Harks*. Words Charles Wesley ("Hark the herald angels sing"…), music anonymous, preserved widespread in aural tradition, line 3] It is so often at line 3 that both poet and musician turn the structure outwards. Wesley's plodding stress is met with (again) steady pulsation of chords in sequence, I to IV, V to I, classic folksy or Handelian song routine, with (again) a running bass figure. (The lightness at this point is in strong contrast to the standard Victorian setting, words adapted to a chorus by Mendelssohn, where "peace on earth" gets a kind of trumpet blast or call to arms). We are suddenly, momentarily, in a children's game/dance-song, with an adult chuckle underlying it.

Moments galore: *One star alone of all the plain / For ever and for ever more* The most telling figures are so often turned towards the sky and/or a sense of the horizon's vast extent supported by an upsurge of musical rhetoric. *Night's terrific shades give way / Rise to adore the mystery of love / Joyful all ye nations rise, Join the triumph of the skies... // May peace and glad tidings spread over the land* And a bringing together of these aspirations under a lyric cover thus a quite wild hope of unity: */ Ten thousand thousand are their tongues, But all their joys are one.* These are the aspirations of early socialism too.

Moment upon moment until there is nothing else. *Join the triumph of the skies* There are pieces with what you might call galloping fuging, like the one known as *Curly Hark* [Wesley's "Hark the herald angels" to anonymous music fully preserved only at Eyam, Derbys.] where the refrain goes into a closely echoed four-part imitative structure, remarkably dense and fluid, one four-note motif printed all over a musical tapestry, constantly echoed and re-echoed among the parts. Not the long running fugues of the Baroque, but more social, more of a madrigalian texture, a block of close mutual echoes. Padstow has a piece of similar effect, *Zadok*, with American connections, and there are others, both American and native. In these pieces, which embody the most sophisticated part-writing practised in this tradition, the sense of the music *wrapping itself round* the singers is particularly strong, not projected outward to congregation or audience or God, but curving back ("curly") to the first-person plural, the extended realm of participation to which the words are directed.

But there are also hymn-like chordal pieces which refine the whole process into a seamless item in a more orthodox way, 19th century, but not the ponderous stepping-stones of the great Victorian hymns, rather march and dance rhythms. Like *Awake Arise Good Christians* [words anon., music attributed to William Mount of Worrell, which is one of the Sheffield villages still involved, before 1880]. You should hear the mob from Dungworth still belting this one out at the Royal Hotel every Christmas, glasses clinking, tenors partly out of control... with the gallery band transformed into a kind of Blackpool Tower electric organ routine... And it is the speech of angels: *Awake, arise... Fear not... all with a joyful mind...* And the angels and the shepherds both get merged into the carol-singers themselves, wandering from door to door with good news, transhumant pastoralists coming back with the food from common land. *And like unto the shepherds, we wander far and near...*

While shepherds watched… There are songs of simple praise, and some generalised nonconformist /Here comes Santa/ Merry Christmas/ mishaps, there are even some secular pieces, but there is nothing of the "little baby Jesus in the snow" routines; these carols have been described as "gutsy", Nativity anthems rather than what we now call "carols". I notice eventually that there is a strong focus on the annunciation to the shepherds – all other items of the "Christmas story" are normally absent. This selection must be the choice of centuries of turning out in driving snow to sing from door to door in moorland villages, as they still do in one or two of them. And of being there and passing the hope on, increasingly abstracted – the resigned and persistent optimism of a northern working population which has always felt itself displaced from power, a constant inner resistance, a defiance, when the steelworker is on the stage as both shepherd and angel looking out into the depth of the Universe. Nahum Tate's "While shepherds watched…" was by far the most popular text to initiate and be fed through this process of participation. There were hundreds of settings of it. The Sheffield moorland singers still know about thirty of them, including quite monumental creations: *Pentonville, Old Foster's, Liverpool…* In most of these the transforming stress is, by various devices of upsurgence, on line 3, "The angel of the lord came down…" echoed at "Glad tidings…" and "Good will henceforth…" And in these northern versions (but not in the south) the actual details of the good news can be omitted. "To you in David's town…" etc., verses 3 to 5 of the hymn-book version: this may or may not be there. All that happens is that the sky comes down and speaks: "Don't worry." That's it. Then straight into the Gloria.

4

What does song do? In the first place it confirms where you are and in what company you belong. It does this whether it says, "God rest ye merry gentlemen" or "Exilde for ever Let mee mourn". There is no question of social alienation – whatever it says everyone agrees to it, otherwise it would not be musical. The sorrowful moan in lyric is recognised and acknowledged as a common fate. Songs of protest and rebellion merely transfer the image to a shifted placement, most of its properties on loan. All lyric is mass lyric, and the dead join in.

This confirmation is theatrical in the sense that it is set up and you enter into it as you draw breath for the first note. You praise God, England, the King, heaven-knows what, without demurral (though persons devoted to singular redemptive causes would no doubt balk at times, at Methodist hymnals as at Elizabethan song-books) because its amplitude is instinctively recognised; there is no space at all for the instrumental adjusting of focused mission. You are simply not in the song the person you are, you stand in for anyone else, and the more remotely you are absent, the more you pass into the lyrical realisation of the human edict itself, its absolute contract with nature and earth, of which death is only one clause.

The wind of 600 voices blows subjectivity sky-high. It flutters under the ceiling reading work-ethics.

Basically, lyric means song-like and is one of the things people do to make life bearable. It is not a problem. It is not something to worry about as if something is being stolen from human commonality into a sole self, or conversely as if the self is being robbed of its autonomy. The self offers itself into the picture as a skill, and vanishes. The first-person is merely the sign, of authenticity, of presence, of initiality. The performance of that sign moves within, but at the edges of, the recognisable.

Events like the Village Carols Mass Sing take place everywhere: mosques, dance halls, political rallies, cathedral naves, football matches, the Haj, clubbing in Ibiza…. thousands of places. And in each you are offered the same uplift and massification, but by and through a particular textual context which determines the value and consequence of the lyric moment : exactly what *formulation* of ecstasis you are lost into, and its channels to the total, if it has them.

"Mindless" too. The self is surrendered into the construct as a property of it, and doesn't contribute a skein of a thought, is absorbed into an act of work. But the worker also "*chooses* to do all he knows". Choices are skills, and the skills are learned from and owed back to, the commonality. Like conducting a working life, which you do for your self but also for the sake of what might be possible at large. The "mindless" act is also, through acts of choice possibly quite minute, a mental participation in the creation of the work, as to some extent the act of reading is of text, is a form of donation. An immense support is offered which it is folly to turn from. Whatever the "personal" lyric is, it can only be a miniaturization of all this.

Bird-song too is hunger and support. Individually it claims a working space in accord with tradition, always most insistent in the early morning and late evening, times of shift. In its mass (flock) form it is the individual maintaining contact with the communal space by its edges, keeping in touch, carolling fear and comfort into the tribe as it moves through time, maintaining awareness of the length of the world.

I don't see that it is so different for the poet, working lyric moments in the absence of music, and thus more and more focused on the breaks in the discourse where the light of difference flashes through, essentially alone but equipped with memories of choral harmony. From being a text for singing, the "lyrical" poem becomes a pre-sung text, sung-in-itself, because it still has to be kept separate; it needs a song-like hood over it, increasingly formed from the language itself, to distinguish it from the unsinging which it depends on, and in a sense serves. Because, I suppose, it also has a duty to entertain, and to draw people into its performance. Its pains of knowledge decorate the space it inhabits. Its constant elsewhere has finally to belong back into the mass it arose from. *And shout in universal song.*

5

The universal that we gain through a group is a local one, it is already there. The sudden, enhancing, glimpse of the starry sky at a musical cadence, as if we have broken through (alone) to a far wider extent than the diurnal can furnish, is also already there. Those stars are above the Sheffield moors where they have always been. There and only there the Star of Bethlehem shines, the forward hope in the lyric moment. It is the field of the self as a potential of virtuous action and reward disguised in all this space, and in the singing it is the reader's recognition of the transcended authorial self, the human image of the optimum.

The group serves to keep vocabularies, not beliefs, alive through long histories, ancient things, courses which have been tested and refined and are handed down to us ready for translation. Thus we gain resources against modernity communally which we cannot individually, and which we need, or all our worth is handed to a mere acceleration. Things like the Sheffield moorland carolling are valuable because in them an extent of image, a vastness of perception, is maintained and handed down attached to ikonic figures from which we become free to detach them. The very grandeur of the concepts, and their slow delivery, constantly referred to terrestrial vision, delivers us from mystical appropriations. The extent of terrestrial space and the rounds of the starry sky are wrapped round us without losing their scale, and our frailty is shared universally in the space opened by slow thought. It is not a redemption so much as a confirmation of what we are capable of, as an accumulated plurality depending for its realisation on the individual moment. Any one of us would "happily die" at the high points of the chorus.

You do not have to go rushing off to The Black Bull at Ecclesfield on Christmas Eve for such knowledge (in fact they would rather you didn't). Experience is crowded with like constructs, group or solo (e.g. reading) which are figures of each other. All that is necessary is to recognise when you can release yourself from a distrusting reserve.

It seems to me to be the easiest thing to translate, on the instant, a Christian ecstasis into a secular one, it hardly requires any thought at all. And the more you are brought up in it, have always had its terms with you, the easier it is to see through it. Myself, early 1950s, school choir, other side of the lower Pennines, annual carol service: *While shepherds watched*, always the same tune, such a pop carol that the music teacher was reluctant to admit it to the service. Handel's *Messiah* every year from local choral societies in every northern town, they still do. "And there were shepherds, abiding in the fields..." We didn't know what shepherds were. They must have been some ancient form of employment looking after sheep. The ones we might occasionally see during trips to the Derbyshire hills weren't shepherds, they were farmers, sheep-farmers at best. They were solitary, with black and white collies, they didn't go out in the winter and no angel would glance at them twice. Later you learn the histories, which also help you see through the iconisation. That in the peasant societies of the European and all other temperate zones the shepherds spent the summer with the sheep up on the open grasslands, and sometimes wandered further in search of pasture, great distances sometimes, and came back with knowledge of foreigners, and new songs. The first announcement was already heading for outside. Christianity can seem to lead you to transgress itself, to smash its own images, to get out of the place and the singular token: Bethlehem in a snowstorm, anywhere on earth, mother and child.

Suppose, then, that the universality we know is there could be recognised across diverse and opposed versions of mass lyric, Christian, Islamic, secular, theatrical, military... How? One way could be by tracing 'folk' structures across Europe and Asia to the culture of peasant farming which unites them and remains the source of most of our terminology for the sublime. All the Biblical imagery of elevation (sky, cloud, hills, river...) is peasant farming, indicating the sources of fertility. Or by casting all that adrift and heading into futurity one by one, into the biological unity, birth death in the abstract with nothing but the natural obscurity of song to keep us in step? Beneficial instincts shared among all creatures? Is such totalisation possible? Attempts become desperate: the gabble of a rap that nobody listens to, the destroyed poetry of the Cambridge intellectuals where words flee from each other in terror, is not all that also a bid for immense and impossible regions? Directly or indirectly, do we reach into the heart of difference for the point where we join together, in what kind of, what site of, what scale of, universal song?

Annex: Tone

I delegate to an annex some suggestions about lyric and tone, arising from these studies and experiences, which remain tentative or unprovable. This also involves delving into areas of musical and literary history which have become badly cluttered with modern intellectual folklore and superstition.

The definition of lyrical poetry as subjective, "the expression by the poet of his [*sic*] own feelings" (Ruskin) is sometimes taken as a premise in academic discussion now, as part of a blanket nervousness about any form of self representation in text. I feel this definition to be no older than 19th century, probably later 19th century, and even there not unanimous. The Shorter OED is ambiguous, giving a main date of 1589 for a wide and changing definition which includes this one, but the only citation is the one I quote, from Ruskin. My reading experience tells me that at any time prior to that the lyrical poem is defined mainly by formal properties derived directly from song, and its content is normally fictive. I'd apply this even to the history of the sonnet – speculations about Petrarch's, or Shakespeare's, love-life strike me as an impertinence. This 19th century shift in definition is contradicted by, for instance, Swinburne's practice, where it is clear that the lyrical poem may be almost any poem which is not cast in dramatic or narrative form; it also manifestly covers a great deal more than self-expression, and can include very long poems (*Studies in Song,* 1880). In that case to justify Ruskin's definition as definitive you might have to bypass Swinburne and prioritise someone like Coventry Patmore. From this shaky beginning the definition has grown in some quarters into an outright condemnation of the lyrical poem and all direct manifestation of life experience in poetry. And yet by a more venerable definition all modern poetry is lyrical.

There is another and parallel popular notion of a change in the substance of music at about the same time, perhaps beginning with Schumann. It is held that a kind of interiorisation took place by which a direct appeal is made to the individual listener's emotional experience, as opposed to a primarily musical sense of what is taking place – a process conveniently classed as "Romantic". Music becomes "expressive" not in its social or theatrical functions but innately, and when involved with text the music is expected to employ stress, elasticity and appropriate dynamics, to emphasise this function and to bear the text company, as it were, by replicating its emotive tenor. The techniques are those of unsettling and interruption, which cast the musical experience to the listener as a questioning, felt as "personal" because of the inevitably threatening substrata of musical disruption. If you start this story from Schumann and carry it on through Chopin, Liszt and the Wagnerians into the 20th century you may well get a sense of a progressive disturbance of formal and tonal properties and irregularity of measure, which a certain definition of the modern condition would recognise as party to alienation of identity both political and personal. But it also seems obvious to me that Brahms' music has little or no share in this process (Berlioz might seem a gift to the thesis but in practice more of a stumbling-block; the same goes for Janáček and Mussorgsky). It is also obvious to me that what can only be called expressivity is an unalienable property of texted and sometimes untexted music during the previous 300 years at least, surfacing starkly for instance in the early 17th century in such works as the solo Lamentations settings, and freely embodied in solo instrumental works of that period, especially the clavécinistes. The techniques of disturbance are the same, though generally over-ridden. The possibility I want to explore is that changes which affected the status of "song" about 150 years ago occurred less in the music itself and more in the performance of music, which is much more difficult to know about, but can be attempted through survivals in folk music, and in west gallery music, which is particularly pertinent as a concerted music. A small amount of evidence is available about the performance practices of the Sheffield west gallery tradition, which although dating from the 20th century, seems to describe a survival which predates the Romantic definition.

The singing was originally accompanied by a "symphony" or band, which played constantly during the singing and often played an introductory passage and a coda, and interludes between verses which could be quite extended. This practice survives still in some villages but reduced to a piano or electric organ, in one case a solo violin, or vocalised by the choir. The recovered band parts seem to indicate a string band of violins and cello or bass, though the Lancashire west gallery bands included clarinets and bassoons. One particularly renowned band was from the village of Worrall, Sheffield, known as The Big Set, consisting of three violins, 'cello and bass. It was a family concern, the Mounts of Worrall, plus outsiders, led from the 'cello by the eldest, William Mount, whose descant playing was especially noted by observers. As a carolling band it was a selection from the 'chapel orchestra' which will have played a wider variety of west gallery music and may have been as many as ten strong or more. Dr Ian Russell, in compiling music from the Worrell repertoire, was able to speak to surviving players from The Big Set and hear them playing, and to collect contemporary descriptions of the performance habits of both bands and singers. This is what he says about the singing:

> 'It is abundantly clear that the singing was extremely robust and uninhibited. The use of expression was kept to a minimum and

most carols were performed fortissimo. Tempo was generally strict, slow, and deliberate. ... There is strong evidence of phrasing, not in the sense of light and shade, but rather through the use of pauses and by stressing a musical phrase or melisma, sets of words or rhythm. The repeat of the final section or the use of a coda, served as a refrain to which the singers would rise with great passion.'

The evidence about instrumental playing style is parallel in many ways: robust and deliberate, with special emphasis on the bass fuging passages, especially in runs. Special note is made of the style of the bass player from the Big Set, Jack Couldwell: "vigorous, positive and rhythmic, due to his 'attacking' use of the bow, rather staccato and in strict tempo, with minimal use of vibrato, and generally forte/fortissimo." The effect, Dr Russell adds, is more of an individual performance than a contribution to a harmony, polyphonic rather than homophonic. It is suggested that a more 'polished style' was developed later.

And it was said that the Lancashire singing (from a quire of about fifteen or possibly involving the entire congregation within a small stone church or chapel) could be heard on the other side of the valley.

These features lend themselves to a "folk" categorisation, though west gallery music is of course not folk music, and the society that produced it was not rural – the musicians were mostly men in the small metal trades of the Sheffield area, file-makers and cutlers; they were not involved in agriculture except domestically. In the Big Set lined up for a group photograph with singers c.1906, every adult man wears a bowler hat. They were gentlemen of trade. Nevertheless the description of unremittingly forceful and deliberate singing style might well call to mind the Georgian and Russian village choruses, who never sing quietly (until fetched into town choirs) or the notorious Aberdeenshire slow-singing traveller-women, who if they could on occasion shrink to a whisper adopted a normal pitch and attack akin to pibroch. The description of the playing of the string bass immediately reminds me of the Transylvanian and Slovakian village bands, with their emphatic and staccato 'sawing' basses. Indeed it is an almost universal characteristic of traditional group music-making to be loud, necessarily so as social music, and to drive the music forwards, with the performers generally facing inwards towards each other.

As it survives in modern documentation, the singing of actual folk songs in the British solo singing traditions shows a very wide range of vocal production, a clear instance of which is provided by Joseph Taylor and George Gouldthorpe, two singers from the same area at the same time (North Lincolnshire 1905, both recorded by Percy Grainger), the one legato and ornamented, the other plain and plodding steadily note by note, but each transmitting as much emotion from the text as the other. Domestic solo singing would not normally be loud, in contrast to the raucous bellowing that took pace when it was banished to the village pub, but documentation of outdoor singing and work songs, solo or group, speaks everywhere of full- and open-voiced singing. It is tempting to speculate on the manner in which the Lancashire hand-loom weavers sang their Handel in the 18th century, or even what London or Italian concert performance of Handel might have sounded like in his presence. Certainly not a steady fortissimo, but neither would it have been the cathedral warbling or salon sinuosity which we inherited from the 19th century. The point about the emotional load is that it is *already there* in the text and the more the music straightforwardly upholds that text the more intact and therefore strong it remains, and the more so as it is felt to be something held in common.

The steady, open, forthright, entirely expressive lyric tone might extend back through centuries of singing, in a common modulation of tone by which the funeral music was not sad but solemn, the jigs and reels not happy but lively, and the love laments not pathetic but strongly engaging. What the singer of a Dowland song principally offers the listener (if there is one at the time) is the musical line as enhancement of the text, rather than the text re-emphasised into music. The point is that your, the listener's, emotional experience does not come into play until it accords with the text. And I hear this continuity finally eroded only at that very point at which it is proposed that song is (merely) an expression of the author's "personal feelings" – if, indeed, any such category of feelings could be honestly said to exist, for is not "feeling" shared by definition, is that not how it is recognised, named and validated? There may be personal or idiolectic language habits, but what is sensed and held in the text cannot be appropriated or privatised. It is common property.

All this is *song*. And it is known as song by its structure. It doesn't change. However far away in time or remote rurality, it is not only social, or theatrical, it is also individual, it also inhabits the solitude of poetry, and it is also recognised as absolute music. What it does not offer is that peculiar "poetical" incompletion by which the audience is disturbed into a necessarily forlorn "feeling" by vacancies and diversions, hesitations and bends, in the construct.

The basis of song is words echoing each other, so it is necessarily a discovery of delight in nature, which makes a narrative memory possible whether it is history or weddings or funerals. Nothing has the power to take away that delight. Protest songs or dirges are grounded in it; Puritan intervention needs it to embody the message. Even anti-poetry is lyrical poetry. You can squirm and howl and shed your own blood but if it is poetry it is lyrical because it places words next to each other by the gladness of their force. You can stop people enjoying themselves with laws or bombs but the dreaming goes on, and song is where it manifests itself, in concert halls or in secret corners of the labyrinth. "Lyre" means an instrument of praise.

Musical Glossary

bare fifth Two notes a "fifth" apart (e.g. C and G) sounded simultaneously without the "third" (E) between them which would change the sound into that of a chord and define the chord as major or minor. It is an "empty" sound prohibited in academic music exercises and rare in written music after c.1500.

contrapuntal or **polyphony/-ic** Musical writing in which different voices have their own melodies to sing, which are made to fit harmonically with each other. Opposite of homophonic.

dotted rhythms in which a note is extended by a half or quarter of its length, therefore jerky rhythms.

folk There is possibly no such thing as folk music, but I use the fiction to refer to music which (a) has been passed on aurally and subject to individual variation, and (b) does not betray a comparatively recent written existence or context stylistically.

fugue / fugal / fuging Contrapuntal writing in which a musical phrase occurs in different voices not exactly at the same time, so that one voice will seem to **imitate** what another has sung. Here spelled fuging rather than fugueing to distinguish it from the contrapuntal practices of classical music. There are no fugues in this music, only sections within certain pieces, in which a phrase is passed from one voice to another before block harmony is resumed. These fugal passages are normally short and simple, but could sometimes become extensive and even dominate a piece.

the Gloria The verse praising God which traditionally ends many pieces of liturgical music and also many hymns and carols.

homophony/-ic Music for choir in which all voices (soprano, tenor, bass etc.) sing their notes at the same time, i.e., in chords. Opposite of **heterophony** (see next note).

lining-out archaic form of congregational singing in which a leader reminds the congregation of the text in a solo chant at the beginning of each line, followed by the chanting of a slow tone-row in which participants do not concur exactly but move individually in proximity to the notional melodic line, and may instinctually harmonise without strict reference to each other, producing a shifting heterophony.

monophony/-ic One line of music, neither harmonised nor accompanied.

part as in "three-part writing" is the same as **voice** – soprano, tenor, etc., each getting their own line of music to sing. May also refer to the sectioning of a piece of music.

pastoral In European 17th and 18th century European music an arcadian fiction was often suggested by a lilting 6/8 rhythm, of six beats divided into two threes. Handel uses it for the shepherds' music in *The Messiah*.

subdominant The note or chord on the fourth degree of the musical scale, i.e. F in the key of C. It is the chord on which the A- of Amen is traditionally sounded.

Bibliography

George Deacon, *John Clare and the Folk Tradition*. 1983.

Roger Elbourne, *Music and Tradition in Early Industrial Lancashire 1780–1840*. 1980.

Vic Gammon, "Babylonian Performances: the Rise and Suppression of Popular Church Music 1670–1860", in *Popular Culture and Class Conflict*, ed. E. and S. Yeo. 1981.

Thomas Hardy, *Under the Greenwood Tree*.

Ian Russell, *Sixteen Carols from the Mount-Dawson Manuscript, Worrall*. 1994

Nicholas Temperley, *The Music of the English Parish Church*. Cambridge University Press. 1979.

Discography

English Village Carols. Smithsonian Folkways (USA) CD 40476.

Three compact discs and ten cassettes issued by Village Carols of Sheffield. One CD is of the mass sing of 1998, all other items are of individual village singings. All have accompanying books of texts, music and commentary researched by Dr Ian Russell.

Traditional Carols from Padstow in Cornwall. Cassette issued by Veteran Tapes of Stowmarket.

The Watersons: *Sound Sound your Instruments of Joy*. Topic Records 12TS346, 1977 (LP).

The Gladly Solemn Sound, *"Repeat their sounding joy"*, Music from a Wyresdale West Gallery. CD issued by the choir, c.1999.

Larks of Dean Quire, *Carols and Festive Songs from Ordsall Hall Museum*, 1995. CDr issued by the quire, copied from a cassette, 2007.

Purbeck Village Quire: *Christmas at Purbeck*. Issued by the quire, 2005.

Coupe Boyes and Simpson, with Fi Fraser, Jo Freya and Georgina Boyes: *"Fire and Sleet and Candlelight": regional and historical carols*. No Masters Co-operative Ltd., NMCD21, 2003.

[ibid.], *"Voices at the Door": Midwinter Songs and Carols*. No Masters Co-operative Ltd., NMCD25, 2006.

While Shepherds Watched: Christmas Music from English Parish Churches, 1740–1830. Psalmody and The Parley of Instruments, directed by Peter Holman. Hyperion CDA66924.

2

Dawn Songs

Preface

An obsession, which started when a Transylvanian village band played at a pub in Cambridge in 1993, led eventually through a lot of travelling and a lot of tapes and CDs and old travel books, to an essay on one of the song forms. It took a long time and it got finished, but the information never stopped coming in. It still hasn't stopped; it arrives piecemeal, mostly emerging from research in Hungarian and Romanian Englished into CD booklets and websites, or further extensions of the thesis develop through books on anything from psychodrama theory to bagpipes. Travel to Transylvania, now generally biannual, always leads to disturbing discoveries and contradictions. But the essay seemed to have completed itself and except for major reversals everything else was delegated to the notes.

Thus following the essay and its footnotes, is a big section of newly developed and unattached notes, 'Additional Notes', which are extensions or revisions to the essay, further topics shooting off at a tangent, etc. A whole new interpretation of one of the main theses of the essay sprouted up unexpectedly at the last moment and is given in the final section.

There is no doubt that the only trustworthy comment on a society comes from those who have lived there and spoken to many people and understood all the internal and external complexities without bias. That's not me. I was intoxicated by a string band in a pub in Cambridge in 1993, and it has led me to write where I have no authority, and don't even speak the three languages involved. I've tried to get involved with sociality only as it creates necessities which condition the music, and I think this is possible. But my final excuse rests on that evening in the rather dingy black-painted pub-theatre, The Boat Race, Cambridge (now, alas, some kind of smart eatery), with the band from the village of Soporul de Câmpie (now, alas, gone to U.S.A.) brought there by a professor from Cluj.[1] It was a rainy evening and there was an audience of about ten. We were told that they had never left their parish before, and they probably didn't know where exactly they were, but as soon as they started playing they found themselves – they were somewhere, and happy to be there. It was obvious that whatever "community" such a band served (which is not a simple question) I could hear them as clearly as anyone in the world, and the opening their music seemed to offer was something I had a right to. I only learned much later the reason for this: that I as much as they inhabit the history within which the music came into being.

Notes

[1] This was in a way a fortunate introduction because the music arrived under a Romanian aegis. I was later to find that 80 percent of available research and comment comes from Hungary and most of it presents the music as Hungarian. Most outsiders are led to this music through Hungary and it can be very difficult to escape from the nationalist agenda; there is less Romanian research, it is more academic, and it is hard come by. It is also equally prejudiced. There is no Romanian "revival" version equivalent to *táncház* music. Hungarian researchers have ignored the Soporul band almost completely while devoting a lot of attention to the same kind of music from bands serving Hungarian-speaking villages in the same area. This could be a factor in what led the band to emigrate. My account of seeking them in their village and attending a dance they played for, is given in the title story of my *The Dance at Mociu*, 2003 (revised edition 2014). The leader, Şandorica, eventually returned to Transylvania and is now active in the area, noticeably stouter.

Dawn Songs [a]

In the repertoire of Transylvanian village bands working for the Hungarian-speaking population is a category known as the 'dawn song' (*hajnali*). In its full social use, which is now uncommon, it marks, in a quite elaborate and extended way, the termination of a dance or celebration, which would normally be at about the time of first light.

The bands normally consist of a virtuoso violin (or two) with a chordal viola (or two) and a string bass, and the players are traditionally gypsies.[1] Their services are required mainly for weddings and a few other festive occasions, dominated by eating, drinking (mainly very potent home-brewed fruit spirits) and a great deal of dancing, and these events can be of great length, 48 hours or more, during which the musicians have to play almost continuously.[2] While basically marking the end of the festivities, the dawn songs might also occupy an interval at the end of the first night. These people seem to be able to drink and dance and sustain festivity to almost superhuman lengths. But at a point just before dawn the dancing and noise stop, the musicians start playing preludial slow airs, and those who wish to sing approach them. One by one they step forward to face the musicians and sing a dawn song. The music may be played continuously, modulating from one song to another as each next singer comes forward. Sometimes a song may be taken up by a small group. This can go on for hours, sometimes involving some final dancing.

Other sources of information place the dawn songs differently.[3] In this version they constitute the formal ending of the celebration, and only men are involved. In the first light of dawn the men process out of the house or yard led by the musicians playing, and, holding onto each other by the shoulders, they walk down the village street singing together, and are thus escorted back to their homes and occupations. As the group arrives at each man's door[4] he sings his dawn song facing the musicians and company, as a form of farewell, until there are none left. This can take hours.[5]

We are talking about a large upland area, a country,[6] of plain, peneplain, hills, and mountains, most of it covered in large and scattered agricultural villages, most of them linear villages strung along roads. It is sometimes referred to, at least in parts, as one of the last true peasant societies left in Europe. This is half true in terms of land ownership and the sufficiency of the family smallholding, but it is very far from a 'classic' peasant society. There are a number of cities and market towns, but this music now belongs to the villages, to landed smallholders living in clusters of farms with a sub-class of

---

[a] Notes to this section may be found beginning on p.53.

unlanded workers, often gypsies, living in small houses on the edges of the villages. In northern Transylvania much of the architecture was recently still of wood, including the churches. The surrounding land, usually hilly, is covered in cultivation strips except for the areas of pasture attached to each village or situated above it on mountain slopes, maintained by professional shepherds. In mountainous areas the shepherds are transhumant, living through the summer on the high pastures with the sheep, or alternatively smallholders themselves move into small "summer farms" on the intermediate slopes. The agriculture is self-sustaining and in the more remote areas still capable of ensuring self-sufficiency. The system of land tenure, which in every generation divides the family's land equally among all children of both sexes, resists the formation of large capitalised farms and has in centuries past, in certain areas, protected the villages from the formation of aristocratic estates. State-enforced collectivization was resisted for a long time, and abolished immediately Ceaușescu fell.

The work is constant and arduous, from daybreak to night at certain seasons though minimal through the winter, highly regulated in extended family units, and people undertake it in full knowledge, these days, of the alternatives, and with a certain resigned fatalism. And surely sometimes, they live lives of contentment and fulfillment which do not need to rest on any form of innovation but only on maintaining a set cycle of necessities against a shifting world with its own possibilities of improvement. Into this duration the two forms of observance, calendrical and occasional, are set as major stations, of which, as in other places, the wedding shows by far the greatest resilience.[7] The leafy nuptial crown, punned with the death wreath and the birth coronet, marks the central node of a concentric economy, however eroded round the edges.

So it is at first light in these family farms, the larger gatherings out in the yards under temporary textile awnings with lanterns, the smaller ones inside the houses,[8] that the enormous expenditure of festive energy and persistence for whatever occasion, reaches at last its point of tiredness, and the movement of the dance gives place to the solitary singer, singing dawn songs. I assume it to be hushed then, I assume everyone to be listening.

It appears that this is or was to some extent an improvised singing, or at least that each person had his or her own song to sing and that its words might be self-composed and have bearing on the singer's own fate. My own conjecture is that song texts were constantly re-composed in preparation for performance, and that during the long periods between celebrations people would, while watching the beasts or hoeing the land or weaving the textiles... have been preparing their next dawn song, by composing or revising words to a known tune. But it is also obvious from the examples given that singers were free to sing pre-existing songs of several (but not any) different kinds on the dawn song platform, and songs could also be put together by taking phrases and whole verses from known songs into a new sequence.[9]

In most oral traditions the singer receives a song from the repertoire as material for re-shaping, re-stressing and re-figuring, both text and music, and this freedom can be exercised in very slight shifts of tone, pace, or ornament, or in radical transformation. It is one of the surprising liberties of supposedly strict self-regulating societies, but one which goes to the core of the structure. And generation upon generation the succession of singers continually reforms the piece, according to their own versions of desirable figuration and their own versions of living a life. An apparent extreme of this condition, which may be commoner than one would expect, is where the text, if not the music, is more-or-less completely self-composed by the singer as a thing wrought from his/her own fate and made public in a specially licensed arena such as the dawn-song. In the notes to the CD of the band from Szászfenes, Kalotaszeg[10] (recorded 1998) László Kelemen indicates that such not only did but in some places still does take place in the social performance of village singing in Transylvania: (my italics) 'The song text can be applied to the melody according to taste or whim, and when our informants sang, *they sang mostly of their own fates, in the old style.*'

In unaccompanied song this means a freedom to re-form both text and music according to your own lights, though the melody would of course have to retain its contours and basic figurations, or it would no longer be an 'old melody' as most of them are described. Accompaniment by ensemble, introduced into this music probably during the earlier 20th century, tends to 'freeze' the piece musically, but with a margin of collaborative extemporisation still possible between singer and band-leader, which will be a lot easier with slow tunes such as dawn songs.[11]

It is also common in Transylvanian village music (as in other traditions) for melodies to 'belong to' individual patrons, who are entitled to demand that the musicians play them on the instant, whether for listening, dancing, or singing. This proprietorship probably has a historical relationship to the practice of personal re-invention of songs, though I know of no evidence for what exactly that relationship may have been.[12]

* * *

It is obvious that anything called a dawn song will, if it fulfils half the potential of its title, face permanent questions of ending and beginning and the extent of the world figured against the daily journey of light. If the Transylvanian dawn song does this, it does it by a relentless focus on diurnal reality projected into a cathartic theatre, thus on working destiny rather than epiphany.

The dawn song functions as a bridge out of the event: at weddings, funerals, christenings or whatever, it marks the end of exceptionality and turns to face the continuing world beyond, returning from the festive island to normality. But this normality is expressed as a condition of fated extremity which remains within the lyric fiction, with the seriousness of a form which has never been allowed to float away from the demands of realism, but has been continually referred back to actuality by the intervention of individual singers in its course of development. Even in the fixed texts that now circulate around the urban 'revival' scene it is possible to sense that the poems have been wrought out of individual past fates which still adhere to them.

In festive space the entire community faces inwards and revolves in strict order round the node at the centre of the birth-death chain, thus confirming its right to subsistence and hope, but also confirming the extent and symmetry of the structure and thus its avenues to freedom. The actual ring-dance is now reserved for the opening of such events and most of the dancing is an elegant, it is said 'court-derived', couple dancing, in which the couples constantly turn this way and that, separate and come together. (The Romanian for the ring-dance, *hore* – also meaning a type of lyrical song – relates to the Greek Χορoζ.) The mutual self-illusioning of festive release is forced to a focus which excludes questions and holds all of history in the present moment, a communal protection. But at the end of that the temple doors are opened by individuals singing their own songs, 'Yes, but the singularities also wield sceptres', and lead us back to uncertainty, loss, and hope.[13]

People come forward at the end of an episode of formalised immediacy, a community hypnosis which steps outside time, and declare in song the demands of necessity, *within the edge* of the festive enclosure, bearing that theatre with them into questions of actual fate. What is created, always anew, in that transitional space thus has the potential of drama, even tragedy, wrought out of the lives that surround it, as the more individual and particular it is the more it acts out a cosmic relentlessness. And that is exactly the sense of the steady pace and harmonic richness of the dawn-song music.

The texts of these songs are for the most part deeply and bleakly unhappy. They deal in personal inadequacy, failure and ill-fate, either directly or more often through the modes of the common lot and its traditional sung repertoire, songs of the acknowledged unbearables: love-loss, economic failure, orphaning, toil without reward, punishment, exile, imprisonment, recruitment,[14] but not death. Or rather only the living-death, the welcome-death, of the self's abandon to impossibility, not the lament for the lost other.[15] And sometimes they figure a totalised sense of loss by singular image (candle-flame extinguished, bird flown, flower faded etc.). Where other communities sing at this terminal point 'We wish you a merry Christmas' or 'Auld lang syne' and send us home full of affirmative comfort, these people show a wound you would hardly suspect to exist.[16]

The ethos of the songs has distinct echoes in (or from) the cultivation of 'melancholy' in 16th and 17th century European 'courtly' song, with which it shares a strong sense of quasi-exilic loss, a refined cultivation of misfortune and undeserved rejection to the point of welcoming death. In the poetics they share an at times extreme hyperbolism involving degrees of wit and even humour, and in the music a relentless steady movement as of a slow march or pavane. The convergence can at times be startling, and some of these village songs could stand alongside some of Dowland's, though I think there are important distinctions to be made concerning the localisations of the dawn-song, and the absence from it of the pastoral distancing of the courtly lyric [see Appendix 4A on p.92]. Where the songs are circumstantial they deal with known realities of life which are felt as integral to a common fate rather than depicting an individual accident or the typicality of a phase of life or a 'character'. Where they are generalised they come closer to some of the more extreme lyrics of cultivated melancholy, especially on the 'welcome death' theme, but tending to cling more to social particulars and conditions, and deploying a minimal symbolised imagery of bird, tree, and flower, which relates to pastures and fields rather than gardens, so that even the expiring moan is a factor of the substantiated locality.

Only through these iterated invocations of the site-specific societal whole is recognition of the species condition approached. Even when it enters the kind of ironic localism which makes fun of itself, it takes on board absolute fatality. The peasant society may represent itself as an inescapable framework (which it no longer is, if it ever was) but by making even the fullest hurt intimate to participation and belonging it transcends small-scale subjective solution, or home-comfort. The loss remains stark, unmitigated and finally terrestrial.

> The bird wanders everywhere, it's an orphan,
> *Bújdosik az árva madár...*
>
> It lands on the edge of every country[17]
> It's an orphan just like me
> Poor thing, of course it wanders.

I'm going to have a house built for myself
But it's not going to have any windows.
When I'm inside they'll cover me with dirt,
Then they won't be able to push me around any more.[18]

These bleak, defeated lyrics are performed head up, full-throated, in consultation with the musicians (who have been playing for two days, their fingers are blistered and they can hardly stand up, but they never falter[19]). And we can assume that rather than actual orphans they are performed, sincerely, by heads of families and owners of flocks and smallholdings, by respected matrons, by village beauties and likely lads, by satisfied grandparents... who sing themselves into the role of the meanest reject of the village, the fool and the luckless, and they sing it as their own song. The whole tone of the event forbids the adoption of a fictive *persona*, where it occurs, to be a distancing or disowning act. What they are singing is human commonality, the fate of one is the fate of all, the figure that opens up the imaginative possibilities of yearning. It is extraordinary for this to be coded so clearly into social or festive custom.

The stately music transfers the fictive lament into a theatre of great poise and deliberation. The desolation is sheer, but held quite proudly before the world, you can sense that it is also smiled at, as something splendid, because it is known for its truth and its belonging, the common recognition of its elevated fatalism. This recognition is bound within the singer's own group, by which the fictive disaster remains in the realm of possible fatality (no one is going to start singing, 'Alas, I am a poor gypsy...', which in some villages would be considered laughable.)[20] The penetrative and destructive excess, the hopelessness patiently born, are intimate to the music with its constantly yearning but dignified tone derived from its complicated, probably partly aristocratic, ancestry. The extent of ever-present potential disaster is viewed from a personal elevation won from history, a distinct and endorsed frame of mind which encompasses the extremes of the possible world by acknowledging precisely the wholeness which shows no mercy.

+++

And I thought as long as the world turns
The candles would still burn

But now I see they are dying,
That they are really dying...

+++

My mother cursed me
                      Engem anyám megátkozott
When she brought me into this world.
                      Mikor a világra hozott…
She cried out in pain
That I should never be happy.

She cursed me again
When she rocked me in the cradle
She put a curse on me
To wander the world and never find a home.

I cannot stay here
The wild rose bush is my shelter
I cannot stay here
The wild rose bush is my shelter

I caused her pain
I carry her curse,
Her curse got me
Because I wasn't her good little girl.

Mountains and valleys, please stop
                      Hegyek–völgyek álljatok meg
So I can tell you my troubles.
                      Hogy panaszoljam el nektek
I have so much sorrow in my heart
                      Annyi bánat a szívemen
I'd have to fold it in half to fit it into the sky.
                      Kétrét hajlott az egeken.

+++

The tears have dug a ditch in both my cheeks
                      Árkot vágott a könny mind a két orcámra…
As the rain does in the mud of the road…

+++

Kicsi madár, hogy tudsz élni
            Little bird, how can you live
Mikor nem is tudsz beszélni
            When you can't even talk
Lám, én tudok beszélgetni
            Look at me, I can talk
Mégis alig tudok élni.
            But I can hardly live.

        +++

My mother's rose bush[21]
            Édesanyám rózsafája
Opened me out the first.
            Engem nyilott utoljára
If only you had never opened,
            Bár sohase nyilott volna
If only I had stayed in the bud, hey-ho.
            Maradtam vón a bimbóba, hateha.

I'm the sort who doesn't belong here
            Én vagyok az, aki nem jó,
Who opens the doors of the clouds
            Fellegajtó nyitogató,
I'm always opening up the clouds
            Nyitogatom a felleget
And the rain becomes my tears, hey-ho.
            Sírok alatta eleget, hateha.

        +++

Street, street of sorrow
            Utca, utca, bánat utca
Paved with stones of sorrow
            Bánatköböl van kirakva...
My sweetheart paved it
So I would walk down it in tears.
I don't walk down it in tears,
Let who paved it, walk down it.

On my way home
            Mikor megyek hazafelé

The sky divides into three
>	Hasad asa ég háromfelé
The stars cry on me
>	Sírnak reám a csillagok
Because they know I am alone.
>	Mert tudják hogy árva vagyok
I am alone like the bird
>	Árva vagyok mint a madár
Riding up there on a cloud
>	Ki a felhön odafenn jár.

I am the one who is no good
>	Én vagyok az, aki nem jó
I open the doors in the clouds
>	Fellegajtó nyitogató
I open up the clouds
>	Nyitogatom a felleget
And weep under them.
>	Sírok alatta eleget.

+++

The bird has flown away, its cage is empty.
>	Elment a madárka…
It left a message saying it would be back in the spring,
But already the wheat is ripening and it isn't back,
And if it's not back when the grapes soften, it'll never come
>	back.[22]

+++

Sorrow, sorrow, I was born only to sorrow.
>	Búra, búra, bubánatra születtem
My mother raised me in sorrow.
>	Édesanyám búban nevelt fel engem
Raised with sorrow and lived in sorrow and now
>	Búban nevelt búban éltem idáig,
I'll live on in sorrow till they close my coffin.
>	Búban éek koporsóm lezártáig

+++

The raven washes its young on Good Friday,
                          Nagypenteken mossa holló a fiát
This world has called me snake and frog.
                          Ez a vilàg kigyót-békát rámkiált
Say this to my face –
Who have I offended in my life?
Mother, what is that jingling in your pocket?
Even if it's only small change, please give me some.
I'll use it to have a coffin made of marble,
With moons carved into all four corners.

                +++

Mother, what have you got in your apron?
                          Édesanyám, mi van a kötényèben?
Red apples. Give me one.
I don't get to eat your apples now
Because I'm wearing the uniform of the Romanian army.
I don't ever get to eat your bread either,
Because I'm carrying the weapon of the Romanian army.

If I go out to the cemetery hill
I'll throw myself on my Father's grave.
Dear Father, please get up from your grave,
Your one and only son has become a soldier.

                +++

Transylvania is fenced round
                          Erdély be vagyom keritve…
But still I shall leave it
As I'll leave this beautiful girl
For whom my heart will ache for ever.

Mother, my dear old mother,
My dear nursing mother,
I was your last born
But still you let me be taken for a soldier.

The cemetery gates
Have been open for ever.

They'll carry me through them
And put me into that black grave.

On both sides of my grave
They'll plant roses.
The best girls of Köröstö
Will plant them there weeping.

+++

I would like to be a tree in the forest
                      De szeretnék az erdóben fa lenni…
The one called oak tree
Because the oak burns with a blue flame, without smoke,
My heart is never without sorrow.

Come October the soldiers get out of the army
Every mother waits for her son to come home
But my mother isn't waiting for me
Because she knows I already lie in my grave.

I'm resting, mother, I'm resting in Romania,
Come to me in black mourning clothes
You'll find my grave at the foot of a high mountain
Dear mother you can cry yourself to nothing.

+++

River Rákos, where have you gone?
                      Rákos, Rákos, hová lettél…
You have lost your good name.
After us the Hungarian language
Will be as rare as a white raven.

They are sounding the trumpet in battle,
Like eagles they fly to the fight,
My heart hurts as I see this.
Crying, I plow my homeland.

Little brown village girl,
Don't draw water from the Rákos,

Its waters run over Hungarian bones,
And its taste is salty from tears.

+++

I pray to my dear Lord
                      Arra kérem as én jó Istenement…
To heal my poor heart
To heal my poor heart
For it will soon die of sorrow.
But my heart aches and cannot be cured,
And for whom I cannot say.
My coffin lid will soon cure me,
The earth crashing onto it like thunder.

+++

Sorrow rises in my heart
I bend under the weight of dark skies
No more sorrow could I bear
Or my heart would split asunder.

My heart isn't made of stone
Nor as soft as wax
A stone heart will break if it cracks,
And a soft one will melt and flow like wax.

My mother told me long ago
But I never paid attention
Now I wish I could hear her voice again
As tears flow down my cheeks.

They flood my lap and wet the ground,
They soak my grieving bosom,
They pour down my cheeks
Like a torrent in the streets.

+++

Once my mother loved me so
                      Engem anyám úgy szeretett…

She put me in the cradle and rocked me.

I am full of sorrow
Like a pathetic apple tree
With no apples left on it, they lie underneath
But the branches still bend to the ground.

My mother cursed me
When she brought me into the world,
She cursed me saying,
Let the nation and the world be your home,
Be the companion of the gusting winds
And the leaves that fall on the ground.

+++

You'll see, I shall go away
                        Úgy elmegyek, neglássatók…
You'll never hear from me
If you ever have news of me
It'll be my death-notice.

If I were free I'd be
As a bird in the air
If I were so free
I'd be with you night and day

I am eaten by grief
As an old tree by worms
I am as bitter
as the twisted willow.

+++

Sorrow, sorrow, you are so heavy
                    S bánat, bánat, be nehéz vagy
You have lived in my heart for so long
                    Be rég hogy a szivemen vagy
And by the time these [sorrows] dissolve
                    Amig azok eloszolnat
All good things have passed away from me.
                    Tölem minden jók elmúlnak

Grief has eaten me up
As woodworm eats the tree in the forest
The tree killed by heat
My heart killed by sorrow.

My sun my sun my bright sun
      S napon, napom, fényes napom
My star shrouded in darkness
      Homályba borult csillagom
I have wondered all round the earth
      Összejártam a világot
And I have not found happiness.
      Nem találtam boldogságot

The fields must sprout green
If they are rained on every day
The woods must turn dark again
If a new wind blows on them every day.

The wheat must ripen
If the air is warm every day
The grape must soften
If dew settles on it every day.

My heart must break
If sorrow enters it every day,
My face must wither
If tears fall on it every day

And my hair must turn grey
For all the misery that has fallen on it.
My life full of trouble, my days full of sorrow.
I live under black mourning.

    +++

I went out onto the road to cry
And nobody came to comfort me.
Let all mothers have mercy
And not bear any more children.
My dear mother I am going away
Lift up all your worries from me.

O God, my daughter Magdó
Is this how I must say goodbye to you?
When Magdó was a little girl
She had a lovely black braid.

I will build a house
With no windows in it.
It will have no door and no window
And no one will come calling there.
I want to live in the soil
Then no one can shove me around any more.

+++

Stream of cold water
                           Pârâuts cu apă rece
God let it dry up
                           De-ar Dumnezu, sa sece…
Only the mud stayed
As I stay with my love
Only the dust stayed
Like the problems that stay with me.

Play, gypsy, when I tell you.
Don't hang the fiddle on the wall.

+++

Lord God, you who made me,
                           Fă-mă, Doamne, ce mi-i face
Change me into a big block of salt
                           Fă mă-un gruz mare de sare
For the ewes to lick
                           Să mă lingă oile
The girls to mourn for me
                           Să mă plângă fetele
For the rams to lick
                           Să mă lingă berbecii
The young men to mourn for me.
                           Să mă plângă feciorii

Little leaves and tiny flowers
                Frunzuliță, flori mărunte
Wind blowing in the mountains
                Suflă vântul peste munte
It brings great desire
                Și-mi aduce doruri multe
Blowing into my heart.
                Mie sufletul mi-l umple.
God, don't punish me too much,
                Doamne, nu mă bate tare
I also am your creation.
                Că-s ș i eu-al Dumitale.

+++

Don't leave me, God, to die, God,
                Na mik Devla kokola, o Devla le
Until I've lived my life out.
                Dzsi kaj me na cseljuvav
Where can I go, where can I stay
                kaj de dzsav, kaj te phirav
To live in the world?
                Ande lume te maj dzsav

God, don't punish me too much, God
                Na mar Devla kokola, o dela le
Until I've lived my life out
                Dzsi kaj me na cseljuvav
Where can I go, where can I stay
                kaj de dzsav, kaj te phirav
Ay, God, I am dying.
                Ajaj, Devla, szar merav.

+++

By the Danube there's a mill
                Dunaparton van egy malom
That grinds worries into little bits, hey-ho.
                Búbánatot őrenek azon, ejeha!
I have so many worries
I'll take them there to be ground, hey-ho.

+++

Worry and unease
      Supărarea si urîtu
Seem to be gathered by the wind.
      Gândesti ca te-aduna vântu
Unease and worry
      Uritu si supararea
Seem to be swept together by the stream.
      Gândesti ca t-aduna valea

+++

I'll go away, don't know the route
      Duce m'as, nu stiu drumu
Worry, teach it me.
      Învata-ma nacazu
I'll go away, don't know the path
      Duce m'as, nu stiu carare
Sorrow, teach it me.
      Învatsa-ma suparare

+++

May the world all around me
      Cata lume 'n partea mea
Burn till nothing is left.
      Ardear de n'ar ramanea

+++

Forest, don't let through the wind,
      Mai codrul'e nu da vânt
I am weary of the world.
      Mnie ura pa pamânt
Forest, don't let through the mist,
      Mai codrul'e nu de ceatsa
I am weary of life.
      Mnie ura pa viatsa

+++

> The moon shone between two trees
> > Két fa között a holdvilág
> I am like the camomile flower:
> > Olyan vagyok, mint a pipitérvirág
> Half red, half white, half of this and half of that –
> > Fele piros, fele fehér, fele más –
> I shall die of so much weeping.
> > Mëgöl engëm a sok köserü sírás

+++

These are some of the words sung,[23] which – whatever their particular origins – have become learned and repeated texts, verses swopped around from song to song, adopted and modified by particular persons, families, villages, but never absolutely finalised so as to be closed off from further development until they emigrated. They were and are sung, or parts and aberrations of them, on other occasions too: folkloric festivals,[24] school classrooms, recording studios, international concert halls…

The words set up a theatre of loss or despair cohered by wit and transgressive imagery. In performance the theatre rebounds to the community, as it is sung from among the congregation, facing the musicians, and the particularities it touches are known things: failures, rejections, falls into the impossible, which stand all round the singer as he/she sings, known in present company or personally owned by the singer – fatal possibilities, emotions inhering in the entire condition, communally recognised. It not addressed "out into the world" and no responsibility towards that entity is entertained. The minimal possession, the life itself, is thus absolutely fixed in the person whether it hurts or not.

The music houses the whole thing in a sense of relentless but dignified cosmic movement, as much so as the sun, seeds and ropes carved on the village gates. Such songs sung as unaccompanied solo in a domestic setting, which they may originally have been, would reach that ecstatic condition on a basis of intimacy, but with the string band in the social event the wholeness of the concept is immediately public. The sufferings and dangers it touches on cannot be set aside as aberrations because they are structured from the centre and owned imaginatively by all present.

The music itself guarantees the weight and moment of what is sung, new or refrain, especially in the fullness of ensemble which we suppose to be so rare in village music.[25] The fiddle (or two) carries the same tune as the singer but ornamented, virtuosic trills turns and other figurations moving constantly in and out of the melody line[26] (which the singer will also traditionally ornament in a less florid way, always keeping the principal moves of the tune very clear). The bass supports the whole thing steadily from below, emphasising the movement and also tending to follow the melody in its basic moves. So in a way all three: singer, fiddle and bass, are pursuing the same course, moving along to the same set of tones which they variously stress and elaborate but are fundamentally bound to. The chordal violas in the middle flesh out the whole thing, realising and enriching the harmonies set from the bass, re-emphasising the movement and forming an almost orchestral fullness of tone – the conservatoire ear thinks of a viol consort, though the harmony is at once simpler and more hazardous[27] and the texture more baroque than polyphonic.

The fullness of history stands in the viola chords[28] over which the bird-song fiddle, always fluttering round the notes of the song, is like a soul trying to escape. A figure of loss and failure sings in its own central clearing, and a court fills the space round it with promise of justice, while a kind of nonsense, a kind of cynicism, an out-of-tune bass, runs after the entire procession shouting 'Wait for me!'. A peasant, a work-destroyed body, commands the entire cosmic diagram, and sits outside it weeping.

No one person creates this possibility, though the validity of the realisation rests precariously with the individuals concerned.

It is difficult to speculate now on what it was like when and if the singers really 'sang their own fates'. That is, what exactly was the nature of the license operative on the tired and dizzy border of the festival space, what it allowed people to 'say' in their singing, and how we may presume it to have been an accepted and renewing creative process, since its terms passed into the artistic continuum. Henry Stahl's book has examples of 'primitive' village courts or fora in Romania, not structured from outside, in which every single member of the community was free to state their case and expected to. [29]

But must it not have been a courageous thing, to undertake this performance in its authentic personalised fullness? There where you are known, is it not to lay your life on the mat for what it's worth? – as they do in the improvised funeral laments, declare their final terms against the dead mother in front of everyone: lament, adore, but also confess and blame. And not only in the words. The inflexions of the dawn-song music by singer or violinist are an account drawn against fate. Extension and refinement of a form going back centuries create the theatre in which this summation is possible: the solo moment crosses the historical total and resolves into distinction. And of course it is performed without prior 'artistic training' (though not without study and practice) – the recognition of the form throws it open to anyone, what you mainly need is to be there. I have heard the grating, tobacco-scarred voices of old men soaring through these songs as an entirely proper and successful act, because they have the right.

Like the village manners and traditional generosity and hospitality of the region it is a function of the structure, while at any instant that structure is maintained or denied by individual acts. The protection offered by structure is that one failure does not destroy a continuity which can only be seriously threatened from outside. As in other creative acts, the performers know that they participate in this trust through the techniques of their crafts. The singers of Transylvanian dawn songs know without any doubt how they are singing themselves through the self into the borders of the conditions.

The conditions are abrupt. The rules of toil and attachment permit no duplicity in gender formation or the commitment to succession, though there is plenty of leisure and plenty of choice. Things must be as they appear to be or the whole thing would fall apart. Subjection to man or nature is assumed to be a necessity of survival on the spot, greatly resented if it is further inflicted from outside, as by the state. So there is a fatalism which openly exhibits its melancholy within the festive cycle on such occasions as the wedding transfer and the greatly extenuated periodicity of mourning. But the dawn song is unique as the expression of the diurnal power of this melancholy, where it actually strengthens continuity by contemplating the in-built negation, and gladdens the heart by confirming a participation in earthly and eternal conditions of uncertainty, in a unification of exceptionality and commonalty. The rest follows: how by seeing to the depths of the conditions within a musical construct representing the universe there is a liberation.

Which isn't just theirs, it is also anyone's – it is ours as much as any 500-year-old painting in Venice or product of the 16th century London theatre is ours. You can't build a conceptual wall round a 'community' and forbid 'outsiders' to listen; if there were such a thing the music would never have come into existence. But it won't be ours if we don't accept its open evidence as our purpose too, as of any 'art' – to decorate existence in its local colours, and make of the earthly condition a bright regalia on the shoulders of the labourer, something to say, 'You are not such a poor thing'. In this way success offers itself to misfortune, declaring both to belong within the same necessity.[30] And in this way you escape from success and from where you are and from necessity, into a sheltering enclosure, the only true clearing or break in harm, a figure of the world as it truly and secretly is.

Notes

[1] Gypsies have been a musician caste of Transylvania for a century or two, working originally for the gentry as well as the villagers [see Appendix 4B, pp.99–121]. At village ceremonies the function of the gypsy band-leader can also extend to that of master of ceremonies, presiding over the proceedings to make sure that they are conducted in accordance with custom. But it is not their music or their custom: they are employed to furnish and assure it. This has not prevented the music from being sold as 'gypsy music' on the rare occasions when it features in the so-called 'world music' market.

This at any rate is the basic situation. There is of course a gypsy contribution to the creation of the music since they are its bearers, which seems to be a matter more of style and delivery than substance, and will be most evident in the music played for the gypsy communities. But basically the peasants employed the gypsy bands as purveyors of their, the peasants', own music, and it is said that in certain zones, notably the areas of eastern and southern Romania where the gypsy 'tarafs' operate, the customers kept a strict guard over the music to make sure the bands did not 'gypsify' it. As that grip has relaxed recently the more successful tarafs have tended to stop performing the extended ballads and to have generally moved their music towards the București/Budapest gypsy 'restaurant' style of virtuoso playing, notably the exported artificial group Taraf de Haidouks. On the other hand the comparatively new freedom of a band such as Szászcsávás to play whatever it wants on CDs and to foreign audiences has brought forth an increasing quantity of 'gypsy' pieces which they never used to play for Hungarian or Romanian patrons, but only 'for ourselves'. [All this is further explored in 'The Last Gypsy', pp.166–169.]

The only people locally to treat the gypsies as an ethnicity are their enemies. There are two distinct classes. "Gypsy" translates the local terms țigan / cigány, basically meaning all such, but the gypsies themselves distinguish between these and "rom". "Rom" are a lower class of labouring or wandering people whereas "gypsies" are better off and more independent by means of trade. The musicians are all of this latter category, and they would not want to be called "rom". The two classes merge in practical terms: out-of-work musicians have to take the meanest of jobs such as mud-brick making or have no income, but they do not thereby become "rom" even temporarily, as they are distinguished by lineage as well as occupation. I use both words without upper-case initial – "rom" translates as "people".

[2] I use the present tense throughout this essay for practices which do probably continue in some places in more-or-less modified form, though the music and lyrics later referred to are kept alive in a variety of ways in both countryside and town. Even in the most isolated and resistant zones such as Maramureș, I don't think a wedding now ever lasts any longer than a day and a night, and while the

customary village music is played for the extra-ecclesiastical ceremonial parts of the wedding, the all-night feast and dance is more likely to have a modernised and amplified version (sometimes played by the same musicians) with hired singers. [On duration of events see also additional note I.]

[3] Most of this documentation is from CD booklets reflecting recent research in Hungarian but with an increasing quantity of translated articles. The subject is not treated by the old folklorists, nor by ethnomusicologists such as Bartók who were mainly interested in the ethnic implications of the melodic lines, and very little in the occasions. There is a growing body of research from younger Hungarian and Romanian ethnomusicologists (who are not normally on speaking terms with each other), some of it translated into French, German and English.

[4] or rather the gate, itself a richly decorated cultural artefact which would become a significant backdrop to the song. Each 'house' is a smallholding entered through the door of a large gate into a yard. If we assume (as seems likely) that the traditions of wooden architecture and carved (formerly painted) decoration extant in Maramureş were at one time widespread across Transylvania, we can then further assume that the dawn-song singer at his gate stood before a representation of the ordered Universe, in the cosmic signs embellishing the uprights, tableaux and cross-beams of the gate: sun moon stars, the soul of man, the rope signifying continuity, and the grain of wheat, set in a formal harmony. This back-drop is particularly significant in relation to the projection of the dawn-song text which, as we shall see, is a theatre of the local, and the specific, at the extremes of possibility.

[5] I have seen a rough-and-ready version of this form in practice involving a group of half a dozen men singing together (Kalotazsentkirály (Sancraiu) 2001). The drunken raucousness of the renditions was reminiscent of the worst effects of English village singing after it was banished to pubs. It is doubtful that any other version still survives, though the individualised songs on the recording from Szászfenes suggest it might. I don't know why there are these two distinct definition of the occasion of the dawn song, especially as I find them both in the CD notes of one of the principal Budapest exponents of this music, the Ökrös Ensemble. Their CD 'Blues at Dawn' is a finely staged compressed reconstruction of a dawn-song session lasting one hour, using both village and professional singers. Dawn songs seem in fact to be more often sung by women than by men in the available recordings.

[6] Transylvania was briefly an independent princedom within the Ottoman Empire in the 17th century, and has since been contested between Romania and Hungary incessantly, being awarded to Romania after the 1914–18 war and

again after the 1939–45 war, by way of punishing Hungary for being on the wrong side (notwithstanding that Romania had switched sides in 1944 after participating under German pressure in the Nazi mass murders of Jews and Gypsies). The population is mixed Romanian and Hungarian, fairly equally until the balance was deliberately tipped in favour of Romanians by enforced population movements imposed by 20th century nationalist regimes. There is also a smaller population of gypsies, one of the largest in Europe.

[7] The details in this paragraph probably only fully apply now to certain valleys of the area known as 'the historical Maramureş', a mountain-ringed enclave in the far north, where domestic wooden architecture, for instance, is still in use in many villages. But most of Transylvania, including Kalotaszeg, the home of the dawn song, only falls short of this conservation by degree, and generally retains strip cultivation with its associated land tenure system, horse transport, and professional transhumance. Or simply retains poverty. But there are also areas where, although the collective farm has been abolished, its structure remains. Romania's application to enter the European Economic Community depended to some extent on the eradication or at least containment of traditional agricultural practices which hinder the progress of capital. The results of entry at a local level have yet to be clearly seen. This 'peasant' structure is starkly absent from the neighbouring parts of Ukraine which were one territory with Maramureş before the 1918 division.

Style is divided into 'peasant' and 'rural'. In dress for instance, a home-made elaborate 'traditional' style which probably replaced plain peasant gear in the mid 19th century (bright earth colours, heavy ornament, strapped leggings, fulled woollen jackets, flounced skirts, etc.) is reserved in most places for special occasions, and everyday wear is a duller factory-produced ensemble (thin-rimmed hats, headscarves, black or flowered flounced skirts, white shirts black trousers etc.) which nevertheless clearly marks the person as a villager.

[8] Or more often now in the village hall, with amplification. This building was introduced during Communism and is often called the House of Culture. Its use in weddings seems to make no significant difference to the course of events, and only the final and longest section of the wedding, the feast and dancing following the church ceremony, is regularly removed from the family house. It should be realised that the dancing and singing with a 3- to 5-piece string band normally took place in the principal chamber of a farmhouse, something like 10 metres square and able to hold about thirty people. The acoustic impact of the band was therefore unmitigated by any distancing, and good modern amplification, with close mike for recording, actually gives a better sonic picture of the occasion than does transfer to an unamplified stage.

When not taking place in the house, the music would be outdoors in the yard, with or without awning, and regular Sunday afternoon dancing took place in an open space in the village. The acoustics here would of course be very different, but the very low ambient noise level (by 'western standards') would facilitate clarity, especially during the night. In many of the photographs I have seen of outdoor events the dancers seem to keep close to the musicians, but in an atmosphere untainted by constant air traffic or passing lorries this is not really necessary, and photographs or films of Sunday dancing before 1980 show (for instance) a big circle of about 50 dancers with a three-piece string band in the centre...

[9] The firmest aural evidence of the reality of the dawn song itself is given on the CD of Pici Aladár's band (first in the series Új Pátria, Fonó 1997) on which about six of them are performed instrumentally by a village band from Kalotaszeg, and on a cassette of part of the repertoire of the violinist Sándor Fodor known as 'Netti' (or 'Neti') issued for study purposes by Néptáncosok Szakmai Háza, Budapest, where he plays the melodies of 21 of them. In both cases they are identified only by the generic title, since the words for any particular performance would be variable or interchangeable, and Netti makes it clear in his interviews that he first learned them as textless melodies. Melodies and texts of all kinds generally have independent existences, and in principal a given text may be sung to any melody which fits the metrics and is otherwise adjudged suitable, as in just about all oral lyric traditions, early Renaissance courtly song, etc.

[10] No. 13 in the Új Pátria series.

[11] Extemporised singing still takes place in Transylvanian villages, and if in lyrical pieces it is restricted to surviving practices in small corners, it is much more widely practised in other forms, of which the commonest is *strigatura* (Hungarian *csuijogatás*), which is a rhythmic and pitched declamation (shouting-singing) of rhyming couplets against instrumental dance-music, still common on many occasions, especially weddings and calendar ceremonies, and carried out with great verve. The substance of these improvised and semi-improvised couplets stretches from political satire to erotic jokes, and is free to refer to present company.

A very different improvised singing takes place in connection with death and burial, when half-sung lamenting is performed during the wake and funeral rites and was at one time elaborately extended. It is extemporised in a formulaic framework, to a free-er melisma than the songs, in either rhymed couplets or a formal prose. It is even more likely than the dawn-song to be a personal statement, a final confession and declaration of terms vis-à-vis the deceased, either directly or dramatised as the deceased speaking. [See Kligman, especially Chapter III and Appendices C and D, and Nixon Appendix V which describes a rather de-formalised performance suggesting the decadence of the practice]. Instrumental versions of lament music exist as dance preludes, as they do of dawn songs.

It may seem rash to assume that anyone in a Transylvanian village was capable of these degrees of creativity, though it may be equally rash to assume that anyone was not. The evidence given by Kligmann for Maramureş is that certain persons were recognised to be particularly good at extemporised performances and were most frequently asked to sing, sometimes on behalf of the person who would normally sing. And yet the formalised lamenting at funerals was, at one time, a duty of the nearest women relatives which could not be omitted or delegated. There is a moving account at Kligmann pp.187-8 of a teenage granddaughter lamenting at a funeral for the first time, clumsily but correctly, supported by her mother.

Extemporised or re-composed singing occurs, of course, in many musical traditions, and notably among Romania's neighbours in the Balkans and Greece. It is normally thought to be a traditional feature of long standing, and often involves improvised 'duels' in sung poetry. And indeed improvised oral poetry exists all over the world. But in most cases the extemporisation is very much a performance, done by semi-professionals or experts, and does not carry the kind of personal declaration of fate implicit in dawn-song texts. But there are many instances of a non-professional and more intimate nature. One of these lies in the history of the Portuguese fado, an urban ex-rural and ex-maritime music which has been greatly refined and variegated through the 20th century. Here the professionals do perform extemporised displays, including duels, but there is a 'back-street' fado in Lisbon which cultivates directly extemporised personal declarations within the formal demands of the song. Sessions of this kind are described in Vernon's book on fado – he mentions for instance a man of 85 who came along and sang about the proximity of death. This kind of fado seems to have been introduced or reinvented quite recently, but is also said to be of rural origin. The connection between extemporised lyrical song and melancholy is widespread, to the extent of suggesting a fixed global association between the freely formed slow song and existential sorrow. [See Appendix 4A and additional note J, p.138]. The following quotations, referable to this and other aspects of the Transylvanian dawn song, are from Amhraín Sorcha Ní Ghuairim (1911–1976), a singer from Connemara, as printed in the booklet of her CD:

> When I was growing up, we had great evenings of singing in the house, and my mother and father, God be good to them, often sang, especially if they were sad or troubled in any way.
>
> [...] Everyone had their own version of this lullaby long ago. Like the lament, everyone put their own words to it, as it suited them.
>
> [...] When she heard that her brother had drowned, she did not shed a tear until she had composed this song.

At the old-style occasions in Transylvania the dancing itself is organised on similar principles: individually conceived and performed in direct communion with the musicians, with the participation of the company. Most of it is couple dancing and the couple nearest to the musicians (occupying the 'first position', known in Maramureș as 'under the neck of the violin') leads the dance, and the music played is 'their' music, which must modulate when another couple takes over that position. These 'personal' shifts in the music are mainly contained in the lead fiddler's ornamentation or descant, and rubato, but may involve the 'rhythm section' too. There is no question of the entire dance-floor moving together or in formation; couples do what they want to in accordance with the character of the particular dance. From time to time one of the male dancers may indulge a virtuosic solo performance involving leaping and calf-slapping (sometimes physically supported by his partner to make the more complicated leaps possible) and here he too will *turn to the music* and dance in constant eye-contact with the lead violinist, like the solo singer. See the article by Lucy Castle on the mutually creative relationship between musician and audience in Maramureș until recently, and Jacques Bouët's close analysis of 'elastic form' realised within the occasion, in the playing of Oaș violinists.

It is somewhat premature to my argument to note at this point that most of the 'court' dancing in Europe in the 16th and 17th centuries was individual dancing (solo or couple), performed as a demonstration of skill and participation in a refined ethos, by courtier and royalty, and to note that Louis XIV himself danced solo at the Versailles balls to the music of his own musicians, and was indeed particularly admired for his ability as a dancer. The only other kind of dancing at such events we would now call set dancing. [See further additional notes D/ii-v, pp.128–134.]

[12] Proprietorship of melodies is firmly documented wherever the music still has or had a true social function (including Transylvanian town society, see additional note R, pp.151-2) and it is one of the lead musician's most important tasks to know the tunes peculiar to his many customers and perform them at a moment's notice. Others may request them too, as long as the original proprietorship is acknowledged. The violinist Sándor Fodor 'Netti', in the interview on video, when asked 'So everyone has his own tune?' answers –

> 'Yes. At a wedding lots of people will ask me to play their tune, and if I don't know them, they'll say, "Don't have Sanyi here any more."' (Sanyi is the less used of his two nicknames). He adds later that during the Ceaușescu period the local 'milicista' (military police) superintendant was fairly lenient with him, because 'I knew his tune, and would play it for him.'

Such proprietorship was at one time widespread in local music-making, which includes the former music of courts and city salons, and is almost certainly reflected in English practice circa 1600, with surviving pieces bearing titles such as Lord Lumley's Paven, Lady Cary's Dumpe etcetera. Similar tune names are common in music from most of the European renaissance centres, not to mention Scottish and Irish rural music, though sometimes the names attached to tunes are those of the musicians who invented them. [see additional note R]. Many Romanian titles, especially from Maramureş, have the possessive 'lui' in the middle, followed by a name.

[13] Something resembling a dawn-song occasion in Hungary in 1929 is described by Walter Starkie, in *Raggle Taggle* p.20 thus: [After a particularly wild dance and at the end of the proceedings] 'The *Primás* immediately began to play a slow lament to bring the people back to normal life and lull the Dionysian god to sleep.' He goes on to compare this to what he wrongly calls 'the *peripetaia* or 'fall' of Greek drama', the final reconciling hymn, which became a feature of almost all subsequent tragedy. This seems to me an entirely just comparison in spite of the difference between a wild party and a tragic action, and typical of the flights unacademic scholars like Starkie could make before their hands were tied behind their backs by demands of academic propriety.

He goes on to characterise what happened as, 'Oedipus had disappeared down the grove of Death and the chorus sang their final hymn on the inscrutable ways of the gods.' I can't work out exactly what he is referring to, but the short chorus texts at the ends of both the Oedipus plays – 'Count no man happy till he dies' / 'All rests in the hands of a mighty power' – are well in tune with the dawn song, as an exit which drags fate with it into the diurnal future, more so indeed than the Shakespearean version, which tends to emphasise exceptionality. (See additional note Y on the rurality of Greek tragedy).

The occasion in which Starkie participated took place in 1929 in the Lake Balaton area of Hungary. There is no mention of any singing. Starkie, a professor at the University of Dublin, walked from here across Hungary and Transylvania to Fagaras in the summer of 1929 bearing a rucksack and violin, in a thoroughly Romantic quest for 'gypsy' music and experience, showing at least as much interest in flirtation as in music during his journey. He entirely missed the village music of Kalotaszeg and Mezőség, through which he passed, by sticking to major towns and main roads, and focusing on 'gypsy' experience, as a kind of latter-day Liszt. He never witnessed a formal village dance and failed to relate the music to dancing at all; the one flute-player he found was a beggar not a shepherd. But he did have the courage to go, sometimes at great risk, where his instincts directed him, and left some authentic accounts of music and life in Transylvanian towns.

[14] Recruitment, which took place annually in October, was a particularly painful subject to the Hungarian Transylvanians because on top of the loss of the young men of the village, some permanently, it was recruitment to a foreign army, first Austrian and then Romanian. (Previously it had been a particularly painful subject to the Romanians, conscripted into an Austro-Hungarian army). This

annual event became a form of ceremony, allied in some respects to the wedding ceremony, during which the young men of the village sang, while dancing in a circle, a medium-slow melancholy song, the recruitment song, which could be substituted for the dawn-song. The occasion was essentially a sung and danced farewell in the knowledge that there might be no return. An older genre is called 'Song for Accompanying the Soldiers', that is, sung to them, perhaps chorally, as they were marched out of the village. The 'Soldier's Song', which is basically a lament at a distance for the loss of home and love, was another viable substitute for the dawn-song.

The origin of the recruitment dance was a music introduced into the villages around 1800 by the Austro-Hungarian recruiting teams, who brought musicians with them for the purpose, which was intended to help entice young men into joining the army. It was called the *verbunkos* (from the German *werben*, to recruit, first documented 1793, Romanian *barbunc*) and was originally a lively dance in alternating slow and fast sections, danced in a round under the direction of a 'verbunkos corporal', with much leaping etc. As the recruits increasingly had no choice in the matter of being enticed, the music was taken over by the village using their own musicians, and transformed. It was slowed down to 4/4 time, becoming the quite melancholy round-dance, sung and danced by the departing conscripts before they left, referred to above. This continued until quite recently and there is one shown in the television film *Beyond the Forest*, 1991 (at Szék, the footage probably predating the film by several years). The *verbunkos* passed into the village dance repertoire as a men's dance both solo and/or group and in the process recovered some of its speed and variety. It ended up as a stately dance with individual episodes of virtuoso display, often used by the Hungarians to open a dance set, replacing the old graceful couple dance of courtly origin. *Verbunkos* also passed into the nationalist urban version of Hungarian music in the 19th century as a composed folk-form, alongside the csárdás.

The association of recruitment with song and dance seems to have been widespread in old Europe, described for instance in Tolstoy's sketch 'Singing in the Village' where, as elsewhere, the 'merrily' singing and dancing recruits form a procession analogous to the wedding procession. Tolstoy has one of the bystanders remark, 'Sorrow weeps, and sorrow sings!' [1909–10, Maude translation in *Three Days in the Village*, 1910.]

[15] As implied in footnote 11, p.56, the dawn song is distinct as a genre from the lament (in Hungarian *keserves*) though similar in tone and content. But the lament is slower and heavier and in its funeral use involves a lot of extemporised singing. The dawn song proceeds to a slow rocking rhythm in 4-time. In the archives of band repertoires from Kalotaszeg which the Hungarians have collected there is a common instrumental sequence which goes, with variants: Lament – dawn song – slow dance(s) – fast dance(s). It is difficult to accommodate the traditional role of the dawn song to this accelerando, which must represent

a license to extract both laments and dawn-songs from their true occasions and incorporate them into the dancing repertoire, as preludes or interludes, sung or not, between dances. [Further on the lament see additional notes O/i-iii, p.142-4 and Appendix 1, p.73.]

Compared with the Lament the dawn-song is danceable, or stands poised between listening music and dancing music. It is not impossible that behind the solo dawn-singer a number of couples may have at one time continued to dance the slowest and most elegant version of the Transylvanian couple dance, in which the man and the woman constantly come together and depart turning from each other, ending in courtesy but not embracing. This dance has also been interpreted as a display by the man of the beauty and grace of his partner, turning her constantly this way and that. [See additional note D/ii, p.128, on the possible derivation of dawn song from slow couple dance.]

[16] The tradition of the 'last waltz' strikes me as similar in tone, as a farewell which is a misty sign of both ultimate departure and the return to necessity, but rather more wistfully.

[17] or in another version, 'It lands on the edge of the forest', meaning in both cases that it belongs in neither one world nor the other.

[18] It is important to note concerning 'they won't be able to push me around any more', that this is not a society where people are generally pushed around, such as the feudal or industrial, but one in which people act independently within highly structured groups, pushed around mainly by necessity itself. The persona of this song occupies a social extremity which is a constant danger rather than a diurnal burden. Generally, of course, the gypsies had a great deal more to lament in their daily existence and were a great deal more pushed around, than the peasants they accompanied. See footnote 23, p.64, for comment on the selection and versions of quoted lyrics.

[19] 'I myself once played with 'Netti' for three days at a wedding, which resulted in cold pack treatments for inflamed hands because of the many hours of playing...' – László Kelemen, in the notes to the CD *Transylvanian Portraits* by Ökrös Ensemble. Also Béla Kása in *Transylvanian Musicians*, on meeting the viola player István Sándor (then aged 73): 'He was so exhausted after playing continuously for two days and a night that he could neither eat nor sleep. He just sat in the kitchen smoking.' According to Emily Gerard, in the 1880s a Romanian-Transylvanian wedding lasted seven days (but with breaks). (See additional notes I/i-ii, p.137.)

[20] It is thus too a very different thing from the 'blues' of the southern states of America, with which Budapest groups such as Ökrös and Muzsikás insist on

connecting it in their CD titles. In the 'world music' scene any melancholy song from anywhere on earth is liable to get labelled 'blues' in order to assist its sales, a form of globalization. I'm sure the word has been applied to Dowland but I don't know where.

The blues (as it was developed through the recording industry) was the song of the professional outsider, projecting a solo alienation which at its most serious claimed the unbearable as a theatrical asset. Compared with it the Transylvanian dawn song is hardly solo at all and certainly it is the song sung from *within* the community, and the *désolation* it finds there is thus inescapable. The enactment of individual gestures which transgress the decorum of the form is thus irrelevant, though there is plenty of space for creative movement within it. 'Race label' music is not a place to seek parallels to the dawn song, because it is a music derived principally from printed and recorded sources, and sung by roving professionals, increasingly roving towards a microphone. As in any popular music patronised by working people there is a tone of steady resignation in some of the songs of the older songsters, and in the southern States this probably relates to the lost music sung socially and chorally in slavery. There the song is of course held absolutely within the group, and the basic musical condition is choral. The fate of one is the fate of all.

The professional outsiders in Transylvania have been principally the gypsies. In a widespread, perhaps semi-global, tradition, gypsies (or other groups in similar conditions of social demotion) became the purveyors of instrumental music as a caste (cf. the genre epithet in Afghanistan for instrumentalists, dancers, barbers and suchlike, the 'Born of Others'). The other outsiders, the Jews, also purveyed instrumental music in Transylvania, when they were there. But in this non-industrial context personal misfortune is declared as a true fate, thus liable to all, rather than as a distinguishing mark either racial or social. Hungarians (vis-à-vis Romanians, and vice versa), are outsiders as a community, delegated to that position socially by national and international forces, from a former elevation, whereas Gypsies are outsiders from the start. The outsiderness of many dawn-songs and ballads in both Hungarian and Romanian is one which is integral to the entire society inhabited in its relationship to the world, the condition known as 'peasant'. Over 50 percent of the world's population still falls within this category. What they are outside is not society (they are it) but privileged and non-local forms of power. This condition is certainly present in the dawn-song repertoire without necessarily being definitive, for there is also the reach for a near-total human condition which mocks temporal attainment.

No one *except a gypsy* is going to start singing 'alas I am a poor gypsy.' That gypsies may have done precisely this on a dawn-song like occasion with appropriate music is a recent discovery, explored mainly in Section 5.

[21] This particular verse is popular and widely distributed, and has served several different functions including dawn song. The song as quoted can be heard on

several táncház CDs and sung by Erzsébet Dezsö of Magyarszovát village on the CD 'Magyarszovát – Búza' (Fonó 1997) (where it is labelled as a soldier's song), and on Ökrös' CD "Blues at Dawn" by Mrs János Simon from Kalotaszeg. The verse also occurs in outlaw songs and prisoner songs, usually as the second verse, after the situation has been established.

The tune to which this song is most often sung is also used for two other functions, with the same lyrics or others. There are love song versions, one of which opens with the two verses as quoted intact, followed by five further verses of rejected love –

O the road is long and wide
On which my sweetheart treads
Turn back from your long path, sweetheart,
Remember what you promised on Saturday night…

The last verse returns very much to the spirit of the first two but insists in its last line on the specifying function of the love lyric –

Mother, why did you bring me into this world?
Why didn't you throw me into the churning River Tisza?
The Tisza's water would have swept me to the icy Danube
And now my heart wouldn't ache for a young man.

It is as if the dawn-song might have been created by subtracting specifying factors from the love-song and others, producing in this case a text of stark elemental imagery which is an apotheosis of the genre. It is indeed a possibility that all dawn songs are transfers, adaptations or reductions of other types of song.

Édesangyám rózsafája is also liable to occur at a particular stage of the wedding ceremony, the 'farewell to the bride'. The traditional Transylvanian wedding, on which there is good documentation available in French and English (see especially Kligman and Cuisenier) is for most of the major participants the occasion for floods of tears, especially for the bride and her family and friends. The whole occasion is from the traditional bridal viewpoint close to a funeral (or a recruitment!) and the shouted and sung lyrics prior to the churching are close to lamentation, but for ironic and erotic sub-texts. It is all very seriously meant: the departure of the bride is recognised as a loss of youth and liberty, a removal from a known to an unknown (to a land without pity, see Appendix 2) which figure it as a form of death. The dawn song's link to this point of the wedding reveals its aspect of farewell, perhaps specifically a farewell to the artifice of festivity and return to the time structure of the continuing and practical world.

The music for the wedding processional, 'accompanying the bride', is frequently a rather plangent piece, moving somewhat quicker than the dawn-song and to a more determined rhythm, which can seem intimate to the lamentational tone of the bride's departure from home, notwithstanding that the occasion is basically a joyful procession. It also seems to be a tradition in many places for the fiddler to play this piece without ornamentation or variation: strict repetition many times over of a quite short piece in relentless machine-like movement (viz. especially track 8 of the Mociu Band's self-produced CD).

[22] This verse can occur without specification as a symbol of pure loss, but it can also occur as part of a wedding song indicating, again, the departure of the bride. The messenger-bird which never returns also occurs in outlaw songs and ballads, usually sent into the wilderness by the outlaw's mother or sweetheart.

[23] Most of the English versions are taken or adapted from lyrics given in CD, LP and cassette notes, some of which strive very hard to rhyme in English. I've tried to eliminate the resulting distortions by comparing different translations of the same lyrics where possible, by recourse to my own minimal understanding of Hungarian and Romanian, and sometimes just by the exercise of common-sense. The detail *poesis* is my own, worked in something like the spirit of Gennady Aidi's *Salute to Singing*, but unless something has gone wrong there should be no reason to suspect any poetical figuration in these texts to have come from anywhere but the originals. Where available the incipit is quoted in its original language, as are other lines in some cases. I'm grateful to George Gömöri for checking translations and Hungarian orthography.

Most of the texts come from songs specifically identified as *Hajnali* in the Hungarian repertoire, but to restrict the selection to those would be misleading since many kinds of song can be pressed into service for the purpose, and there is a great deal of trading of 'floating verses' from one song to another whatever their original genres. As well as unspecific slow songs from Kalotaszeg my selection includes parts and wholes of recruitment songs (which were particularly favoured for dawn song use), love songs, prison songs, a historical song, laments from Gyimes and lyrical and dance songs from Maramureş. Romanian and Rom songs which had no dawn song function are included to indicate the existence of traditions of melancholy song in those languages and suggest transfers across linguistic barriers. This contribution could have been greatly augmented by inclusion of texts from the Romanian *doina* repertoire, but as rhythmically free melismatic melancholy songs (or vocalisations) these are closer to lament than dawn song, though they too have undergone regularisation into strophic melancholy songs. The relationship between the *doină* and the dawn song remains uncertain to me. The italicised lines were shouted rather than sung, which could not happen in a dawn song and they come from dance songs, where terms from the repertoire of slow melancholy song can easily and to us surprisingly occur in an up-beat context. I have included some variant translations of the same Hungarian texts, to show implications of meaning as heard by native speakers, e.g. 'Én vagyok az, aki men jó', strictly 'I am such a one, who (is) not good' comes as 'I'm the one who is no good' but also 'I'm the sort who doesn't belong here'.

The pronoun Én = I is normally understood and so is emphasised when it is enunciated, forming an exceptionality, which justifies the variant. The union of exceptionality and commonality is one way of seeing the dawn song's particular force. It is fairly unlikely, though not impossible, that any of the texts given were extemporised or personally conceived for a particular performance, though those sung by actual villagers are at least likely to have changed in some details since they were last sung.

[24] Centralization of local and communal culture during the Communist regimes became spectacularised under Ceaușescu, with televised mass song-and-dance routines covering entire mountain-sides etcetera. When all that was cancelled, and collectivization with it, and family land rights restored, village culture moved into a limbo of hesitation which remains to this day, whereby most major rites subsist in a selective version hovering between former strict models and the 'modern' or metropolitan alternative which says that no observance of any kind is actually necessary, take-it-or-leave-it. In the north many calendar events have been converted to, or attached to, 'festivals' which remain local but in which the principal active agents are children, singing and dancing on small stages in the village centre (sometimes accompanied by intact village bands distorted by worst-quality amplification equipment). To an outsider this appears as spectacle, but these children are presenting what they do mainly to those who already know it, and rather than trading their local identity against a touristic currency, are confirming where they are under a shifted aegis. But this leaves something of a mystery: that the adult population who know these dances and these songs to heart, do not dance them and do not sing them, but sit and stand and watch while the children do it instead. And the singing is projected out to them with the music supporting it from behind, instead of being performed from within the community, facing the music. At least one front row of dark-suited officials is obligatory, who seem to act as a barrier between the people and the performance, and whose opening speeches are an intrusion from the national exterior which can delay the start for over an hour.

These festivals are direct and little-changed descendants of the Ceaușescuian rural spectaculars (the levels of participation and exclusion are about the same). This is particularly evident in a thing like the 'Prislop Hora', a mountain-top event on the border of Maramureș every August which attracts thousands and is the original of most village festivals, including those which have been converted from calendrical rituals of great antiquity. The speeches now praise the region and the nation without specific reference to state ideology. The music dance and costume are village-specific but standardised. It has all become 'folklore' and is vaunted as such, and so it is sharply displaced from where it is, made acutely aware of its own provinciality.

Lucy Castle-Hotea has suggested (in conversation) that the village people are increasingly ashamed of their music and dance as something which marks them as displaced from the modern world. This would apply less to the Hungarian Transylvanians, who have had the support of a youthful cultural movement in Hungary encouraging them to retain their inherited forms, whereas right through the 20th century Romanian peasant culture has generally been ignored in the cities or seen as a joke. But musician schoolteachers, among others, are determined to keep things alive, even if they cannot pass the arts on in the customary participatory and spontaneous ways. What this means will only be revealed as the children grow up.

[25] The use of instruments in the European villages in the 19th and 20th centuries has been much more affected, or determined, by the procedures of classical music than the singing has. The commonest instrument, the violin, reached the more northerly countries from Italy only by about 1700 and the largely diatonic music of its dance repertoire was a product of its classical credentials, variously folklorised. In many places it supplanted the bagpipe, as can still be heard in the dance music of Gyimes and Maramureş, but it normally did this by a blending of the demand for a familiar effect from the villages with "country dance" repertoire established in assembly rooms of the towns.

The English folk-music movement in the early 20th century focused on two distinct categories, not always on amicable terms: solo singing and dancing, the latter a completely separate musical repertoire using fiddle or concertina. There were plenty of other instruments on the premises, included basses, 'cellos, flutes, clarinets, bassoons, dulcimers, accordions, mouth-organs… only some of which were likely to have been used in dancing, though all of them except the fixed-reed instruments could have found a place in church galleries. But the genre 'folk-song' has remained separate from all uses of instruments, here and across Europe. Where they come together, in the accompaniment and arrangement of folk-songs, is most commonly in the urban or classical zones under the aegis of nationalism, as very much happened in Scotland in the 18th century (see Johnson 1972) and in Hungary in connection with the end of the Austro-Hungarian Empire. Folk-song melodies were then collected adapted and invented, and fitted out with full classical harmony, with the inevitable struggle to fit diatonic harmony to non-diatonic melodies which both Haydn's Scottish arrangements and many of the Transylvanian band versions show.

A lyrical song is not going to be harmonised and accompanied if it is sung in private; such enhancement is for a social occasion, whether casual or ceremonial. In places like Romania and Georgia this manifestly took place in a highly developed way producing a strong tradition of harmonised singing by choir or accompanying ensemble, but it seems to be absent from the British traditions. This may to some extent be the result of collectors' preferences back-fed to the countryside, for there are tantalizing traces of evidence for it, along with unanswered questions. There is occasional suggestive evidence from tune-books, such as the one John Clare compiled when he hoped to earn a living as a fiddler. This contains mostly dances but quite a lot of songs, of which the majority are dance-songs but some are not. His transcription of 'Black Eyed Susan' seems to show the violin playing an 8-bar prelude, continuing to play through the song, and repeating the prelude as a coda. The unanswered question is whether somebody would have sung at the same time. Similarly the repertoires of Irish fiddlers and pipers contain many slow airs, all titled as songs and in many cases with the full lyrics known. Again the unanswered question is: when and why were these airs played on instruments, and did people sing to them, and if not why not? I think myself they were probably played as interludes between sets of dancing, but that doesn't answer the questions.

These instances represent monodic renditions of song melodies on instruments. The provision of harmony under the melodic line was not unknown and may have been more common than the evidence suggests. In English dance music there were probably sometimes improvised second and third harmony parts based on west gallery music, and this texture could have been used in accompanying lyrical songs. In north-east Scotland the fiddler used to play with a second violin 'contra' part. In both these cases the introduction of a harmony instrument (accordion family and piano respectively) may have taken over from something approaching a string-band sound. [These opinions *verbatim* from experts at the London Fiddle Conference 2006.] This would be quite distinct from the concert performance of national airs with classical ensemble, piano etc., though possibly influenced by it.

Compared with most European countries we know almost nothing about how music was created socially in England, or even so much as what went on at a village wedding. One reason for this may be the collectors' almost exclusive interest in solo singing, but even their interest in dancing was largely divorced from any interest in the social occasions of dancing. Another reason seems to have been the English gentry's and clergy's inability to keep their noses out of things, and, when they get their noses in, their predilection for putting a stop to things – complaints to the Bishop about erotic songs being sung at weddings, village girls being allowed to witness animals mating etc. Research in the better documented area of parish church music has revealed a great variety of instrumental and choral activity, albeit rather late in the tradition and under direct influence from urban centres. [See further additional note M, p.142].

It is a striking fact that for most of Central and Eastern Europe a large proportion of surviving or preserved rural song is categorised as specifically for use during the protracted wedding ceremonies (whether also performed at other times or not) – collections issued during the Communist-Nationalist periods from Serbia and to a lesser extent Bulgaria seem to consist mostly of wedding songs, and many of the working village musicians were and still are categorised as "wedding bands", probably because whatever else they did the cash available from weddings far exceeded any other source of income. But the wedding is also the principal focus of communal identity and continuity in what I usually refer to as the "real" village. I do not think I have seen a single item of English folk music, song or instrumental, which has been categorised as in any way associated with the wedding procedures of the English village, whatever they were.

Eugen Weber's book gives, in chapter 26, comparable information from France (where enclosure took place nearly a century later), emphasising the ubiquity of singing in French peasant society and its integral association with work. Instrumental music was only flute, bagpipe and hurdy-gurdy, until the intervention of urban-style bands playing fashionable dances in the middle of the 19th century. These were professionals (though not gypsies) and rather than enhancing the existing music of the villages introduced an entirely new music. Village bands in England, which accompanied dancing and played in church, seem to have been amateurs, trained locally (like the church choirs) either by music masters or by each other, and their repertoire mainly ex-urban 'country dances'. The comparisons of England and France bring out not only the far greater involvement here of the town and its regimes, and the eagerness of the Protestant church and the gentry to participate in, and regulate, all social life, but also the absence of an aristocratic involvement in village music which might have acted as a conserving factor, or a manorial class more practically or congenially involved in the agrarian community. Or a structure outside the Anglo-Norman feudal heritage. Even into the mid-twentieth century (see Woodfill 1953) the 'peasant' class are assumed to have been unskilled in music and /or uninterested in it.

Another reason for our ignorance of instrumental music in England is the fact that in the early decades of the 20th century Anglo-American and German recording companies were willing to send recording engineers to the far reaches of Mongolia, the heart of sub-Saharan Africa, Easter Island or Patagonia (all this literally) to record the local music and sell it back on 78 rpm discs to the local population along with the gramophones, but never thought for a moment of sending anyone up the road to Chipping-in-the-Marsh to record what was going on there. This means that we know more about local musical activity in the 1930s in Trinidad than in Shropshire. Only continuing dance traditions do anything to bridge this gap, and to a far lesser extent surviving traditions of pub and traveller singing.

I would expect Transylvania to have been visited by producers of 78 rpm records in the 1920s and 1930s, when English and German recording teams were active in neighbouring countries to the east and south, including Hungary, but I have seen no evidence of it. There are Hungarian 78s of the 1920s–40s of the urban 'gypsy orchestras' which have quite strong rural and national elements in their music but remain distinct from village music, mainly in the qualities of vocal production. Even Romanian musicians in exile in U.S.A. do not seem to have got onto 78 rpm discs, though many from Poland, Ukraine and Slovakia did, as did East European Jewish musicians. For these periods we rely on early 'field recordings' (by Bartók, Kodály and others) which can be misleading, because their content was liable to pre-selection by the collector, in a way which the 3-minute shellac disc produced by a disinterested sound engineer was not.

But collectors' preferences can shrink the account anywhere at any time. Even in the mass of devoted collection done, mostly by Hungarians, in Transylvania, it is noticeable that the 'pure' string band is favoured above the intrusion of the accordion, though this has been common for some time (see additional note #Z, p.163) and the recent addition to the bands of clarinet, tarogato, saxophone, guitar, keyboard, drum-kit, etc., is fairly methodically ignored. Not all such additions are recent. There is a photograph in the booklet of the CD of József Lunka (Magyarpéterlaka in the Fekete Antal series), of him and three other musicians at some kind of celebration in 1938, one of whom is holding what looks like an alto flügelhorn. This would have been imported from the military band, as a number of other instruments may have been.

It must, however, be admitted that if, like Sharp and Bartók, what you are interested in is strictly 'folk music', solo singing is all you really need. Pretty-well all European fiddle-based dance music in 'folk' context, derives from classical music or at least was conceived within the technical range of classical music, and the Transylvanian string bands with their harmonising violas do not have to be considered as strictly folk music at all, but rather, since they do not use sheets of paper and this has certain stylistic results, as a folklorised form of classical music. This does not of course mean that the folk song remains a pure and uncontaminated rural inheritance, as it is commonly assumed to be. The heavily literary nature of the texts of many Irish songs might, for a start, suggest otherwise, crowded as they are with nymphs and cupids and classical gods. This is not the case with Transylvanian songs, but how and by whom such songs as the dawn songs were originally composed remains unknown, while on the evidence of structure and musical vocabulary it seems likely that they came into being at least within earshot of a classical milieu.

[26] The fact that there can be, and often are, two violins performing in near-unison means that the elaborate and high-speed ornamentation is not normally extemporised but learned. In fact a lead fiddle had to learn by heart not only a large repertoire of tunes with their arrangements, but also the ornamentation given to each tune, of which there might be several different versions specific to the various villages and groups regularly serviced. But the second fiddle of the Szászcsávás band reported that on certain special numbers he had to 'stay back' to leave the lead fiddle free, presumably for a more spontaneous handling of the melody. This referred to the *doină* and table songs in general, thus should apply to the dawn song. There is also a great deal of extemporisation by the lead fiddle during long engagements, when individual dances can last half an hour or more; this can be heard well on the CD of Icsán's band from Szék in 1972, and a tape of Netti's band at work at a village dance in 1988. Unfortunately the now ubiquitous amplification is eroding this faculty since it precludes the rapport between fiddler and dancer/listener which empowers variation.

[27] The harmonic rationale of Transylvanian string bands is, as stated, melody-based, meaning that the bass line tends to follow the melody at the unison, and first-position major chords are built on the principal melodic notes or their closest relatives. This procedure is of course tempered towards classical European procedure, especially at cadences and increasingly in town-influenced music of a newer stratum, but usually remains noticeable, spiced by a very skilful use of seventh-notes in transient chords. The harmonic concept is simple but it works, and it was probably common at one time all over Europe in the unwritten darkness behind court and concert music. It could be inferred as a development from faux-bourdon on the one hand, and/or near-eastern parallel top-and-bottom procedures on the other, but it may also have descended as the memorisable form of a more complicated harmonic system in the courts and salons. It is present in American nonconformist congregational music of the 19th century, but not in the equivalent English reformed parish church music. Even Schubert used it in moments of his songs, perhaps as a *Volkslied* element, as at the end of *Gondelfahrer* (D808). The 'false relation' of moving a major chord up or down a third, as here, is a typical signal that this system is in operation. But the closest harmonic practice I know to the Transylvanian bands, and it is sometimes very close, is the secular music of the north Italian courts circa 1500, known as *frottole* [see Appendix 4A, p.92].

The most common tonal structure in the fully harmonised pieces such as dawn songs is a bitonality by which a piece shifts between the key of the major tonic (e.g. C) and the relative minor (e.g. A) without being definitively placed in either. This is presumably caused by the application of triadic harmony to a modal melody of the kind known as 'aeolian'. The final cadence cannot be said to define the tonality of such pieces; in fact it is quite common for most of a melody to be harmonised in the major, shifting to the relative minor (often with sharpened third) only at the final cadence of a section. This represents a very effective solution to a dilemma in the harmonisation of folk melodies which is widespread; the Scottish 18th century faced exactly the same difficulty in harmonising 'Scots' tunes and never found quite the right answer.

The bass was probably the last instrument to join the string bands, replacing the 'cello which is still used in some places, and which plays within and reinforces the harmony whereas the bass hovers outside or on the edge of the harmony, sometimes sounding 'out of tune' because of this. It is explained that the bass's principal function is to supply rhythm for the dancers, hence a certain disregard for pitch, but I personally find the resulting souring of the texture a problem and am not satisfied that the bass was ever entirely successfully introduced. Certainly the leaders of the best-known and exported bands, including those which established a substantial reputation over an extended local area, have all made sure that the bass is in tune. The string band with 'cello which still survived recently enough to be recorded in several places results in a much more consort-like texture.

Incidentally, Bartók was active in all these regions in the 1930s but took little interest in the 'gypsy' string bands, which he viewed as a music largely determined by intrusive urban factors, and thus ethnically insignificant, since he was at that time mainly concerned to identify the stratification of Hungarian music and insisted quite rightly (as did Cecil Sharp) that the older or original music must be unaccompanied singing. The string bands have indeed been formed not only through the court music of the Transylvanian princes or whatever, but through two or three centuries of urban café entertainment, and classical music. The various versions of the Rákóczi March they play include one which is unmistakably Berlioz's, albeit simplified. The Szászcsávás band now includes two of Brahms' *Hungarian Dances* in its repertoire. It is never very far to a town in Transylvania and some of the villages most renowned for the survival of this music (such as Méra, Soporul de Câmpie, Bonchida, Szék) are within thirty kilometres of the major city of Cluj. The village musicians have often known what was being played in the towns, including the concert halls, and have sometimes doubled as restaurant or theatre players. The history and social spread of the music are discussed in Appendix 4B (p.97) and see additional note K/i, p.139, on the sophisticated connections of Kalotaszeg music in particular.

[28] The first violin, the *primás*, is in every obvious way the leader of these bands, and is also usually their manager, agent, and coach, and may in addition be an authority on the correct traditional ordering of the events at which they are employed. Yet it is sometimes said that the first viola or 'kontra' player, whose function is entirely harmonic and rhythmic, in some way 'leads' the music. This is mainly because he sets and maintains the exact pace of each number for the dancing, but it may also represent a recognition of the fact that the role of the violas is what really distinguishes this music, and is also what marks it, however 'sophisticated' it gets in harmony or figuration, as distinct from the urban restaurant bands. In fact the viola is a 20th century innovation, replacing a second-violin with flattened bridge, and before that a normal second-violin double-stopping, which is what is still used in string bands within the same tradition in neighbouring parts of the Carpathians (the town music uses an accompanying second violin playing quite normally). Some of the most attractive playing I have heard has come from bands reduced to violin and kontra only. The consort-like sonority produced by violin viola and 'cello may or may not relate to the music's ancestry in the music of the Transylvanian Princes via the Hungarian rural gentry.

[29] This is of course in 'Romanian' Romania whereas the dawn-song zone is 'Hungarian' Transylvania. There are occasionally other instances (compare Appendix 2, p.82) where these distinct and even inimical territories become one. I prefer not to get involved in the bitter internecine controversies as to what exactly is Romanian, Hungarian, Transylvanian etc., though with this music it is impor-

tant to try to define what is 'gypsy' and what is not. Racial and national forces are undoubtedly powerful factors of the music, but the most interesting and creative performance and listening goes on not outside but in the interstices *between* these constructed categories. 'Village communism' in one form or another is anyway a pan-European phenomenon in peasant culture (except English).

[30] I have avoided the whole business of Transylvanian witchcraft, werewolves, vampires, and so forth as largely a product of Bram Stoker and the American film industry, and anyway no more integral to Transylvania than any other part of the Balkans and many other places, and now hardly extant at all. But there is a lesson (derived from the book by Harry A. Senn) bearing on my final moral, which is that in places such as Romania and North Africa, places untouched by the Inquisition, mediaeval witchcraft was defined not as a demonic intervention in the world, but as an accident of fate, a product of 'misfortune', something that happened to people who could not for whatever reason function well where they found themselves, and thus in its way a necessary defining factor of the total social and cultural condition. This didn't stop it being opposed with violence; it threatened communal thriving with a substitutional alienation and so had to be suppressed. But it was understood as the devolved condition of normality and when science revealed vampire and other such belief as a misunderstanding of physics it disappeared without a pang. It left no experimental poets in its wake.

Further on sociality and music, see additional note #Z, p.163.

Appendix One: The Gyimes Laments[a]

Gyimes (in Romanian, Ghimeș) is one of several edge-zones to Transylvania to the east and north, with distinctive instrumental musical cultures, all involving drone accompaniments. It is a small area of pastoralists known as Csángós whose language is a dialect of Hungarian, though all are now either bilingual or speak Romanian only. They live in high valleys of the mountains on the eastern edge of the country but also further east in Moldavia. Their status is contested. The Hungarians claim them as kin, asserting that their culture retains archaic central-Asian elements from the Magyar migrations. The Romanians, or some of them, claim that they are really Romanian and were taught to speak Hungarian by Franciscan missionaries in the 13th century. Unprejudiced musicologists say that their music and dance dialect both have more in common with Romanian music and dance to the east than with Hungarian music, but the words they sing clearly belong to Hungarian Transylvanian culture. Nationalists have moved into the area from Hungary and are trying to take control of its culture, organising youth groups, managing the village musicians, attempting to stop the villagers from speaking Romanian. On the eastern edge of this zone, in the centre of Romania, they have set up notices saying, 'Welcome to Hungary'.

The instrumental music here is mainly a matter of virtuosic ornamental violin playing, though flutes are also important, accompanied by a thing called a 'gardon' which looks like a crude 'cello but is a rhythm and drone instrument, played by plucking the four open strings, which are officially all tuned to D, and tapping them with a wooden stick. The gardon player is often the wife of the violinist and they are commonly gypsies. The violin is usually played in a bravura style with double-stopping of open fifths at phrase endings, and chordal flourishes, and there is an extra resonating string running under the fingerboard which enriches the tone and emphasises the drone.[1]

Romanians in an area not far away to the north-west (Bicaz) have a quite similar but distinct music using a version of the gardon, which is difficult to account for if, as is claimed, the Gyimes music represents the survival of a Magyar/Székely music once practised all over the big Székely area known to the Hungarians as Csík, whence the Csángós moved up into the mountain pasture zones in the 18th century. In fact the most evident features of Ghymes music are not demographic but instrumental, it being the closest in the whole country to an earlier bagpipe music.

---

[a] Notes to this Appendix may be found beginning on p.80

Most Gyimes instrumental music is for dancing, and most singing remains domestic, but there is a genre of laments (*keserves*) with a similar function to the dawn song since they are most likely to be played at the end of a dance event such as a wedding, thus often at dawn, to mark the end of the proceedings, and it seems that they may also be used as preludes to dance sequences. They are songs, but learned basically by the musician as melodies, some with text and some without, or to which different texts and verses may be applied, all within the ambience of regret and melancholy which pervades the dawn song genre. In fact verses sung in Kalotaszeg and the rest of the Hungarian culture-zone in dawn songs or other categories, recur abundantly in these laments, sometimes in identical textual formulations.

The Gyimes laments may be connected to particular local persons, who have the right to command them and to demand particular texts for them. But it is the violinist who does the singing, while playing, and for this he cultivates a vocabulary of lyrics, formulae, and movable verses. Possibly the proprietors of these songs at one time performed them, and created at least some of the text however much else was borrowed or quoted. But this would have to have been before the professional violinist intervened in the process. It would indeed be difficult for anyone not well versed to sing-along to this music, for it retains telling features of a true lament, especially quasi-improvisational flexibility of rhythm and phrase-length, *parlando* delivery, a general sense of suspended movement. It is very much like an unmeasured free singing which the violinist duplicates on the instrument with ornaments and flourishes. For a practised performer immersed in the idiom it would certainly be possible to perform thus in close collaboration with the violinist, though I have seen no mention of this still taking place – the professional musician seems to have displaced the village singer completely. The gardon is not played during laments in Gyimes[2], and the music is clearly not for dancing. Fiddlers were until quite recently hired to perform this same lament music at funerals as a farewell to the dead, accompanying the lamenting of the family, or replacing it. I have heard one 2-minute recording of Gyimes funeral lamenting which is clearly being done by close relatives of the deceased but accompanied by at least two violins (*Hungarian and Gypsy Music and Customs*, formerly available as a Folktrax CD, issued before 1964)[3]. For reasons of their own the (Catholic) priesthood have declared the music unsuitable for funeral use and banned it.

The musical material is varied, some of it archaic, some of it transferred from elsewhere with traces of sophisticated harmonic thinking, and includes dance tunes, but wherever it comes from it is all transformed into the Gyimes lament with its characteristic suspended rhythm and melodic meandering, violin trills and flourishes running alongside. The music is anchored in the 'minor third' tonality: usually given at the start as a violin flourish and never seriously departed from. In the absence of the drone accompaniment the drone-note is constantly iterated, the plangent sense of the fundamental key-note never escaped from. The first phrase of the melody, usually short, may descend, sometimes precipitately, towards it, or hover uncertainly on the third- to fifth-notes zone, then settle down to the fundamental, and succeeding phrases will venture further, with suggestion of modulation to a 'major' or 'dominant' tonality, always undermined by constant back-referral to the minor-third tonic, to which of course it returns. (There is a slight similarity here to Indian 'alap' procedures.) Dawn-song melodies on the other hand tend to rest on the major-third tonic (i.e. on C rather than A in piano white-notes); and even when they do end on the minor-third tonic this tonality is not emphasised throughout but rather turned to in the ending phrase, sometimes quite unexpectedly. The string-band harmonisation favours major chords, indeed sometimes knows no other, so that even when the melody falls to the minor third keynote at the end the chord is likely to get a sharpened third. The sustaining (through pace, phrase, emphasis etc.) of sad tone through a dominantly major tonality is one of the features of dawn-song, though not definitive.[4]

Only one recording has been issued which demonstrates what the Gyimes lament is. This is of the blind violinist János Zerkula from Gyimesközéplok (with the occasional intervention of his wife Regina Fikó), who was one of the two acknowledged senior violin masters of Gyimes music, recorded in Budapest in July and October 2000 and issued by Fonó as no. 16 in the *Új Pátria* series. Here we can witness Zerkula putting laments together textually with a range of verses from all over the saddened aspects of Hungarian-Transylvanian song and possibly beyond. Very few seem to be local or unique and there is a sense of a large ethnic or geographical pool of lament available to this local intensity.

As with dawn songs, while remaining 'laments' the songs have texts which derive from different genres which are sometimes intact, sometimes completely fragmented, sometimes proceeding within their own genre and then switching to a verse from somewhere else. Within Zerkula's performance there are complete songs of forlorn love, prison songs, soldiers' or recruiting songs, and others, not to mention a completely inappropriate bucolic song, and there are formulae or episodes of these genres mixed in with other material or with each other. There is a sense that the formulae might be improvised into the substance of each lament, but there is also a sense that these are the words he always sings, give or take this and that, to a given tune, especially when Regina joins in. There is never a sense of randomness: couplets and quatrains spring up from all over the place and even recur from one lament to another, but the resulting poem is always at least coherent and sufficient. As in most songs in oral tradition, the lacunae formed by formulaic composition are transcended by acts of recognition which destabilise the occasion and refer it to a larger and so more strongly felt condition.

Sometimes the textual condition is the same unrationalised, untypified, totalised fatality which marks the Kalotaszeg dawn-song at its most complete, using the same words –

> Sorrow, sorrow, how heavy you are,
> > Bánát, bánát, de nehéz bánát
> How long you have been in my heart
> > Be rég, hogy a szívemen vagy
>
> Tell me, sorrow, where can I go
> > Mondd meg, bú, meere menjek el
> In order to leave you behind?
> > Hogy töled maradjak én el.
>
> Everywhere I go to live,
> I live with sorrow.
>
> God why have you struck me
> Even if I deserved it?
>
> Why have you struck me more than another
> When I am no more to blame?
>
> Street, street of sorrow,
> > Utca, utca, bánat utca
> Paved with sorrow's stones
> > Bánat-köböl van kiravka
>
> My sweetheart had it paved
> For me to walk down in tears.
>
> I'll go to live in the ground
> > Olyan házat csináltatok
> Then no one will push me around
> > Ablakot rá nem vágatok

No door and no window
> Se ajtója, sem ablaka
And no one comes knocking.
> Sem aki vagyok idevaló

Only one couplet here attempts to tie the lament down to a situation of lost or betrayed love, and that is a quotation like all the rest. Textually this could be a dawn song, and it contains at least three of the major formulae of dawn-song texts, versions of which I have already quoted. There are many such elements throughout Zerkula's performance which are immediately recognised by anyone familiar with the dawn song: the bird that has flown away and will not return, the 'orphan' theme, 'Where I go even the trees are weeping…', 'My sorrow would have to be folded in two to fit into the sky…' 'My tears fall like rain on my chest and onto the ground…' …and there is a version of Édesanyám *rózsafája* / 'My mother's rose tree', or at least a song beginning with that quatrain which then goes into hints of a departing recruit's song among several general lament formulae. Its melody is the standard one, though not easily recognised without careful attention in the elasticated delivery.

One motif which gets stressed by Zerkula rather more than it does in the dawn songs is the direct address to sorrow as a haunting presence: 'Sorrow tell me where I can go to get rid of you…', 'Virtuous sorrow, say something to me…' and in one particular song, which I quote entire, this becomes an elaborated symbolic structure –

I was in Gyimes last night,
> 'Zeste a Gyimnesbe jártam
I met sorrow there.
> A buvál megtalálkoztam.

It made a contract with me
> Oly szerzödést kötött vélem
Never to leave me behind
> Hogy ö el nem marad tölem

Tell me sorrow, where I can go
To be without you

Wherever I go to dwell
I live with sorrow there.

My dear soul, my shining sun,
                    Édes lelkem, fényes Napom
My star covered with haze[5]
                    Homályba borult csillagom
The one I've lost will never be mine.
                    Kit elvesztettem, nem kapom

Before every crimson dawn
                    Minden piros hajnal előtt
I wash myself with my tears.
                    Könnyemmel mosdom meg előbb.

which, notwithstanding what I say in footnote 20, p.61, distinctly recalls a theme of American 'blues' songs, such as

Good morning, Mister Blues,
    Mister Blues I come to talk with you
Good morning, Mister Blues,
    Mister Blues I come to talk with you
Mister Blues, I ain't doin nothin,
    an I would like to get a job from you.
            (Otis Harris, *Waking Blues*, 1928)

Early this morning the blues came walking in my room
Early this morning the blues came walking in my room
I said Blues, please tell me what you are doing making me feel so blue.

They looked at me twice and smiled but, yes, they refused to say
They looked at me twice and smiled but, yes, they refused to say
I seen them again and they turned and walked away.
                (Ida Cox, *Rambling Blues*, 1925)

Now the stars really are shinin – clouds look awful grey
Now the stars really are shinin – clouds look awful grey
I believe to my soul my blues and trouble are goin' to carry me
                                            [to my grave.
    (Little Brother Montgomery, *Tantalising Blues*, 1936)

The blues also tend to arrive at dawn, and greatly overstay their welcome, and can be reached through the image of star or sun occluded, and make of the grave a welcome refuge.

I wonder if the professionalism of the Gyimes musician, acting as both singer and accompanist, has by some common mechanism produced these echoes, projecting the acknowledged condition into a more theatrical mode than when the villagers do their own singing. But it is best not to speculate on distant echoes – you can find popular songs of Han China saying 'I'll love you till all the rivers run dry.' Perhaps it would simply be strange if you couldn't.

Many of the same formulae (or whatever you want to call them – chunks, autonomous modules etc.) which link dawn song and Gyimes lament have been recorded from the far western side of Hungary and everywhere in between, though rarely so intensified as in Transylvania. I've seen very little signs of their translation or re-creation into Romanian, in spite of the virtual identity of Hungarian and Romanian instrumental music in Transylvania.[6] As hinted previously, and no more than hinted now, we do seem to uncover a pan-Hungarian melancholy, evidenced in widespread lament formulae, perhaps more of the transferred or staged lament than the actual funeral lament, which is clearly not a textual source or emotive focus of this concentration of folkloric seriousness. It dwells more widely in the present tense, the lives lived and the sense of what people are.[7] The Gyimes laments are laments in music only; textually they are dawn songs. But the comparison of these two forms brings out the fact that they share very similar texts and tunes, or tone-rows, but have very different modes of musical expression, because the Gyimes music is far less touched by classical procedure, especially when not being played by gypsies.

Listening to János Zerkula creating his laments is a revelation. This is such a tiny zone; it is basically the valley of the River Tatros (50 kms long) and its tributary streams, high up in the Carpathians over the eastern watershed, flowing towards Moldova, a blank zone on the map with one proper road through a mass of forest and mountain. And for all the attention it may have had from Hungarian folk-fascists, and all the inquisition from Romanian urban fascists, it has maintained its own unique features through all the wars and oppressions of central Europe. It could so easily have gone under. And this extremely localised culture produced a distinct instrumental sound resembling no other, combined with a completely undistinct textual repertoire, echoing melodies and texts from a thousand kilometres away. Each of these factors holds elements of distance and proximity differently meant. What is not allowed to change is what connects furthest, that is the actual 'folk' factor.

But such distinction is not of itself the quality of these acts. János Zerkula and others[8] work within a highly developed and demanding musical tradition of which they are absolute masters. One wonders how many more such there must be on the earth, pockets of persistence working according to the full contract of human creation – the agent's disappearance into the act. Flourishing in forgotten perpetuity, or about to be wiped out by developmental intervention.

Notes

[1] The duo of melody instrument and gardon (or something like one) has been around in Transylvania for a long time, first documented in the 17th century. Although there are signs of the professional (gypsy) musician having taken over musical functionality in these villages, as elsewhere, there are also non-professional and non-gypsy musicians, as in Maramureş. These play mainly flutes but also sometimes violin. They would typically be smallholders who learned the flute as shepherds when young, and gained a reputation which enables them to earn extra income by playing for social occasions. On a small sampling, when playing the violin they perform with less bravura and less elaboration than the gypsy professionals.

[2] The gardon is used during laments in Bicaz, where it is known as 'doba', the Romanian for drum, but in a *tremelando* manner, which is the way the guitar and drum are used in Maramureş for slow *doina* type songs.

[3] In this the lamenting is done to a very freely melismatic descending tone-row, as is the unaccompanied lamenting on the previous track, the singers overcome with emotion but keeping to the rules. Interestingly, the violins do not follow this line but seem to be doing a kind of descant melody to it, which rises and falls while the lamenting only falls, and has episodes of rhythmic repetition, though supporting the lamenting voice cadentially. I don't know what this means, but the tempering of lament with measure exists in the same kind of ratio in the professional or secular Gyimes laments.

[4] The best-known instance of this in western art music is probably the lament in Gluck's *Orfeo e Euridice*, but it is quite common among the *frottole* (see Appendix 4A, p.92), far from unusual in Tudor song, and so on. The entire assumption that the major key or chord conveys a happier emotion is probably a modern romantic ruling.

[5] It seems uncertain whether the address in these two lines is still to Sorrow, or to the speaker's soul itself, or some other entity. It is not a turn of address to the lost lover, who is referred to in the next line. Kati Svorák sings a version of it among the 'Songs from Gyimesfelsólokból' on her CD 'Eclipse' –

> My sun my sun my bright sun
> > S napom, napom, fényes napom
> My star shrouded in darkness
> > Homályba borult csillagom

The paradoxical address to the sun as a concealed or shrouded thing suggests to me that this is or was originally an address to the rising sun and/or the morning star in a funerary context.

[6] A few are quoted from Maramureș songs at the end of my textual selection on page 49(17). But it should be borne in mind that these are from a selection recorded by Hungarians for issue in Budapest, and the selection favours melodies which are popular in the Hungarian *táncház* movement, and which might originate from the formerly larger Hungarian population of this zone. I have not come across such formulae elsewhere in Maramureș music, though the Romanian *doina* is always likely to throw up phrases of comparable intensity.

[7] There are of course echoes in peasant song from anywhere on earth, but these Hungarian texts have a modernity about them as well as a peculiar intensity. Having been, and sometimes still, recreated on the spot out of people's individual fates, their terms and imagery tend to be immediate and specific.

A possible reconsideration of the link to death on a quite different level of comprehension is suggested in Appendix 2, p.82.

[8] Zerkula and Mihály Halmágyi (both now dead) were the two best known violin masters of Gyimes. Both of them probably worked latterly as much outside Gyimes as in it. There is also a developed tradition of flute playing, which is to be expected from a community whose economy is chiefly pastoral. The flautists are not professionals and not gypsies and sometimes also play the violin in a much plainer manner. The playing of the accompanying gardon is no mean art, requiring a delicacy of touch which is rare among imitators. Most of the *táncház* groups do an occasional Gyimes number, well enough with the best groups such as Téka, but the difference when a whole life has been concentrated on this kind of playing is unmistakable.

Appendix Two : Zorile [a]

There is another structure, which survives, or did, recently enough to be documented,[1] among Romanians further south.[2] In the village there will be a group of women, normally three, sometimes more, who are called upon to sing at funerals and during the period of lying-in before them. This function with its texts and its melodies, is passed on to younger women one at a time so that there will always be the same number. They are called *Zorile*, the vocative form of the Romanian for 'dawn' which is a plural noun; they are the singers to the dawn(s). They arrive at dawn on each of the three days normally appointed between death and burial and sing in the yard facing the rising sun, then enter the house and sing facing the open coffin, holding candles.[3] On the fourth day they sing again at several points of the funeral procession, and finally at the graveside as the closed coffin is sunk, and the earth thrown noisily onto it.[4] Their function is parallel to that of the priest, and they are paid on the same terms as he. The songs they sing are not personal and not improvised; neither are they laments or dirges. They are to be sung 'cu glas fărâ durere' – in a voice without sorrow, and they must not be sung by close relatives of the deceased. They are ceremonial songs concerning observance and the meaning of death. Their texts are rich in active imagery and are said to be some of the most archaic European texts known. The music[5] bears a harsh beauty, something beyond the ancestral, something as modernist as the dawn-song. This[6] is one of the songs they sang at dawn in Dobrița, Oltenia:

> Ieri alataieri
> D'e-acas' am plecat...
>
> The day before yesterday
> I left the house
> And I met
> When I looked up
> A cock who roared.[7]
> He shook my hand,[8]
> He took my voice away
> He stole my eyes.
> You, loved woman,
> Get up[9] and ask
> Strangers and neighbours

---

[a] Notes to this Appendix may be found on pp.85–87.

To do something for you
To leave aside a while
Their daily work
Their sleep at night,
Ask them to lead you
From one country to another,
From a country with pity
To a country without pity[10]
From a country with sorrow
To a country without sorrow.
The thread, the thread
Of the leaf of the rose-bush[11]
Why have you delayed?
Why haven't you flowered?
I have delayed long enough
To detach myself
From my mother and my father
And the whole world
From brothers and sisters
From the flowery gardens[12]
Of my neighbours.

This is in fact a kind of modern compendial version (by the village in question) of the *Zorile* form, which abbreviates and substitutes for a whole set of funeral songs with distinct content and function. There are *Zorile din casă* (in the house), *Zorile din afară* (outside), *de fereastra* (at the window), *al luminarilor* (of the candles) and several emphasising particular figures of the poems – of the fairies, of the road, of the departure, of the rose-bush… There are also, paradoxically, *Zorile* subtitled *la amiazi* at noon, and *de seara* in the evening.

The song sung at dawn with the candles is the first, and is basically a preludial address to the dawn personified as fairies or siblings (being plural), begging that daybreak should be delayed until *dalbul de pribeag* – the pale wanderer, the deceased – finishes a long journey he or she must undertake. This undoubtedly connects to the wedding candle-song, which delays the departure of the bride with a solemn dance round her by her female peers holding candles, while her hair is being bound up into the sign of maturity.

The next is The Dead Person's Song, sung at the coffin, which dramatizes the dead person speaking of the experience of death as inanimation and invasion (the black crow etc.) and thus excusing the inability to thank and greet friends relatives and neighbours as they arrive.

The most important song, The Song of the Journey, originally sung during the funeral journey itself, is the one that urges and instructs the dead to set out on their journey and gives directions. I quote entire here Alexandru's summary of such a song –

> The traveller is urged to set out, *Cu roua-an picioate…* / With dew on his feet / With mist at his back / On that long road / Long, without shade… He must follow the road to the right *Càtre mîna dreaptâ / Câ-i calea curatâ* / For it is a clean road / Ploughed by white oxen /Sown with wheat… Not the road to the left *Câ-i calea stîngâ / Ci bivoli aratâ / Cu spini semânatâ* / which is a difficult way / Ploughed by buffalo / Sown with thorns… He is advised to make friends with the otter who knows the streams and the fords, with the wolf who knows the secret paths of the forest, and he will meet the *Samodiva* or *Gia–Samogia* who writes down the names of the living in red ink, and the names of the dead in black.

And there are others: at the grave, at the burial… which continue and extend this treatment of death as a new life. An entire theatre is constructed in these songs offering a post-mortem landscape combining the familiar, the mysterious, and the paradisal, relenting of nature (as long as you keep 'to the right' or 'straight on') and the grave itself is finally depicted as a house with little windows through which light and fruit will come. Such posthumous spirit-journey narratives could well lie behind all the inflated Transylvanian stuff about vampires and were-wolves.

This death journey takes us far from the dawn song, even if departure is one of the dawn song's commonest narratives. And the music is very different from that of either the dawn song or the lament, except that a falling line is common in the latter.[13] But in the appeal in many dawn songs to an obdurate 'God' (and Mother) who sometimes seems more bonded to physical earthly necessity even than Zeus, some kind of faint echo might be felt of the address to the dawn on behalf of the dead, which begs the ever-new light to guide the victim of earth through the labyrinth. In that case, in the dawn-song's modernity, the transport through Hades is reinstated on earth as a figure of necessity, the shadow of personal and social fate.

Notes

[1] A monumental collection of *Zorile* texts edited by Kahane and Georgescu-Stanculeanu, was published for the Bucharest Institute of Research into Ethnology and Dialectology in 1988. This megalithic compilation, typically of earlier East European ethnomusicology, involves a vast amount of musicological classificatory analysis, and almost nothing on the occasions on which the songs were sung, or even the significance of their texts. A short sequence of them is rendered into English as the last item in Brâiloiu 1984. My example is from Cuisenier, chapter 15.

[2] Basically southern and western Romania: sub-Carpathian Oltenia, the Banat, Hunedoara and southern parts of Transylvania. Cuisiner's example is from the village of Dobrita, Oltenia, 1974. In Oltenia epic or ballad singing still took place at weddings in the 1980s (Beissinger 1991) and Zorile may possibly survive there still. Generally this practice had already ceased by the 1970s, though traces of its text sometimes remain in laments and 'funeral songs' sung by relatives during the wake.

[3] In the brief account given by Emily Gerard (1880s), where they are called merely 'professional mourners', they sing *to* the dead, one of them placed each side of the head of the closed coffin, at ear level, where special small holes are drilled through the wood.

[4] Those who have witnessed a 'peasant' funeral know that the whole thing, although entirely solemn, is far from an occasion of hushed propriety. The roar of the withdrawing of the ropes after the coffin has been lowered into the grave, thunder of clods of clay falling on it – these are the acoustic climax of a long process of mounting lamentation, formal or not, which is silenced only during the comparatively brief intervention of the church. See my *The Funeral* in *The Dance at Mociu*, 2003 (revised edition, 2014).

[5] The quite long texts are sung to a short chant-line repeated many times, a more or less extended cadence with a vocabulary of 3 to 6 notes, or to a longer line which itself comprises the repetition of such a motif two or three times with variants. The cadence is always a falling one, normally onto a base note of minor-third tonality, from the fourth above it. But sometimes the base tonality is major, and sometimes an apparent major tonality gives way to a minor tonality at the last moment. The singing, as annotated, is comparatively lightly ornamented for this part of the world, with plenty of grace-notes, mordants, slides etc., but keeping the principal succession of notes clear. Sometimes the fourth degree is augmented, either consistently or in passing, sometimes by less than a semitone, as is normal in the songs of the areas in question. Brâiloiu says

they are normally sung antiphonally by two groups of two or three women, but Kahane and Georgescu-Stanculeanu say that the norm is three, sometimes more, but always an uneven number. I have not managed to hear a recording, but the delivery is sometimes described as 'shouted'. The north Transylvanian 'long song' (hora lunga, cântec lung etc.) is musically similar to the Zorile chant and is usually delivered fortissimo.

⁶ My translation of Cuisenier's French with dictionary reference to the original Romanian. It is a useful example as it combines poetic elements of two or more genres in the repertoire of funeral ceremonial songs, all sung by the *Zorile* but only one of them at dawn. Most of this version is redacted from the songs sung to the dead and as if by the dead, which were performed during the course of the funeral journey.

⁷ Literally 'belled'. Variant versions introduce a black crow at this point, who 'pierced my eyes / darkened my face / glued my lips.' (Brâiloiu 1984).

⁸ This hand-shaking [*sic*] with a bird or other animal at the end of a fictive journey occurs in quite different contexts, even possibly as a joke, but anyway as a persistent if rare signification of a final condition where species identities dissolve. In this truncated version the function of the animal guide in the journey of the dead is omitted. To some there is a distinct 'Egyptian' feel about the *Zorile* imagery.

Compare a Romanian song from Ieud, Maramureș, described as a 'march' and which could be used as a love song or a recruitment song –

> The road I've set out on is long
> > Drumu-i lung, pa el ma duc, ma.
> I will never reach the end.
> > Capâtu nu i-l ajung mâ
> If I get there
> > De-as ajunge capâtu', mâ
> I can shake hands with the cuckoo,
> > Dau-as mîna cu cucu. mâ
> But not with you, my dear.
> > Si cu tîne mîndrâ, ne, mâ
> I can shake hands with the thrush,
> > Dau-as mîna cu mierla. mâ
> But not with you, my dear.
> > Si cu tîne mîndrâ, ba', mâ

⁹ This imperative to the relatives to get about preparing the funeral is compounded with an address to the dead (distinct in fuller versions) to get up and start the journey to the land of death.

¹⁰ This is identical to the formula used in wedding songs as a term of the bride's transition from her original home to a home among strangers, but the subsequent clause is not. Brâiloiu's text has a third couplet 'From a land with love / to a land without love' prior to these two.

¹¹ 'Rose-bush' is Cuisenier's interpretation of an unusual Romanian contraction. Possibly his 'thread' (*firule*) should be 'bud' (*fire*). The connection of this episode to 'Edesonyám roszafaja' is obvious. Both dawns' song and dawn-song refer the unbearable to custom and structure through the imagery of floral retension – we are the buds which never fully open into the possible world, and eventually detach themselves and fall into the unknown. Another funeral ritual song, from the Banat, begins –

Fire, fire, trandafire,	Bud, bud, rosebud
Dar to ce te-ai zabovit	Why did you wait so long
Si n-ai înflorit?...	Before you opened?

These could be interventions of parts of lyrical songs into the *Zorile* text, but the theme, 'If I had known (about life/ about death) I would not have grown and ripened' is also present in texts of The Song of the Pine (*Cintecul Bradului* or just *Bradul*). This is another funeral ceremony song sung (by the Zorile?– this is not clear) only at funerals of the young unwedded, when a small decorated pine tree is set up at the head of the grave, as it was the custom to set up just such a tree at the gate of the new house when a couple got married, thus a "death-wedding" element. The song speaks in the voice of the pine tree, which laments the use to which it has been put – 'If I had known / I'd never have risen / If I'd been aware / I would never have grown.' (Brâiloiu – the quatrain occurs four times in his text, as a refrain.)

¹² Most 'gardens' in this society are what we would call kitchen-gardens, growing vegetables for the table rather than flowers. 'Flowery' might then indicate 'flourishing', implying that from the perspective of death the necessities or rewards of the world appear as ornaments or preliminaries.

¹³ The very connection to dawn might be misleading, for it has been suggested that the term *Zorile* is corrupt, its contracted form *Zori* equivalent to *Zêne*, 'fairies', by which the *Zorile* may be identified as Fates and their singing the Song of the Fates, which might bring us back to the dawn song. There too there is no conceptualisation of dawn, which is hardly ever mentioned, and the generic title is largely fortuitous: they are called that because that was when the songs were usually sung because that was when the celebrations tended to draw to a close.

Appendix Three: Enter a Peasant, Drunk

In Chinese classical poetry the character normally translated drunk, intoxicated, [JIU / zuì,] has a more precise meaning in the poetry, or at least a traditional poetical modulation of meaning. It indicates a particular level of intoxication which was specifically valued and carefully cultivated, because it was considered an optimum condition for creativity. James Liu characterises it as 'mentally carried away from ones normal preoccupations'. Its achievement is a signal to take up the ink-brush, tune the zither, start imagining the poem, or prepare to sing. This may be a purely solitary occupation, or the zenith of an occasion: a group by the stream at night, say, with lanterns, turning at a fixed point to music and poetry. I would suppose this condition to be attained not just by a certain amount of alcohol, but by particularly favourable brews consumed at a certain probably slow rate in combination with other factors in a suitable milieu, with or without contributory food and company. And I'd expect it to be the purpose of the occasion rather than a felicity incidental to having a good time; I'd expect it to be part of a meditative process in a very broad sense. And it will surely reach its apotheosis very late in the proceedings, after both stimulant and repressant alcoholic effects have levelled out, possibly close to dawn.

I understand this carefully measured process as a means of attaining a state of mind attuned to the particular terrestrial melancholy of a major strand of ancient Chinese poetry, which so much sets it apart from Western poetry, that sense of the person at risk on the surface of the wide earth, correlating extent and intimacy from a peculiarly poised and elevated frame of mind, set apart from (or in exile from) the social centre, out among the lakes and mountains, compared with which almost all European poetry before the late eighteenth century took place in rooms, and was interested in very little beyond contractual human relations (emotional, social and political) or the same transferred to the Deity.

This unprotectedness set the Chinese sage, poet, civil servant, administrator, etc., imaginatively in the same zone as the peasant, toiling in the fields, barely self sufficient, subject at any time to wars and other directives of the State enforcing immense loss. Thus the ink-painter sketched the peasant in his wide straw hat bearing some load, which the European painter before, say, Courbet, would have conceived as a grotesque or comic subject. Thus the old Chinese court or classical music drew on peasant music and programmatically depicted peasant life. In Europe, court or society musicians made fun of peasant music by depicting it as moronically simple, repetitious, and out of tune, or bracketed in a highly artificial 'pastoral' mode and so not quite real (though there was a more serious attention to popular and rural music from such musicians as the English virginalists, Monteverdi, Telemann and Haydn, informing the innovations of their own music). So the Chinese poet sadly noted the peasants returning exhausted from the fields, or the fishing boats returning to harbour, as figuring his own condition and a wider one. Gray might have been the first to espouse this tone in British poetry, and normally the peasant was cast as some kind of quasi-human codification of the baser or sillier habits of the children of the metropolitan upper classes. Even the Dutch 17th century genre painters seem to have been completely out of touch with rural reality, depicting 'Rural Courtship' for instance, as a drunken man in a dirty room with a woman on his lap, fondling her exposed breasts. Peasant courtship is of course the most formalised and rule-bound procedure, a thing of strictly enforced propriety, though not without adventure. But the European metropolis has always had a deep need to depict the people it exploits to gain its food as subhuman, and no one has been more ready to assist the process than the artists and poets (such as Shakespeare).

From Rome onwards it was mainly 'innocence' in the pastoral mode which rendered the European peasant invisible – a relic of the prehistory of the civilised psyche, an idea of purity allied to stunted mental growth which acted as a cautionary mirror to sophistication. The lives actually lived in the fields and villages were either taken for granted or were so incompatible with the pastoral mode as to be uncontemplatable, not really there, and remain unrecorded. Chinese officials were sent out by the Emperor to listen to what the people were singing and report back on the tone of the times, for it was a unity. [Birrell 1988 p.15]. In Europe the peasants sang their own fates, in a way only they knew but with an unsuspected richness of resource out of the entire condition they inhabited.

The European pastoral mode is not an isolable phenomenon, and you do not have to refer to sheep and goat husbandry in order to evoke it. The word 'love' in Renaissance lyrical poetry and drama is itself a pastoral reference, invoking a theatre aside from more serious concerns. The rendering of the food producers as 'clowns' is integral to the delegation of love to youth and the constant concern with contractual terms. It seems that Chinese classical poetry relished much more the condition of solitude as a comprehensive marker of the conditions.

So on some ancient Chinese occasion, the person is stirred into creativity at a point where this wholeness, and this sadness, rise up before the mind as a field of action, an access to forms of beauty that matter in the world, so an opportunity not to be missed. And this could sometimes happen even in public, under the gaze of others and for their sakes, as long as all the technicalities of the instrumentality could still be grasped faultlessly, and the customary inhibitions, the reluctance to elevate the self into a performance, can be set aside in an act of trust, assisted possibly by the balanced and controlled ingestion of a certain amount of alcohol...

The way I speak of this implies spontaneity, or even the improvised singing 'of your own fate'. For the most part, of course, I am speaking in very general and even fictionalised terms of a cultural continuity spanning many centuries, a 'court' culture in which composition is strictly prior to performance however elaborated the performance was, as everywhere else (though I believe that Chinese poets used to consider a poem completed when they could sing it, prior to committing it to paper). But close to the beginnings of Chinese poetry, at the start of the Han Dynasty when there was a cultural break which brought about a kind of new beginning in the arts, there is documentation of a new song and poetry deriving from spontaneous practices. It is still a 'court' occasion in which certain persons (courtier, lady, aristocrat, prince and the Emperor himself) were entitled or obliged to perform songs, alone or accompanied, which are characterised [by Diény 1968 pp.41–46] as *l'improvisation pathétique* – personal statements created on the spot, sincere and simply worded expressions of emotion, and invariably melancholy in tone. There are precise accounts of two emperors (Kao-Tsu and Wu) performing thus –

> In the winter of 195 B.C., when emperor Kao-tsu was on his way back to the capital, he stopped in the countryside at P'ei in the region of former Ch'u state, where he had begun his politico-military career. At a banquet in his honour, overwhelmed by the occasion with its memories of hardship and triumph, he composed a spontaneous song, 'A Great Wind Rises'. Accompanying himself on a stringed instrument he chanted it. Then he formed a choir of some 120 local boys who joined in and repeated his song while the emperor danced, weeping with grief. [Birrell 1988 p.16]

Comparison is made with accounts of 'spinning evenings' among the ladies or harem of the palace 'where each sang for the others her disappointments and griefs [*ses déceptions et peines*].' [Diény 1968 quoting the *Han chou*].

It is suggested that these practices were widespread, going beyond the confines of court and aristocracy and that they may have formed the basis of a new form, the *shih* in lines of five characters, which became the standard form of most subsequent Chinese lyrical poetry for about a millennium. Eleven Han poems survive which might be authentic records of such performances (because plain in style and not artistically crafted) and many others which may represent literary developments arising from these originals, an increasingly crafted and prepared song form. It is suggested that the 'Bureau of Music' set up by Wu might have included among its many functions the collection of these personal songs – that people might even have gone there and sung them for transcription – but also to go out and collect songs from all classes all over the empire, and to effect the development from them of a sophisticated song-poetry. It has left behind a large collection of what are known as *yueh-fu*, 'Music bureau songs', which remain anonymous and are described as 'folk-songs', but the bulk of them are clearly more of a classical product, from the repertoires of professional singers.

The melancholy songs are only some of the forms included in these collections and in the poetry succeeding them, but the melancholy tone can be quite pervasive and the genres included in Birrell's 1988 collection notably include anti-war songs and ballads, songs of yearning for home, love-songs of a yearning nature and various songs of misfortune such as orphaning and the fate of the cast-out youngest brother in the Chinese aristocratic family. The songs of 'spinning evenings' could perhaps be related to the popular poetical genre of the song of the lonely or deserted woman, of which the definitive collection is the *Yü-t'aihsin-yung*, 'New Songs from Jade Terrace' [Birrell 1982]. For being left alone seems to have been the dominant condition of most of the palace women, harem or not, as the officials they loved or married were constantly being sent somewhere. I am only prevented by my ignorance from suggesting that the melancholy and yearning tone, the tone of the exile and the wanderer, which pervades so much Chinese lyrical poetry as we have received it, might have its foundations in these areas of anonymous and extemporised creation. Emperors, or deserted dancing-girls at the close of the season, soldiers longing for home, banished court officials… I would happily have assumed them all to be theatrical or fictionalised representations in the repertoire of court song, were it not for the example of the Transylvanian dawn-song.

Appendix Four: My mother cursed me...

(a) The Court

O mia cieca e dura sorte
Di dolor sempre nutrita,
O miseria di mia vita
Tristo anuncio a la mia morte.

Più e più infelice
Son che alcun che viva in terra.
L'arbor son che il vento atterra
Perché più non à radice.
Vero è ben quel che se dice
Ché mal va chi à mala sorte.
  O mia cieca e dura sorte…

La cagion di tanto male
È fortuna e il crudo amore
Per che sempre de bon core
Servit'ho con fé immortale
La qual hor sicato ha l'ale
E badita di ogni corte.
  O mia cieca e dura sorte…

Perché un viver duro e grave
Grave e dur morire conviene.
Finir voglio in pianti e pene
Come in scoglio fa la nave
Ch'al fin rompe ogni suo trave
Poi che un tempo è stata forte.
  O mia cieca e dura sorte…

Piglia exempio ognun che vede
Scritto in la mia tomba obscura
Se ben son for di natura
Morto son per troppo fede
Per mi mai non fu mercede
Pietà m'ha chiuse le porte.
  O mia cieca e dura sorte…

O my blind and hard fate
Always feeding on sorrow,
O misery of my life
Sad forecast of my death.

More sorrowful and wretched
I am than any living thing on earth,
I am the tree that the wind casts down
Because it no longer has roots.
Truly as the saying goes
Things go badly when fate is against you.
   O my blind and hard fate…

Fate and cruel love
Are the cause of so much trouble.
For always with a good heart
And ever faithful I served
Her who has cut my wings
And banished me from every court.
   O my blind and hard fate…

Since my life is hard and bitter
Hard and bitter will be my death.
I must end in tears and pain
Like a ship driven onto the rocks
Which breaks all its beams
Because it cannot yield.
   O my blind and hard fate…

Pay attention all you who read
This writing on my obscure grave
For I have left the world
And died for too much loyalty.
There was no pity taken on me,
Mercy closed the door on me.
   O my blind and hard fate…

These, the anonymous words of a song by Marchetto Cara (c.1465–c.1525), are the closest in spirit I can find to the dawn songs in Continental courtly lyric. It may be no coincidence that the harmonic rationale of the music is also quite close to that of the more sophisticated of the Transylvanian string bands and there are resemblances too in other musical respects: rhythm, formal structure, close relationship of song and dance, the rule of one note to a syllable.

These songs, known collectively as *frottole*, sprang up under the patronage of Isabella d'Este in the Mantuan court circa 1500 apparently out of nowhere. In fact they must have been to a greater or lesser extent refined out of the aural tradition, and are about the first instances of 'static' or 'vertical' (chordal as against polyphonic) harmony in the official history of western music. They are said to reflect the new humanism of the Italian courts, as against the scholastic art-polyphony of the North. The harmonic structure is based on a limited repertoire of first-position chords, with a tendency (more marked in some pieces than others) to move them around in parallel much as the Transylvanian bands do [see footnote 27, p.69] and when they are performed accompanied by the *lirone* or *lira da braccio* or *viola d'arco* (which I think are all much the same thing), an instrument of the middle tonal range designed for playing chords in 3 or 4 parts, the sound becomes distinctly Transylvanian, to some ears.

The proximity of these words to those of the Transylvanian songs is obvious, but what gives the game away, of course, is the second stanza, which provides the *singular occasion* of all this despair: the rejection of the ardent lover. This makes all the difference, and spreads like a colour-dye through the whole song: the painful condition is disowned at the same time as declared. Rather than a participation it becomes a spectacle in which the audience views a crisis which, no matter how intense the performance, it is protected from. It becomes a special case, but typical of a particular, probably youthful, condition. This mode, which is a form of pastoral, dominates the *frottole* texts almost completely. It is present in exactly the same way in many Transylvanian songs (and songs from all over the world) but I see it as a distinct feature of the central dawn-song ethos that this closure need not take place, but the plaint may be left open. And the bearer is then not protected in the same way – the dawn-singer's 'fate' is too widespread to be remediable or softened into experience. Indeed I am not sure that they really complain at all, in the sense of entertaining any possibility of redress. There is a sense that life is simply 'like this' rather than that life has 'gone wrong'. Neither does anyone in the true dawn-song repertoire declare him/herself to be unjustly dealt with, by God or man, only to be bearing sorrow as an unending weight. 'Others are better off' hardly enters into it. The fate of one is the fate of all.

LACRIMAE

Flow my teares fall from your springs,
Exilde for ever: Let mee mourn
Where night's black bird hir sad infamy sings,
There let mee live forlorne.

Downe vaine lights shine you no more,
No nights are dark enough for those
That in dispaire their lost fortuns deplore,
Light doth but shame disclose.

Never may my woes be relieved,
Since pitie is fled,
And tears, and sighs, and grones my wearie dayes,
Of all joyes have deprived.

From the highest spire of contentment,
My fortune is throwne,
And feare, and griefe, and paine for my deserts,
Are my hopes since hope is gone.

Harke you shadowes that in darcknesse dwell,
Learne to contemne light,
Happie, happie they that in hell
Feele not the worlds despite.
       (Anon., set by John Dowland,
        The Second Booke of Songs or Ayres… 1600)

These lyrics are more inclusive, and the music is more sophisticated than Cara's, with a longer periodicity and greater opportunity for irregularity and suspension in the structure. It is also more dramatic, projecting the declamation of the speaking voice, especially in lines 11 and 15 (though the *frottole* context includes separate pieces, with more weighty texts by poets such as Virgil, which stand at the origin of recitative). *Lacrimae* uses a new melody for verses 3 and 4, and another for the last verse, which is repeated, these three melodies corresponding to the normal three sections of the slow dance form the pavane.

    Some of the more sophisticated dawn-songs can hold their heads up in the company of Dowland, and have the same stately pavane-like pace which songs such as *Lacrimae* obviously demand, court or village notwithstanding.

They also share a fondness for shifting the tonality between what we would now call relative major and minor. The customary ornamentation of Dowland's melodic line by the singer, the terms of which are now lost to us, might well have brought the two kinds of song even closer. The normal accompaniment is for lute and bass viol but can be freely adapted to available resources, and if it were customary to employ the lyra-viol or the tenor viol played 'lyra-viol way', either of which produces chords in 2 or 3 parts, the final effect would be distinctly Carpathian. I've never heard this done, but lyra-viol technique is considered appropriate for music of Dowland's time.

As for the words, it is as if they would achieve exactly the dawn-song total melancholy if the love-situation narrative could be withdrawn [cf. footnote 21, p.63]. Then the desolation and refusal enunciated would be able to spread into anyone's understanding of life without being mitigated by the pastoral theatre of innocence. Some of Dowland's stanzas in isolation seem to be very much in the same area –

> From silent night, true register of moanes,
> From saddest Soule consumde with deepest sinnes,
> From hart quite rent with sighes and heavie groanes,
> My wayling Muse her wofull worke beginnes.
> And to the world brings tunes of sad despaire,
> Sounding nought else but sorrow, griefe and care.

Probably the love-loss rationalisation remains implicit here, and the remaining stanzas posit a cause in an external contrariety which is quite likely to derive from an unmentioned 'she'. The religious version frequent in *A Pilgrims Solace* rests despair on an unspecified sinfulness, but it is dubious whether even here the narrative quite releases itself from the delineation of a case, unless solely by the force of the music.

When the dawn-song specifies the occasion of its despair it also transcends it. It may be a song of despairing love but the music is dawn-song music and moves into the whole dawn-song ethos, whereby the love lost is always lost, because it is what happens, it is what it's like for anyone, if not in love then in some other infliction. Or the transferability of textual components echoes the song out of its occasion. Thus we have

> It's Autumn, the wind is cold,
> The leaves are falling.
> Many a mother would pick them all
> If she could save her son from the army.

which is plainly a recruitment song and we know where we are. But in the same repertoire we also have –

> In the Autumn when the leaves
>   Ősszel, mikor a falevél
> Turn yellow, the wind blows them away.
>   Megsárgul, elhordja a szél
> This world made me tired
>   Ez a világ csak fárasztott
> And brought sorrow on me.
>   Engem ily bánatra hozott.
>
> Sorrow, sorrow, great sorrow,
>   Búra, búra, nagy bánatra
> I wish I had never been born to feel it.
>   Bár ne születhettem volna.
> When I was a boy, my mother
>   Vágy az anyám kis koromba
> Should have locked me in a coffin.
>   Zárt volna a koporsóba.

and this is a 'pure' dawn-song text which we can't delegate, and so the sorrow of recruitment participates in a wider loss. And the generalised text also, reciprocally, invokes the Octobers of recruitment without mentioning them, and/or, it invokes the songs of love-loss. There are always reasons for this melancholy; there is simply no avoiding it.

The Transylvanian dawn songs remain an almost unique figuration of a stark human predicament which few of our philosophies and fewer still of our poetries dare to approach. But the melancholy music of slow dignified accession, proud agreement to the inevitable contract, in the slow music of Cara, Dowland, Josquin, Lawes, Handel, Haydn, and black American 'spirituals', to name a few out of many, is in exactly the same place.

(B) The People [a]

Some time around 1880 Mrs Emily Gerard, the English wife of a military officer stationed at Sibiu, and author of *The Land Beyond the Forest: Facts, Figures and Fancies from Translyvania* (1888), visited Klausenberg [Kolosvár, Cluj] and attended the Easter carnival ball there, which was a function of the

---

[a] Notes to this Appendix may be found on pp.106-121.

upper classes of the city, principally involving the daughters of high-ranking citizens and young army officers. Klausenberg was a major commercial and social centre, of German origin but later a centre of Hungarian culture in Transylvania; it was more than a provincial market town and its annual society ball was a very long way from a village dance. But most of the things which struck her about it are strangely familiar to those who have studied and witnessed the village festivities. The music was provided by 'Tsiganes musicians' and consisted almost entirely of csárdás.[1] The dancing lasted for the three evenings and nights of Monday to Ash Wednesday (much to the annoyance of the clergy) and was virtually continuous for the twelve hours 8 p.m. to 8 a.m. And the whole thing was carried through with extraordinary enthusiasm. Every time a csárdás started everyone rushed onto the floor, and they tried to get as close as possible to the musicians, indeed crowding round them and 'almost stepping on their toes' while two-thirds of the dance-floor remained empty. It was said that the gypsies only played the csárdás with 'real spirit' when crowded in this way.[2]

All this is very close to what went on, and occasionally still does, at a village dance in Transylvania. Dancing and playing go on tirelessly for days. The dancers crowd close to the musicians (though in the farmhouse rooms there isn't much choice about that) and dance and sing in direct communication with the band. There is no sense that the musicians simply supply the music in the correct dance rhythm and the dancers get on with it; a lot depends on exactly who is dancing or singing and how; it is a collaboration. Sometimes the playing is focused on a particular couple at the front, or is directed to an individual dancer.[3] The virtuosic male leaping dances are always done face to face with the lead fiddle, and this is the position from which the dawn songs and interludes would have been sung. And of course, given the length of the event, the individual dances are much longer than the versions presented on stages and CDs and involve extemporisation on the part of the leader, which to the patrons, as connoisseurs, is a major factor of their participation in the music.[4] (By all accounts, the pre-recording days of New Orleans jazz were not unlike this.[5])

The Klausenberg ball ended in the early morning of the fourth day with a final gallop, after which the couples retired to an adjoining room for cabbage soup and everyone prepared to depart. But after this, while they were awaiting their carriages, Mrs Gerard tells us that the Tsiganes started playing again, this time not dances, but 'wild fitful strains and melancholy national airs, addressed not to all, but to now one, now to another, of the listeners grouped about.' The only difference from the ending of a classic village celebration, then, was that individually addressed patrons did not, on this occasion at any rate, come forward and sing their own dawn songs.[6]

Apart from participatory singing, at this point or elsewhere, the other thing apparently missing from the Klausenberg ball which would have been expected at a village dance was the ritualistic procedure by which the local social order was strictly represented on the dance floor, principally in the opening promenade. I assume this to have been absent since Mrs Gerard makes no mention of it, though such procedures can be part of a middle-class 'society' ball, and were *de rigeur* in much court dancing.

* * *
* * * *

It is good to think that 'even peasants' can create a sophisticated melancholy song music as well as any other group, and certainly they have maintained one in the 20th century in Transylvania, and it has become their own. But to hear the music as definitively rural is a mistake. The musical culture from which the dawn-song arises is a larger thing than a 'village music', it derives from the whole historical society of Transylvania, and did not become exclusively rural until, probably, it was isolated from town and gentry by the new dispensation of 1923[7] or even later.

This at any rate is the sense I get after a frustrating attempt to survey its history and sociology, both of which are tantalisingly incomplete and confusing, partly through lack of documentation but mainly because of the conflicting accounts put forward by Hungarian and Romanian commentators, both with vested interests in claiming it as their own music.[8] In fact I think the precise historical origins of the music are lost in obscurity – where it came from, when it was originally played, where, for whom, in what strata of society or ethnic group, how it did or didn't change in the last 300 years – all this is a mass of uncertainty and most of it hardly matters. The music has, by the skin of its teeth perhaps, survived to the present, and it is obvious that as it now stands it is steeped in the conditions of a rural peasant society. You only have to glance at the photographs of musicians in Béla Kása's book and it is obvious that we are dealing with real poverty. And yet one of the perfectly obvious things about it whatever its history is that it is a hybrid of classical music and folk music.

At some time gypsies moving in from wherever they were last flung out of, gradually took over just about the entire music business of the eastern side of the Austro-Hungarian Empire, and converted most of its music to string-band music. They probably arrived in the 15th century and by the 20th had become the principal musical providers to almost everyone except the habitués of symphony concerts. The princely aristocracy had maintained a court music long before this, employing Italians when possible, and this tradition was in some measure maintained in the following century, certainly in Hungary, as at Eszterháza. The cities of Transylvania maintained a musical culture much like other European cities in their salons, concert-halls and cathedrals. Charles Bonner, travelling in the 1860s, noted that even in the villages the Saxon clergy, who were educated in Germany, maintained contact with 'mainland' European culture, and were in touch with recent literature and music (he mentions Beethoven). The gypsy band may not have infiltrated this specifically German high-culture zone but neither was its music bound exclusively to the lower end of society. One theory is that its origins lie in the estates of the Hungarian rural aristocracy.

There is no doubt that the gypsy bands (or some of them) were at one time seriously tied to the big Hungarian landowners. 'Almost every Hungarian noble-man in Transylvania had a gypsy violinist or locksmith on the premises' (document of 1683). (This was probably the dual role of one person, the gypsy violinist becoming a separate profession in the 19th century. Donegal fiddlers retained the same dual function of musician and blacksmith into the 20th century, including the making of metal fiddles.) As described by Mrs Gerard in the 1880s they were close to being retainers: gypsy musical dynasties descending alongside the noble dynasties and passionately aware of this link extending through centuries. Apparently Magyar nobles valued the music very highly and had a strong emotional relationship to it, which could lie at the heart of the 'special relationship' between player and patron which still applies in remote villages in the hills. To the Count they were 'my gypsy band' in a very special way. Perhaps there was some kind of essential reaction here which determined the central nature of the music. It was a meeting through music and dance of the extremes of society: aristocrat and gypsy, highest and lowest, but both free agents. They played Hungarian music – it has always been the duty of the professional gypsy musician to furnish the music of the group played for[9] – probably itself highly loaded emotionally for this rather isolated and besieged nationhood. (There is a saying quoted by Mrs Gerard: 'All the Hungarian needs in order to get drunk is a gypsy band and a glass of water.') They would have brought to it their fiery performance technique, the spirit which made flamenco out of Andalusian music, with a very rich development of ornamentation, not the 'grace-note' ornamentation of the conservatoire but one which leaves hardly any note free of trilling and turns, moving in the freedom of extravagance almost to transcend the musical line. And they enriched it with a pulsing harmonic structure which made it impossible to stand still. It is at least imaginable, that something in this context, including the sharp eye-to-eye confrontation of master and free vagabond roped together into song and dance and entirely dependent on each other for the duration of the piece, made this music irresistible, wherever it was played. The derivation of the music more directly from village song and dance remains a possibility, but one which would make it difficult to explain the manifest classical vocabularies of the music.[10]

But the Count's band was not in his employ, they were not (as Haydn and his orchestra at Eszterháza were) servants tied to the establishment, they were hired under contract for a limited period,[11] and they never became exclusive to the aristocracy. They also worked in the towns, for the merchant classes who had been there for centuries and must always have had their music. And they worked in the villages, hired there as anywhere for weddings, funerals, dances etc., and probably the villages became the focus of their work as the aristocracy declined. They would then find themselves playing for a number of different ethnic groupings and having to incorporate their various demands into the repertoire, as innovations or as adaptations of what they already did for Hungarians.

Hypothetical origins aside, it does seem that in its hey-day, which I place in the earlier 20th century, the gypsy string bands served the whole of this society – that they played for all classes of gentry, merchants, professionals, smallholders, villagers, serfs, gypsies… basically they all got the same music. Possibly even the highest aristocracy used them for dances, employing others for the salon, opera and church.[12] And they played for all kinds of dances from 'card' balls to village hops, also weddings, christenings, funerals, grape harvesting evenings, pig butcherings, sheep-milk measurings, recruitment ceremonies, Sunday afternoon village dances, personal serenades under windows, evenings in taverns, or standing idly by the roadside… And they did this for Hungarian, Romanian, Saxon, Székely[13], Gypsy and Jewish communities.

In fact the various ethnic groups at village level also had their own musicians, described by Emily Gerard, for the Saxons, as 'out of time and out of tune'. These were evidently a lot cheaper and less professional, though said to have been sometimes preferred because they were 'our own'. Bagpipes were the principal instrument of these musicians for Romanians and perhaps others.[14] The gypsy bands were generally preferred when they could be afforded, especially for weddings, which were extremely important occasions for which no expense was spared, and still are.

While the bands played for this near-total social spectrum, the repertoire shows very little real discrimination as to music played for different groups. Basically it is one music. I think this is a sign of its grace and strength, that it had the resource, within its own momentum, to subsume social and ethnic identities (without suggesting for a second that it was able to operate as a social good on any scale). So in the repertoires there are pieces, especially dances, labelled Hungarian, Romanian, Gypsy… but this principally means pieces to be played *for* Hungarians, Romanians, Gypsies, many of which must have derived originally from the songs and dances of these three groups. The string band integrates these distinctions, until any of these ethnically labelled pieces can be played to any of the groups, with exceptions and some acknowledgement of their proprietorship, varying in degree from place to place. Some can still be sung to the original words in the appropriate language including Rom, but are perfectly acceptable to other groups with new lyrics or as instrumentals. The music may also be transferable by relabelling: 'What we play as a lullaby to the Romanians we play as a recruitment song to the Hungarians of Kalotaszeg.' And most of these distinctions are delicate – an outsider can hardly hear them. They concern preferred melodies and versions of melodies, dance-forms, even ornamentation, but they do not change the central nature of the music any more than preferences operating from village to village or person to person do. Ethnicity is reduced to a colouration.[15] This assimilation *within* the music contrasts with widespread (but variable) ethnic and class subjection in Transylvania, directed especially towards the gypsies throughout the 20th century, in spite of which there was never any of the 'ethnic cleansing' experienced in other countries when the bonds of an eastern block country were loosened. This has been attributed both to prevailing 'peasant' attitudes and to the 'civilising' influence of Romania's long association with France.

So much for race and nationalism in peasant music.[16] As for 'class', Bartók said that the closer the gypsy bands got to 'cultural centres' the more their music changed towards the city style of playing and away from peasant music, and Mrs Gerard said that in the towns they played a more 'refined' music. It is far from easy to gauge the extent of this deviation since the bands were increasingly cut off from their better-off patrons from 1923 onwards and since 1945 served the villages almost exclusively. But I don't think this was simply a sliding-scale between village oompah and the quite sophisticated urban popular music of the Budapest and Vienna gypsy bands[17] and/or pan-European ex-courtly dance music, for there was also an inner or even native refinement. It is more likely that a distinctly Transylvanian music traded in the towns with both Hungarian and European musics. The band Mrs Gerard heard in Klausenberg probably belonged both culturally and musically within a Transylvanian continuum secure enough in its own localism to be able to pick up forms from as far away as France and England (and, for political reasons, to reject Viennese forms). Certainly any 'refinement' involved in playing for a society ball was not seen by the musicians as a superiority, for the leader of the band told her that although his band was the only one locally which played 'in society', it was not actually the best. We don't know what the basis of this qualitative definition was (presumably it was technical and affective) but it replaces the central focus of this music back in the villages. Whatever shifted as the music descended the social scale there was no question of it getting *cruder*.

But in considering the quite severe and serious emotive force accessible within this music to the dawn song and the lament, it is natural to question whether such sombre statements have any place in the context of the town ballrooms, in a society which would presumably look elsewhere for its seriousness – to the theatre, the book, the Protestant church, the string quartet from Vienna[18] – and might also have a quite different sense of the channels of fatality. That depends on the extent to which peasant and aristocrat represent human sub-species, with entirely distinct cultural 'languages'; it seems quite likely that, in some perspectives, in Transylvania they were more united than we would assume.

* * *

25 kilometres north of Cluj, just off the main road north to Dej and Baia Mare, is a village called Bonchida[19]. This is on the central Transylvanian Heath, open countryside of rolling hills, cultivated or grazed for centuries and almost bare of trees. In the absence of field boundaries it is easy to imagine migratory hordes or invading armies travelling freely across the landscape (whenever I attempt this for England I see them stopped at traffic-lights). This was the headquarters of one of the country's biggest noble families, the Bánffy, and their palace, once called 'The Versailles of Transylvania', still stand there in ruins. These were one of the aristocracies created at the end of the 17th century when Transylvania seceded from the Turkish Empire and was incorporated into the Habsburg one. György Bánffy was in fact appointed by the Emperor Leopold as the first Governor of Transylvania. According to Károly Kós, these new counts (there were about ten of them) relished their new status and set about accumulating the wealth appropriate to their titles; they acquired big estates and cultivated all the trappings of central European nobles. Their leanings were very much towards Vienna, and they opposed the senses of Transylvanian collectivity and democracy which had distinguished the Principality. They were instrumental in the transference of power to Vienna and the political reduction of Transylvania to an outlying province, but one enjoying comparative peace and prosperity for the next two centuries. The characteristic architecture of most Transylvanian towns and mansions was established in this period in the Viennese baroque style. The Bánffys were at the top of this structure, with one of the finest estates in the country and a particularly famous herd of horses. Most of the counts were statesmen and passed constantly between their estates and business in

Budapest and Vienna. These families were stripped of their estates by the land reforms of 1923 which gave most of the land to Romanian smallholders, but many continued to live in their houses and retained some power and status until the new reforms of 1945. The Bánffy mansion was devastated and emptied by a retreating German army in 1944.

The village has a mixed Hungarian, Romanian and 'Hungarian Gypsy' population, and from this last were at one time drawn a large number of bands (eleven by one account; another refers to there being at one time two dozen fiddlers). Of these there survived recently a dozen musicians of which four 'primás', forming themselves in two generations into two bands and then one. These musicians, particularly the Pusztai family, claimed direct descent from those who played for the Banffy family in the 19th century. They were recorded by Zoltán Kállos and others in the 1960s and 70s, photographed by Béla Kása, and the primás Béla Kolbasz was interviewed by Speranta Radulescu in 2003 (Radulescu 2004). Around 2000 the remaining band was still playing for Hungarians, Romanians and Gypsies in the area.

There is something special about the music from Bonchida, but it becomes very difficult to say exactly what it is, or why. It is in some ways a 'classic' central Transylvanian string band music with all the usual forms (including at least one dawn song, which are not typical of the region – the centre of Kalotaszeg is some 100 kms to the west of here). The ethnic mix is marked in the repertoire, which indicates a history of playing for Hungarian, Romanian and Gypsy occasions, and having done so for a long time, so that the various brands of origin have to some extent become common property and the labelling mixed, pieces 'for Romanians' labelled 'Ţiganeste' or 'Magyar' and so forth. Most of the forms as issued on archival recordings are Hungarian but there is enough 'Romanian' music to fill one of the cassettes (where it is labelled 'Hungarian-Romanian Folk Music'). Singing is included in both languages, frequently of tunes played by the bands, but the singers were from a different village, and typically of the older archival recordings the vocal and the instrumental are kept entirely separate.[20] All this indicates a music formed to serve villagers, including gypsies, as may be expected of any Transylvanian band's repertoire.

But the old Bonchida band has unique features some of which suggest its aristocratic function. It includes a cimbalom, not typical of the region, which here is a sign of Hungarian mainland connections. There is also a greater familiarity than usual in Mezöség with the upper strata of town influence, leaning towards normal 18th century harmonies, with the bass liberated from the melody line. Pizzicato is occasionally used, which is rare except in recently upgraded bands aimed at a wider market. And it was even in the 1960s a large band, with up to three violins, as a band playing for well-off patrons would have been. Previously the musician population of the village had been capable of supplying an orchestra with six or more violins such as are mentioned in 19th century accounts.

But what mainly makes the Bonchida music different is something less susceptible to itemization. It is simply a sense of elegance, or delicacy, or lyrical poise, perhaps suggesting a whiff of Vienna in the playing of a csárdás – difficult to describe but unmistakable to the ear. "…we cannot help but think of the dances of the 18th century nobility" as Ökrös' notes put it – as if the tone proper to the minuet had been brought to country dances. [21]

"Country dances" is exactly it, and we might be here very close to the original conception of this music, as something forged between uppermost and lowest social forces. It is indeed said that one of the Banffy's imported some kind of musician specially from Budapest (perhaps in the 19th century or earlier) to teach his gypsy band. Since musical styles spread widely in the country while retaining local character, the resulting innovation, especially if practised in other estates, could have been a significant factor of the formation of the music we hear now.[22]

It is said that the particular manner of Bonchida music spread to the villages of the area and was particularly well preserved in the Romanian repertoire. I cannot guess as to why this should be, but it is certainly true that through all the regions of Transylvania the dance sets labelled 'Román' or 'Romanește', that is, 'for playing to Romanians', evince exactly this sense of elegance more than the Hungarian sets. At the time of the Banffy prosperity the Romanians were utterly marginalised and, like the gypsies, condemned to poverty. They were living on the outskirts of villages in 'huts'. Yet it seems to have been these who, wherever it came from, insisted on a degree of sophistication in their dances and to some extent in their songs, which can still be heard.

I finally state quite subjectively that I do feel with this band the possibility of the strong tie across the social scale between Count and gypsy, the spark flashed between Hungarian power and melancholy, and gypsy energy, which established the 'special relationship' of player and patron[23], without denying the possibility of an equally strong force-field, transferred or generated, between fiddler and peasant, sympathetically or antagonistically. There is also a sense that the Hungarian aristocrats were anyway not entirely distinct from the peasantry. They were all farmers, and distinctions might sometimes have been of scale rather than kind. Kós mentions the distinctly unostentatious life-style of the Transylvanian Princes of the 16th–17th centuries, who might live in castles which were little more than strengthened farm-houses, and of 18th century aristocrats who chose to restrict their living quarters to just two rooms of a mansion, while the lesser gentry were outwardly indistinguishable from smallholders.[24]

Always with the history of this music you end up guessing. My guess is that the music found its main home among some middle stratum of the Hungarian gentry and gained its initial definition there out of a considerable prehistory, but, being purveyed by unattached gypsies, always knew the various peasant and smallholding societies of Transylvania, and whatever it did bore the melancholy of a border zone on its back. After the land reforms of 1923, and in acceleration from 1945, the gypsy bands were cast entirely on the villages and were deeply involved in the peasants' conditions (including conditions of quasi-aristocratic pride and rectitude) as they sought increasingly to be indispensable wherever music was called-for.

And somewhere along this course the dawn-song happened, quite possibly not reaching its full realisation until the 20th century, when, as the music began to decline,[25] its more concentrated involvement with the working peasantry brought these old songs out into this modern fulfilment. Nothing is more sophisticated than the dawn-song, and nothing is more intense; at its best it is the perfection of song itself, but with its tone and substance now intimately related to the society of the peasant, which represents, after all, a majority of the earth's population. Possibly a final democratisation stripped what became the dawn-song of societal requisites of self-protective pastoral, the suspended animation of wistful regret inhabiting airs of farewell, and raised it to a kind of hymnody, just when the harmonic second violins transformed into the richer sound of the violas. Possibly quite deep parallels of the total conditions of life and death, enjoined from the Romanian side of things, the pre-Enlightenment cosmic machine, solemnised a sweet melancholy to a tragic chorus.

Notes

[1] But also some game dances, a wild gallop at dawn, a 'cotillion', and an 'écossaise'. This last she describes as 'in reality a pot-pourri of several English country dances'. Nobody could tell her how this musical material had arrived here. If her account is at all complete the minuets, waltzes etc. favoured by the Viennese were conspicuously absent.

[2] By the third day Mrs Gerard was exhausted just from watching. Her informant, a young woman, when asked about tiredness replied, 'Of course we are tired. But when you hear the csárdás starting you can't help yourself, you have to get up and dance.'

[3] Pongracz, the band's *primás*, at Klausenberg, said of a bad dancer, 'If I did not play at him, and send my violin to his feet, he would not be able to get round at all.'

⁴ Some recordings of these extended live performances are on CD. They were recently rare enough for me to list, but as more and more CDs are issued long dance-sets have become quite plentiful. The Scászcsávás Band, plays a set of four dances lasting 43 minutes on its CD from Figuras (Switzerland) but the Palatka band holds the current record with a Romanian couple dance (not a set) lasting 50 minutes on a CDr issued by the band (at first entitled *In Memoriam Martin Codoba*, 2002, then *Magyarpalatka Banda*, Palatka Records 2003).

⁵ See especially the early chapters of Shapiro and Hentoff, *Hear Me Talkin' To Ya* (1955).

⁶ The duties of the gypsy band did not end here, for the ball was immediately followed by a succession of parties, about two per day, with these and other musicians playing for dancing towards the end of each.

⁷ This was a Romanian land reform in which land was taken mainly from Hungarian and other non-Romanian estates and redistributed mainly among Romanian peasants as smallholdings.

⁸ To the present day two completely distinct histories of Transylvania are available, written by Hungarians or Romanians. In both cases the one is the rightful, natural or ancient possessor of the country and the other is an invading and intruding alien guilty of oppression and cruelty, and of diplomatic double-dealing in securing overall control at various times. This animosity extends to areas of study which in western Europe are normally considered free of political animus, such as church furnishings. Transylvania has been politically torn between these two neighbours since the creation of Romania in the mid 19th century, and any chance there might have been of freeing it from them has been denied, principally the decision of the Treaty of Trianon 1920, in the aftermath of both the European war and the collapse of the Habsburg Empire, to deliver the country wholesale to Romania, a decision repeated in 1945. It is not a conflict which could ever be resolved unilaterally because it holds the seeds of a major cultural conflict: Hungarian Transylvania was a spearhead of Enlightenment (Reformation, Scientific) culture extended towards the East, as against the (primitive, peasant, Orthodox, oriental etc.) culture of Romanian Transylvania. The long-standing sophistication of Transylvanian-Hungarian culture can be seen in a visit to the Teleki Library at Tirgu Mureş (opened to the public 1802), which displays editions of Goethe and Newton translated into Hungarian in the same decade as first publication and printed in Tirgu Mureş, alongside the first ever Tibetan-English dictionary created by one of the locals after a very long walk... The street it is in is named Bolyai after the father and son who in this same now poverty-stricken, decayed, and atmospherically polluted town, rose to international prominence as mathematicians in the 19th century, mainly

for work in non-Euclidean geometry. The Romanian contrast would be a small Gothic wooden church containing ikons of basic human figurations (mother-and-child) rendered as celestial, the walls heavy with frescoes of miracles and sacrifice, the whole thing dedicated to what cannot and never will be known or understood. Each of these implies the eradication of the other, which means that power should have been handed to neither. But the possibility of Transylvania as an independent country would not have been considered on account of its smallness. Such a country, if it could have existed, might have been forced to structure itself as a harmonious multi-ethnic society, which locally, in 'peasant' pockets, it has been. The U.S.S.R. of course would have gobbled it up in a decade, but it gobbled up both Hungary and Romania anyway.

The official Romanian (Bucharest) attitude, as manifested particularly in the promotions of its embassies, is that Romania is a unified modern state, needing only massive capital investment from the West to bring it fully into the modern world. Gypsies, peasants etc. represent marginal relics which should not be taken seriously. Hungarians are not mentioned. This posing before the Euro and Dollar masks a great deal of corruption and mismanagement. It has normally been a culture of thugs.

[9] Bartók pointed out that the music of the gypsies themselves, the songs they sang in their settlements and camps, had no connection with the music the gypsy bands played. There are in fact clearly documented exceptions to this, which may represent an up-take by gypsy communities of songs the instrumentalists were playing for other groups, but nevertheless some doubt must now be cast on the categorical nature of Bartók's statement, especially with regard to dawn songs. Liszt's reading of what he heard as purely gypsy music was an error but understandable given the lack of information available to him. See additional note P/i p.144 on the historical role of the gypsy musician and 'The Last Gypsy', pp.166–169 on the relationship of the music to gypsy society and the importance of gypsy laments.

[10] Romanian students of the music would be dismayed, or infuriated, by the priority given to the Hungarian population in this paragraph. But the point is that, in a sense, the Romanians were not around at the time. Except in certain special zones such as Maramureş, the aristocracy and the peasant smallholders were *both* Hungarian, and the Romanians are reported as living as many gypsies do now, as unlanded labourers in poor quality housing on the edges of the villages. They certainly had their own music, but on the present thesis, when the gypsy bands started playing for them, maybe not before the 20th century, their music was absorbed into an established way of accompanying and treating song and dance melodies which tended to decrease, but not eradicate, the distinction between Hungarian and Romanian. There might also at various times have been those who viewed themselves as 'Transylvanians' whatever language they spoke, but these are entirely unrepresented in the wars of nationalist musicology.

[11] Liszt says that the leading gypsy troupes would never engage themselves for more than a limited time, always eventually returning (individually or together) to the towns and villages, not to rest but to work there, presumably for much poorer pay. He also mentions that while a gypsy band did stay its personnel would constantly change.

[12] One of the questions I have not yet found an answer to, is who played for dancing at a ball at an establishment such as Eszterháza? I find it very hard to believe that Haydn's already burdensome duties included the direction of music for interminable balls, though he did leave behind a few minuets and allemandes which may have been used for the purpose. It has been said that the Emperor employed gypsy bands for recruitment drives, and to play in his courtyard, and an engraving of an outdoor parade in 1791 shows a group of them (two fiddles, cimbalom and small portable string bass) playing to the side of the processing cavalry. But they do not feature in the Esterháza pay-roll. Haydn's own 'folk tunes' have been described as Croatian in character, corresponding to the area and society he was born into, Esterháza being in the same cultural zone, and it is claimed that there he would have heard these tunes every day. Croatia was incorporated into southern Hungary until 1868. But his 'gypsy' tunes are distinct among these, mainly because distinctly instrumental in character, and the most telling feature is not a tune but an instrumental technique. In a broadcast interview in 2005 the violinist Monica Huggett described the 1st violin line of the second movement of the String Quartet in C opus 54 no. 2 as virtually a transcription of a gypsy fiddler's ornamentation, and when she plays it the resemblance is striking. Other slow movements with less written-out ornamentation could no doubt be performed in this way.

Telemann, in a similar position at the court of Count Erdmann von Promnitz at Sorau (now Zary) in Poland, accompanied his master in tours of estates all over upper Silesia and in the process got to hear a lot of village music of the Poles and Hanaks. He was one of the first 'educated' musicians to be astonished and captivated by this music (which was probably mainly bagpipe music) and he spoke with warm admiration of the extraordinary inventiveness of the players. He learned many tunes and rhythms in the villages, which passed through him ('dressed up in Italian clothes' as he said in his autobiography) into the 'Polish' manner (polonaises and mazurkas) of 18th and 19th century printed music. This manner was at the time no more an exotic or 'folkloric' manner than any other, such as the older German and French forms (allemande, sarabande, courante, menuet, gigue…) though rarer.

There remains Schubert, who in 1824 returned to Zseliz (now Želiezovce in Slovakia) where he had worked in 1818 for Count Esterházy, and there heard and was interested in 'Hungarian' folk music. There he wrote 'Hungarian Melody' (D817) for piano, and 'Divertisssement à la Hongroise' (D818) for piano 4-hands. These involve a number of imitative techniques, including a 'stop-start' pattern in the 3rd movement of D818, some of which can be further traced in his two A-minor major string quartets of this period, known as 'Rosamunde' and 'Death and the Maiden', though some of them may also be traced to Haydn. The left-hand accompanying pattern in D817 can be played so as to sound very like kontra chordal technique.

It seems obvious to me that the written music of court and town which we receive as classical music, had always prior to the 19th century existed in a symbiotic relationship with an unwritten music for the social use of the greater part of the population, a music which lived principally in the villages but was brought unchanged to the towns, and even, possibly, to the courts up to the 17th century. Only scholastic contrapuntal music refused this connection (with exceptions), and rebellions against its dictation, such as Monteverdi's innovations, are invariably infused with 'country dance' factors, the presence of which is never lost sight of in the various developments of subsequent Italian, French, German, Bohemian and English music through the 17th century. But this 'country dance' music was a separate issue from the sung music of the peasant, being normally supplied by professional musicians, some of a separate caste, who may have adapted village tunes but also used music newly composed for the purpose by classically trained musicians. This process is particularly well documented for Scotland [Johnson 1972] and is fairly clear in Hungary. In central Europe most of these dance musicians would have moved between village and town, and maybe also into the court. So it was a music already shared between the village and the town, in different versions and in different degrees, directly or indirectly. The two CDs by the Jánosi Ensemble demonstrate winningly the classical/folk hybridity of Hungarian-Transylvanian dance music, using both written and unwritten sources.

[13] The Székely are a Hungarian-speaking population in east-central Transylvania and beyond, thought to have distinct racial origins

[14] The bagpipe is said to have been formerly the principal musical instrument of the whole of Eastern European (and other) peasantry, made redundant by the appeal of the more sophisticated gypsy string bands (clarinets and guitars in other places), and surviving in a flourishing condition in places beyond the string band's catchment area, such as Bulgaria and Croatia. The earliest strata of string music in the northern and eastern fringes of Transylvania retain drone and other bagpipe effects, as in Gyimes, and Gypsies working for Romanians in the mainland were liable to be required to produce bagpipe effects on demand.

[15] Very little has survived of music for the Saxons, a formerly significant group of high social standing who kept themselves apart and probably patronised conservatory-trained musicians in the towns. They were Germans who, like several other local populations, were settled by invitation in the middle ages with land and special privileges, to protect the Ottoman or Slav borders, and came to dominate

several major cities. They were constantly besieged by Hungarians, Romanians and Turks for nearly a millennium, and during the 20th century most of them emigrated to Germany. They certainly sometimes employed the gypsy bands for weddings etc., and some musicians can still remember ländler and suchlike pieces which were for them. Similarly there are remnants in musicians' memories of the repertoire for the Jewish population which was wiped out during the 1939-45 war. This was a distinct set of pieces marked by Jewish musical features and not so easily transferred to other groups. In fact Jewish bands were in some areas themselves, with the gypsies, purveyors of music both to their own and to other groups, for they were the other 'outsiders' in this society, and musician has in many societies been the optimum outsider profession. The village of Rozavlea in Maramureş used to have a Jewish band working with two violins, cimbalom, bass and drum, which was in demand across the whole area, and whose playing influenced Maramureş music as a whole.

The same village, a large one, had a troupe of Jewish dwarf entertainers, the Ovitz family, sometimes described as a 'circus' but more like a stage show. Their skills included singing, acting, dancing and playing miniature musical instruments: two violins, guitar, cimbalom, accordion and drum-kit, forming a six-piece band. This is not a traditional Maramureş instrumentation and it is not clear from the book on them what kinds of music the Ovitzes played [Koren and Negev 2004]. Certainly by the time they had been through Auschwitz as material for medical experiments and eventually reached Israel they were playing light popular music of the day. But in their early days they must have played at least some Maramureş music, and some accounts talk of them wearing Romanian costumes in their acts. There may have been other such troupes, but I have seen no mention of them, beyond travelling marionette theatres and fairground swings. Indeed reading of the Ovitzes' activities after having become accustomed to the idea of Maramureş as an essentially 'peasant' culture with a highly developed and exclusive form of folk-music is quite an anomalous experience. The highly specific Maramureş music certainly exists, but it was never alone, just as none of the villages is far away from a town, and evidently an 'outsider' group had a range of different entertainment music which it could take up to purvey to the local population. The Ovitz's repertoire was said to include 'melancholy songs', probably of the types which have been cultivated in many strata all over the Carpathians and Balkans.

Almost nothing has survived of the music the Jewish bands played (but see the cassette of the Ukrainian Bukovinian violinist Leon Schwartz), though attempts are afoot to reinvent it from the evidence (CDs by Muzsikás and Di Naye Kapelye). These revivals tend to stress its ethnic Jewish qualities, which it certainly had, though Schwartz makes it clear that it also participated in Carpathian music as a whole.

It is difficult even today to imagine the gypsy string bands playing for the gypsies, some of whom are still nomadic in horse-drawn wagons, and the bulk of whom have for a long time lived in low quality housing on the edges of towns and villages. But they have always had their trades, many qualifying as merchants, and they were certainly among the patrons of this music. Many pieces survive labelled 'Gypsy csárdás', 'Cigány hájnáli' etc., which seem to imply regular engagements for the bands at purely gypsy festivities, for the gypsies were certainly not allowed to dance at Hungarian or Romanian events [see Section 5]. Nowadays there is a small élite of rich gypsies but I haven't heard of them employing the gypsy bands. Nobody seems to remember ever playing anything for the Armenians, a merchant or banker class who were important in some towns on the eastern side of the country.

[16] The internationalism of this music rests partly on the internationalism of the (Italian) violin itself and a long history of imported prestige musicians, but equally in its participation in the innate internationalism of peasant music, such as Bartók discovered for this area in his collecting and research, whereby musical modes and details are traded anywhere within hearing and beyond, especially by non-sedentary professions such as soldiers, foresters and shepherds, regardless of state or ethnic boundaries. This process might normally operate by way of things being 'brought home' but it also reflects the pre-nationalist nature of peasant society and its retention, however remote, of the migratory option. It does not make the peasant a 'liberal' but it does contradict the appropriation of peasant culture as an anchorage to isolationist policies. Bartók got into a lot of trouble with nationalists in the pre-war period. He was accused of falsification by Romanians for finding 'Hungarian influence' in Romanian music, and he was called a traitor by Hungarians for listening to Romanian music at all. His answer to these was the essay 'Race Purity in Music' (1942, in *Essays* 1976).

Nowhere more than in Romania has nationalism used the peasant music to its own purposes, but of course it has always presented the rural music not so much to the nation as to the urban work force as an internalised confirmation, relying on ignorance of its actual diversity. For on the ground it becomes manifestly absurd to present some village repertoire as an emanation of the Romanian soul, when you can move 20 kms down the road and the music is significantly different. National 'folk music' has to be some sort of digest, a reduction of many local musics to a superficial homogeny, whether by political forces as in Romania, or commercial ones as in Ireland.

In the immensely shelf-filling *New Grove Dictionary of Music and Musicians* (2000) there is in fact no entry 'Transylvania', in spite of the fact that the country has a distinct history in both 'art' and 'traditional' music (but then neither is there one for Lancashire, which has one too). In the traditional music articles it becomes a footnote to Hungary as an eastward extension of the country where more has survived; in the Romanian article it hardly exists at all and certainly has no Hungarians anywhere near it.

¹⁷ This music has separate distinctly Hungarian origins, and a different organisation. It was invented out of rural music in the first wave of Hungarian nationalism in the early 19th century with a considerable contribution of original composition. In fact most of the repertoire is composed, often by the Hungarian middle-class customers themselves. But there is some blurring because this town music has constantly influenced the village music towards new melodic styles and harmonies, and the town composers have deliberately imitated features of the village music for coloration. And some musicians must have worked in both fields, especially in the smaller towns. The music does not altogether deserve the disdain which has been heaped on it; even today in the restaurants of Budapest it can be a subtle and charming music with a certain amount of 'gypsy' virtuosic vivacity in the performance. At the time Liszt was captivated by it (as was Debussy) it must have been a stronger music than it is now, perhaps closer to the Transylvanian bands in some respects, especially when played for dancing. There is an equivalent in Bucharest restaurants, deriving from the gypsy 'taraf' bands of eastern Romania but now sounding very similar to the Budapest bands.

¹⁸ Anti-imperial feeling was increasingly strong among Hungarians in the 19th century and by the time Charles Bonner was visiting, Vienna was spoken of almost entirely with resentment and aggression, but I doubt if this would have prevented the gentry from keeping in touch with western 'culture and refinement' and thus German and Austrian music. The culture of the Saxons was oriented almost exclusively in that direction.

¹⁹ In Romanian, Bonțida. I use the Hungarian name here as the documentation is principally Hungarian.

²⁰ The Ökrös Ensemble's CD of Bonchida music has singing in all three languages, suggesting an artistic zone of inter-ethnic freedom under the auspices of the Hungarian nobility. I can only understand this as a retrospective and idealistic construct based on the survival of pieces from Bonchida with various ethnic labels, for it is only the music that actually 'harmonises'. Glimpses of inter-ethnic collaboration in other pursuits exist quite widely in peasant life often at its 'lowest', least urban, niveau, usually at the tops of valleys where they had to work together, and did, but see the CD of the fiddler Ferenc Varga "Csipás" (Antal Fekete series) which was recorded at a wedding in Kalotaszeg in 1977. In this, perhaps due to the comparative sophistication of this zone, the participatory singing and shouting makes it clear that guests included both Hungarians and Romanians. Generally, evidence of ethnic separation and *we/ they* structuring in the smallholder classes dominating Transylvanian villages is commoner. The original Viennese attachment of these aristocrats had probably converted by the early 20th century to Hungarian nationalist anti-Viennese sentiment, which demanded above all 'Hungarian' music for its entertainment,

though the 'Romanian' and 'Gypsy' pieces in the band's repertoire would have been perfectly acceptable, as they still are to the Hungarian smallholders.

[21] There is no reason to expect song texts to be involved in this condition, since probably the music played in Banffy's castle was principally or entirely dance-music and the villages would have adapted existing songs to the Bonchida music. On the small sample available there is a possibility that love songs were favoured; all those chosen by Ökrös are songs of rejected love. One begins to suspect the feel of the 'pastoral', the shepherd lamenting his love-loss, presented to the court as a thing of innocent charm, yet they probably derive directly from the villages. You could hardly say there is a 'literary tone' to the text such as the one which overwhelms Irish folk song. The one song labelled *hajnali* (dawn song, the only one of this genre out of about 50 songs) is actually rather less depressed than most of the others – it shows some defiance within the loss. The theme is 'I'd like to be there in the church when my lover gets married, to hear her perjure herself before God'.

[22] On the other hand it seems rash to assume that however close the gypsy band were to the head of the house, and whatever functions they performed, they were necessarily the only musicians in his employ. One feels that 'the Transylvanian Versailles' must have had more going on in it musically than a gypsy band for dances, however much treasured. Yet the novel written by one of the Banffys, set in the late 19th century, makes no mention of resident musicians, gypsy or other, at Bonchida, and the dancing is all done to a gypsy band in nearby Kolosvár (Cluj), where the Banffys had a town house.

[23] Kása remarks that when he photographed the remains of the old Bonchida band (1976, apparently only two of them left) they were 'always smiling a bit' when they played. I have noticed this myself with other bands (e.g. Soporul) and take it to represent, remotely, the necessary smile of servant to master, but in a privileged relationship without servility. I've noticed it as a quite superior, knowing smile, a delicate and close smile as of fulfilling a contract, and least of all the show-biz teeth-gleam. A less endearing survival of the same relationship is perhaps the irritating habit of 'gypsy' musicians in Budapest restaurants, of walking over to your table while playing and ingratiatingly inclining over your shoulder while rosin dust spreads over your food, without even giving you the chance to request a csárdás rather than 'The Beautiful Blue Danube'. But Walter Starkie's account of Budapest and Transylvanian towns in 1929 strongly suggests that the original point of this approach to your table was, in the city restaurants as in the farmhouse, that you would want to *sing* .

[24] Apart from aristocracy and peasantry it should also be remembered that in the early 20th century if not earlier these musicians earned an important part of

their livelihoods playing in nearby towns, mostly in restaurants though possibly also in other places such as parks, silent-film cinemas and some kinds of dances. Here they would probably have played a repertoire in some degree different and more open to innovation and harmonic refinement, and these elements would have been taken back to the villages, reinforcing in the case of Bonchida the sophistication of the playing. The death-blow to this diversity was the introduction of licenses for musicians in the late 1940s, which most musicians for various reasons could not get, or not afford to get, and so were restricted to 'amateur' work in their own villages while working in factories.

Another aspect of 'special' feel of the Bonchida band is that the playing is much more like that of Kalotaszeg, and what this must mean is not transregional influence, but more likely contact in both zones with urban or international practice, producing more complex harmony, transposition and modulation, independent bass line, etc. and at times a superficiality which is absent from gutbucket village music (see additional notes K/i-ii, p.139, on the urban contacts of Kalotaszegi music).

[25] There can be no doubt that the music is on the way out, and will only continue untransformed while it receives support from outside the villages, and of course this new audience, even the dedicated *tánchaz* sector of it, has different expectations of the music and will tend to modify it into more staged forms. As regards the village string bands, those which survive best are generally the ones which have become ikons of the Budapest revival movement, especially Magyarpalatka and Szászcsávás, and Netti before he died in 2005. As 'star' bands gaining an external audience by national and international touring and CDs they lose any real social function at home, mainly because the villagers can no longer afford them. Their repertoires tend to be reduced to routines and they become liable to add items from other Transylvanian zones, sometimes almost making themselves into *tánchaz* bands.

Extended playing with collaborative extemporisation as at the old full-scale social events must now be rare. I have attended several village dances in Transylvania since 1998 but they have not usually amounted to more than a sequence of 5- or 10-minute dance sets lasting two hours with an interval, as at any English 'social'. A village band playing for one of the many Hungarian summer dance camps, as many bands do, will be expected mainly to play two or three well-known dance sets of fixed length (15 to 20 minutes) repeatedly. On national or international tours, and when playing for the small musical tour groups which are beginning to roam the country, a band will play a series of set pieces, varying the programme by including songs, dancing, and sometimes 'gypsy' pieces, but never letting a piece extend itself for too long. Having participated in such tours with Wim Bosmans, I've learned from him the need to coax from the bands the full range of the repertoire, as by specifically requesting funeral tunes and soldiers' farewells (and dawn songs in the appropriate areas), otherwise the band might be unrelentingly bucolic for the entire evening.

Only international engagements, such as Szászcsávás gets about once a year, are enough to make any real financial difference to the bands. Very few bands get them, only one or two, and even for them this source is not regular or reliable. Szászcsávás musicians have been able to buy themselves out of the 'gypsy village' as a result of one American and one Japanese tour, but as they remain unlanded they depend on continuing well-paid European engagements for their livelihoods, while the younger musicians try to move the music towards a virtuosic 'gypsy' character which in principle should eventually have the same destructive effect it had on Taraf de Haidouks [further on Csávás see additional note P/ii, p.145]. Sándor Fodor 'Neti' for all the take-up he got from Budapest was not able to do much more than get himself out of the gypsy quarter of Méra into a nearby suburban village, in fairly poor housing. Increasingly, band members, especially younger ones, live and work in the towns, playing only at week-ends. The late *primás* of Magyarpalatka, Márton Kodoba, in spite of the band's wide repute and a regular monthly engagement at *Fonó* in Budapest, worked latterly as a refuse-collector in Dej. It seems that true patronage within the village economy when it flourished was more effective than occasional urban bounties. Perhaps the saddest factor is that when a successful musician becomes too old to play there is no infrastructure to support him and he is reliant on the family. Musicians without that support can sink into destitution.

There must be hundreds of surviving unrenowned and unrecorded village bands (and a number of isolated musicians as older band members die and are not replaced), and who knows what qualities they may maintain or for how much longer? Romanian-speaking bands have been particularly under-recorded and under-funded because the Budapest-based surveys tend not to reach them. Only three such have gained any repute: Mociu, Emil Mihai's band (which plays other kinds of music under a different name), and Soporul de Câmpie (who disappeared to U.S.A. for a long time.)

However, the above picture (mine in about 2005) is modified somewhat by the appearance of the Cluj-based website http://traditiiclujene.ro/index.php which has mounted about 50 CDs for free listening, mostly of lightweight *musică populară* but including a dozen 'classic' string bands from villages in the county of Cluj, a large area including the Hungarian zones of Kalotaszeg and Mezöszég. These include no less then two bands from Soporul de Câmpie who did not emigrate to U.S.A., five bands I've never heard of, and, rather cheekily, two bands formerly appropriated by Budapest, indeed emanating from two Hungarian 'musical villages' which have regular Hungarian folk-camps etc. now appearing under their Romanian names of Sic (for Szék) and Palatca (for Magyarpalatka). This is perhaps a sign of a Romanian drive to reclaim the music, though there is nothing defiant about the presentation.

The old cry is still much raised, 'The young people don't want it any more', which is viewed with resignation. In a village such as Szászcsávás neither the young nor the old can in fact any longer afford it (we were lucky to get them at

100 Euros for the six-piece band for one evening). But it is also true that in a sense the young never have wanted it. Like most or possibly all 'traditional' musics world-wide, the music has changed, at times radically, and it has been young people who have enforced the changes. The change from pre- to post-gypsy-band takeover must have seemed to some like the destruction of a venerable beauty. But the old music survived within the new and the demands of youth could generally be satisfied within the received framework. It is a different matter when the old music is replaced by something in a cassette which was recorded in a Los Angeles studio. How much that matters will depend on how much need for actual social music-making continues to be felt, and in Transylvania, unless ones worst fears are realised including the forces of the EU, I think the existing rural society might continue to adapt itself so as not to be taken over. It might, for instance, connect to a western European post-metropolitan cultural development by which it gains by remaining distinct from the metropolitan. If that happens the music will continue, within whatever kind of jitterbug vibration creeps in to enfold it.

Indeed it could be that Hungarian bands in being supported from and valued by the Budapest *táncház* movement are at the same time stopped in their tracks, and in order to maintain that support must disregard a demand for progression which is actually integral to village music. Certainly some of them develop two repertoires or two manners, one for authenticity and one for the villages. Romanian bands do not feel this pressure to the same degree (though it exists for them) and so, depending on where they are, will more freely modernise their music, diversify their repertoires, or go under.

During the Communist period many Romanian village musicians were drawn into conservatoires and thus into organised folkloric ensembles of various kinds, some of them orchestral, where they learned to read music, to understand harmonic systems and to make arrangements. The Hungarian musicians, and Romanians who remained localised, seem to have got through the period on compulsory industrial work and casual or clandestine playing. This experience has affected the music permanently, not necessarily for the worse. In the Romanian musical zones various forms of modernisation have taken place, some so carefully handled as hardly to count as modernisation at all. This happened a long time ago in Bucureşti, before Communism, where the music of the gypsy bands of Wallachia and Oltenia became a vibrant town music for restaurants clubs and dances, led by violin, accordion and cimbalom, and even the sophisticated music of the renowned *chanteuse* Maria Tanase retained strong traditional features. The early work of the Manele heart-throb Nicolae Guţă was inventively and passionately situated in the same, cimbalom-led tradition, though his recent work doesn't sound Romanian at all. No metropolis in Transylvania could rival 'the Paris of the east' in metamorphosing its local music into someone like Maria Tănase, but it is interesting to note how many Romanian musicians continued to develop what they did in various ways for the market while Hungarian musicians stayed with 'authenticity'.

Incidentally, however much concern there is to preserve this music now, its practitioners of course showed no concern for preserving its antecedents. In the gypsies' drive to take over all village public music-making they probably erased bagpipe music, epic singing, social choral singing, and several other forms in most of Transylvania, and there were complaints in some areas that they had even taken over the improvised personal lamenting at funerals and represented it in instrumental versions.

There is a cassette by a Romanian fiddler called Elec Alexandru Lăcătuş of traditional tunes from two valleys in the heart of what is to the Hungarians Kalotaszeg, and some of the same tunes played by Neti and others occur shifted into the mode known as 'Musică Populară', which is the Romanian term for all village or traditional music, the difference being that in the Romanian provincial market the music is not archival, but an entertainment music for social occasions, restaurants, and recording. With Lăcătuş the difference this makes in his treatment of tunes held in common with the Hungarians is a delicate matter. The *primas* line might be the same but for a slight shift into syncopation, a faintly jazz-like triplet rhythm in passage-work, and a more projective or showy violin tone (possibly the work of studio engineers); and the backing is more clipped and rhythmically weighted. Slight matters, but you would never mistake one style for the other. It seems to me to be a quite worthy version of the music but offering nothing like the depth of the Kalotaszeg dawn songs. There are certainly far worse versions of the modernisation or tempering of the music which is endemic to the Romanian scene.

Romanian television in Transylvania has two programmes of *Musică Populară* which seem to run episodically all day long and show almost entirely a series of folk troupes posed in front of the camera in full peasant regalia, singing homogenised and diluted arrangements of village music while dancing minimally – mainly just shifting from side to side with one hand held aloft, and smiling, everlastingly smiling. Sometimes singers and players appear in fields or haystacks with their accordions and electric keyboards. The tone and appeal of these charades, which must be very popular, is indicated by the fact that most of the time there is a text band running beneath the on-screen picture, and customers can, for a price, telephone in messages to be sent on it. The one I understood went, 'Thank you for the cake, mother.' I don't know if these programmes are intended for town or country people but compared with anything happening in an actual village they represent anodyne fantasy. What is mainly missing is the real energy of the dance, which has degenerated into smoothly flowing unemphatic rhythms and infantile minimal body movement (curiously similar to the movement of Tellytubbies). And yet 'the real thing' is not far behind it, for the programme I saw included on older woman giving a quite respectable rendition of a slow *doină*, with feeling and well ornamented, suffering only from strophic rigidity and electronic keyboard accompaniment. Many of the effects of Communist-era massification have passed, sometimes hardly altered, into the demands of the market, but compared with the folksy TV programmes the state ensembles were at least lively. It should be added that these programmes put out Transylvanian music in large quantities, but seem not to allow the existence of Hungarian or gypsy music, musicians, or people.

Being market-led is not necessarily a disaster; it depends what the market serves. There seems to have been a handful of Romanian local musicians who passed through some form of Communist-period centralised control of their music to retrieve at the end a new transparency, reducing the band to two or three bowed string instruments, singing or playing 'straight' but delicately ornamented versions of local tunes over a developed vocabulary of subtly inflected harmonisation, producing a quite melancholy effect, as if presenting a newly enshrined version of a past music. And they do this with considerable skill and eloquence. There might be quite a few of these – the ones I know are the fiddler Efta Botoca from the southern Banat, now dead (see my piece 'Efta Botoca' in *The Dance at Mociu*, 2003, 2014) and the singer Grigore Leșe of the Lăpuș area between Maramureș and central Transylvania. Both have been through conservatoires and/or state ensembles to return to a newly inflected regional 'smallness'. In neither case is the tone ethereal or over-sweetened; Lese in particularly is a strong singer in the true 'unrefined' tones of the village. It could be a matter, finally, of recovering and working in a modern sense a condition of traditional music whereby it is not *made to be attractive* – that is, attractive to an otherness, an audience, an elsewhere, a distribution, but is *made within our attraction*; made for and by us who made it, for our needs and to locate our own condition. Leșe certainly shows that this can be maintained in a post-village arena if you are careful enough. And then there is Ioan Pop.

The music of Maramureș has remained better intact than most other zones of Romania, comparatively free from either scholarly/revival or national/popular intervention. So it has to some extent changed under its own terms, developed and diversified within its own sphere. There are now children's choirs, 'festival' stagings, versions of the music shifted towards jazz, *manele* and even beat (mainly for the cassette and wedding markets) as elsewhere, and there is of course a 'soft' version suitable for backing messages to mother about the cake. Most of the arranged and staged ensemble versions, however, seem to be oriented outside the area, in the national traditional market, so that the performers are aware of themselves as 'folklore' rather than the normal music-making of the place they live in. The range of singing has foreclosed considerably and the regular Sunday village dances are no longer held, but a surprising amount of the music will resurface when an occasion provokes it. And most of these various versions are done by the same musicians, all thoroughly versed in the 'straight' village versions, which continue to hold strong principally for local dancing. There is a seemingly unending supply of musicians, especially virtuoso fiddlers, who seem to lurk in quantity in every village. There are nationally popular Maramureș musicians like the Petreuș Brothers who do a pan-Maramureș music which erodes the distinct modes of particular villages but remains authentic, while others will replicate faithfully musical characteristic belonging to an area of a hundred hectares or less. ('Set any violinist on a chair in front of me and ask him to play for five minutes, and I will tell you which village he comes from.' – Ioan Pop). So in all this proliferation you might get the musician who plays for a village dance event on a Saturday evening in August, freely interacting with the dancers in extended pieces and producing rare old dance measures out of the hat on request, appearing on the Sunday at a festival, dutifully accompanying the school song and dance troupe of his village on the stage. He might (or might not) also do a 'hotted-up' version for cassettes and weddings which require it, or he might do a quite different, national-rural-popular dance music for such occasions. And up to a point, the same quality runs through all these, resulting from a continuity (which is irrevocably lost in the British or 'Celtic' revival scenes).

Probably the most convincing and cohesive musical personality in Maramureş is the multi-instrumentalist, smallholder, entrepreneur and teacher Ioan Pop, who lives in the village of Hoteni in an establishment adapted to accommodate visiting groups and musicians but which remains a Maramureş smallholding. His group, called 'Iza' after one of the major valleys of the historical Maramureş, is an ad-hoc ensemble drawn from the most distinguished singers and instrumentalists of the surrounding villages, all of whom retain their normal occupations, usually that of smallholder, but also labourer, commuting worker or gypsy, and participate in the group when and as they can. It can be quite difficult for Iza to fulfil engagements in October when the pressure of the harvest is on. It plays otherwise when it gets a chance, locally, nationally and occasionally abroad, and for cassettes and CDs. The group doesn't normally play for occasions such as weddings but Popic himself goes out of his way to involve the villagers in his music and will play for them, and with whatever other musicians are lying around at the time, who immediately thus become 'Iza', whenever an opportunity presents itself. There is no question of new high fees cutting him off from where he is. Some of the impromptu local sessions have been recorded and included in Iza's issued recordings (from Ethnophonie Budapest, see discography). The music is simply the local repertoire of songs and dances, a large one, which everyone knows. In most of these respects Iza can be sharply distinguished from the normally gypsy village bands of Transylvania proper, especially in not being fully professional, an advantage in that however welcome what they earn might be, most players are not totally dependent on it for their living. They can thus afford, to repeat my words, to operate the music within their own attraction rather than setting it up to attract others.

Ioan Pop ('Popic') has also been through the Communist era of ensembles and Romanianisation, and what he has preserved from this has enabled him to lead the music forward without detaching it. When he started most Maramureş instrumental music consisted of fiddle guitar and drum working a somewhat shrunken vocabulary of dance tunes, the strummed guitar often keeping to one chord through all the music. Popic has extended the vocabulary of guitar chords to include all the standard diatonic major and minor chords and added a violin or viola playing 'kontra' chords and sometimes a string bass. These moves have both modernised the music and restored it to its former sonic richness and variety (as in the 1973 recordings on Ocora's *Musique de Mariage du Maramureş*, which include bass and a second violin playing kontra. The performances are rough but hint at future possibilities). He may not have been the only one to effect these changes but Iza remains the only Maramureş music I have heard which can extend into a small ensemble without lapsing towards automative costume playing.

Popic and Leşe operate, in their ways, as innovators and conservators in the same breath. Leşe's synthesis produces a melancholic tone which is not integral to such a quest, whereas Popic's music remains bright to the point of fiery, though a melancholy tone will establish itself in the rendering, especially, of familiar old songs. There are probably more such musicians in the country; another is Dumitru Iederan of the Chioar or Forest region west of Maramureş, who has single-handedly saved an entire department of village music from extinction by playing it, training young musicians and manufacturing stringed instruments.

(This footnote last updated 2006. For further updating see the 'Appendix 2006' which was added to the second edition (2014) of my book, The Dance at Mociu. *Further on Iza, see additional note Y on p.160. On the tánchàz scene see additional note V on p.156.)*

(C) ...THAT I SHOULD WANDER THE EARTH...

Sometimes I wonder if I dreamt the whole thing. Did I fabricate all this out of a few hints in CD notes? Or did it really take place? Somewhere up in the hills of the edge of Europe, in a farmhouse room of a village smallholding in one of the Carpathian valleys, or in the open air of the yard with lanterns and awnings, in a pause marked by the incipient onset of first light across the hills, so far from where we think things "happen" – did people really come forward one by one to face the musicians and sing melancholy songs of extraordinary power and serenity? So that I start thinking of Cara, Monteverdi, Dowland, and all sorts of things? I think of the French 17th century solo *Lamentation* genre, of Sainte-Colombe and de Visée, of some of Handel's lamentational arias, of the *Seven Last Words*... of the *ghazal*... Is this actually conceivable? And they were their own songs, versions of known fates personally acknowledged and tied into the common lot, imaginative constructs from worst possible scenarios rolled forth with the slow irrevocability of the turning earth...? And not set out in a proscenium distance but in the round present, taken on intimately by the whole company, an agreed comprehension of irrevocable passage. An 'orchestra'. Did this happen? For if it did happen there, it could have happened anywhere, such as here, in the lost oral histories beyond the light of the metropolis, in the 18th century, when Lancashire hand-loom weavers in remote villages were studying Handel scores by candle-light... The resources were there, the villages not isolated from the towns into time-lapses but participating in the same experiments and the same conservations with their own resources in a real past. Does it mean that the refined, the serious, high lyric was not after all the property of a mere group, casting the rest of the population into silence?

Additional Notes

A.	Dawn, Magic, Police	124
B.	Geography of the String Band	124
C/i + C/ii.	Development of the String Band	125
D/i.	Old Songs with New Harmonies?	127
D/ii + D/iii.	Dawn Song and Court Dancing	128
D/iv.	Dance Sequences	130
D/v.	Dancing and Not Dancing to Dance Music [aside]	133
E.	Accompanied Singing	134
F.	Listening Pieces	134
G.	C19 Hungarian Nationalist Culture and the Csárdás	135
H.	Marginal Zones	135
I.	Duration	137
J.	'Pure' Melancholy	138
K/i.	Urban Contacts	139
K/ii.	More Urban Contacts and 'Gypsy' Alternation	139
L.	Written Sources	124
M.	Diversity of Village Music	140
(Note N was cancelled)		142
O/i + O/ii + O/iii.	The Laments	142
P/i + P/ii.	Gypsy Musicians	144
Q.	English and Hungarian Folk-song Collectors	148
R.	Proprietorship of Melodies among the Gentry of Transylvania and Norfolk	151
S.	Hungarian or Romanian Music	152
T.	How Many Dawn Songs Are There and How Does Neti Remember Them All?	154
U.	Composition	155
V.	Tánchaz	156
W.	Flamenco and Pibroch	158
X.	Tremolo	159
Y.	Electra	160
Z.	Field and Mud	163

#A Dawn, Magic, Police

In the practice of village magic or sorcery attested in places like Maramureș in the 1980s, and not dead yet – I was seriously informed in 2001 that the Romanian government had recently imposed value-added tax on witches' spells – dawn is the prescribed time for the performance of most spells and incantations [Masson 1982]. As a point of transition, dawn figures access to another world at the same time as a return to the diurnal and it offers both relief and danger. It also stands for the transmigration of the soul (see Appendix 2), departure of the bride, enlistment of the soldier, and imprisonment of the outlaw – for dawn is also the time when the 'gendarmes' arrive to make an arrest in the outlaw ballads and prison songs. It is a bridging-point or node at which the world opens and closes.

#B Geography of the String Band
(cf. footnote 1, p.53)

The range of the music is wider than Transylvanian and is best described as Carpathian, both sides of the eastern border of the former Austro-Hungarian Empire, centred on Transylvania. It is sometimes called rather inaccurately the 'Carpathian string quartet style'. Surviving village string bands within the same concept occur in western Hungary, Ukrainian and Polish Bukowina, Moravia, eastern Romania and parts of the Balkans further east, usually with harmonic second violins rather than violas. In several of these places this style is in competition with an alternative band format involving the cimbalom, but this instrument can also be incorporated into the string band. None of those I've heard from outside Transylvania has the particular ensemble quality of the Transylvanian bands, mainly because the central chords tend not to be sustained but struck rather briefly and emphatically on the on-beat. Slow songs are sometimes accompanied by a *tremolando*, which is rare in Transylvania but common among the gypsy *lautari* of eastern Romania. But I have heard Polish bands from the Tatra Mountains and Moravian string bands which come quite close to the Transylvanian sound, not only in slower and gentler pieces. Nothing quite like it occurs anywhere else in the world. It obviously represents a very particular synthesis of classical and folk techniques, the roots of which are hard to trace.

The heartland of the music is perhaps shown by its resistance to the cimbalom, which presses on it from two sides. This, the hammer dulcimer, with an immense ancestry in the near and central East, was very popular in Hungary and was developed there as a chromatic instrument (with pedals) for home and concert use, equivalent to the piano further west. It advanced towards the Carpathians and many bands on the western edge of Transylvania have incorporated it. It was also taken up in Romania proper, and the gypsy bands of the Bucharest suburbs (who are resettled village musicians) and of the villages of Wallachia and Oltenia feature it strongly in their repertoire, which is a music completely distinct from the Transylvanian, more nearly 'gypsy' and with more Ottoman flavour. But the mountain barrier between Transylvania and the Romanian plain seems to have excluded the cimbalom except on aristocratic estates. The cimbalom was followed, of course, as was everything everywhere, by the accordion, which is actually better fitted than anything else to supplying the accentual pace of the violas, lacking only string tone and the edge subtlety of the unfretted fingerboard. It has been used with success in many bands, as have saxophone and guitar, but recently these developments have passed over more to the 'gypsy' or 'hot' syncopated and amplified wedding music style of eastern urban origin which is tending to supplant the string bands in the villages. Here the accordion is played melodically. It's of note that the accordion was introduced to the string bands as a harmonic and rhythmic instrument and so did not, as it or its family did in many other parts of Europe, bring a new repertoire of dance tunes with it.

Another zone where, incidentally, second fiddles are used in a similar way is the Louisiana cajun band (or violin duo) before the advent of the accordion, which is pure coincidence except that this music too has some kind of 'courtly' prehistory in France. I have also heard of harmonic second fiddles being used formerly in the Shetlands and it was probably once a widespread practice in the process of transition from solo/unison playing to a band, but is unlikely anywhere to have approached the Transylvanian 'consort' sound.

#C/I. DEVELOPMENT OF THE STRING BAND

Some accounts say that 'professional ensembles' did not exist before the end of the 19th century, and were at first violin duos. The second violin was replaced by a viola in the 1930s or 1940s and a cello added, later changed to a string bass. This development of the inner instrument certainly did take place, and as recently: no.4 of the independently-issued CDs of the Szászcsávás Band includes a demonstration of it in four stages, all played from living memory: 1) normal second fiddle, 2) three-string second fiddle with flattened bridge (primkontra), 3) three-string viola (kontra) played like primkontra, and 4) four-string viola kontra. Walter Starkie found in 1929 that second violins (stage 1) played chords by use of a primitive and self-made slack bow ('Any little stick suffices') playing all four strings at once, producing 'a crude harmony' probably without much or any pitch change. This could very well be a bagpipe-derived effect, and the invention of the flat bridge a way of gaining a refinement of this effect with a normal bow.

But I am not at all sure that the development of the band was so strictly additive; it is obvious that a full-scale band of at the very least three players was in situ long before the 20th century, at least in town and manor, rather than that the string ensemble rose directly out of monodic village music by accretion of accompanying instruments. A more realistic account says that the number of instruments you got in a gypsy band would depend on how much you were willing to pay, the cheapest being a violin-kontra duo or even solo violin, increasing up to seven or eight players at affluent weddings and the aristocratic balls. In that case the thesis of development from violin duo may represent what was available to poorer villages, especially for Romanians and Gypsies. In the 20th century, as they lost their aristocratic clientèle, the gypsy bands offered an increasingly large ensemble to the peasants at a lower rate. But meanwhile, rather more mysteriously, they filled in the centre of the sound spectrum with a new rich sonority.

#C/II. A Long Time Ago in Hungary

The gypsy orchestras Liszt heard in Hungary consisted of a *primás* (lead violinist) and cimbalom, with or without accompanying band of three or four wind instruments and bass, plus 'as many second violins as can be obtained.' The band of János Bihari, a renowned Hungarian gypsy fiddler (died 1827) consisted of four violins and one cimbalom. The music of these urban bands was composed by the leader or others (including patrons) in a folk-nationalist style which derived partly from the villages. It was also influenced by Viennese serenade ensembles, and this included all the extra bowed instruments. This music could be and was used for dancing but was more often performed in a concert-like situation in restaurants and at receptions and ceremonies. The pieces were formally fixed as 2- or 3-part suites (slow-fast-faster) without the flexibility of the village dance music. This separation from dancing must distinguish their music from that of the Transylvanian string bands, for however much 'urban influence' was absorbed in musical technique, the gypsy bands played primarily for dancing with all the practical adjustments that required. (The Jánosi Ensemble's CD *77 Magyar Tánc* includes some of Bihari's dance tunes played in the current village-band style, i.e., with different instrumentation but great elegance.)

In fact we know far less about the Transylvanian bands employed by the Hungarian landed gentry than we do about the mainland urban bands and have to guess back at their style from the later work the same musicians did for the villages, if indeed there is any distinction to be made there. A more direct influence from urban bands can be heard in the former village bands of central and eastern Hungary, who use the cimbalom a lot, and whose musical structures were more four-square and their tonal vocabulary more basically diatonic. To my ear the Transylvanian village bands breathe a different atmosphere, or at least there is a resistance to unchecked absorption of urban techniques. Occasionally in the places most susceptible to modernising influence, such as Kalotaszeg or Bonchida, an anomalous piece will emerge marked by the kind of banal regularity and simplification of phrase, structure, and rhythm which seems to have befallen most Germanic folk dance music. The musical substance resisting this incursion involves a flexibility of playing and an acceptance of rhythmic irregularity, but only remotely suggests anything oriental. Whether it should be linked to an earlier condition of eastern European court music, which is one of the theses of its origin, is anybody's guess. It could suffice to refer it to the demands of its patrons in the villages, who clearly appreciated musical quality as such independently of suitability for dancing to.

#D/1. Old Songs with New Harmonies?

The dawn song melodies must in most cases be older than the ensemble, and so at some point a monodic music got harmonised. Netti (in his interview on video) calls them 'very old melodies'. Yet in the stylistic succession established by Bartók and others they fall within the class 'new song', introduced at the end of the 19th century, surpassing the pentatonic mode and bipartite form of older tunes. 100 years may be quite old enough for the description, but it is surely also possible that they are much older melodies which did not necessarily arise directly within village culture, but from a milieu more in touch with European music at large, and indeed some Transylvanian village tunes have been traced to written sources in the central European baroque, including church chant. The harmonisation reaches us in such a fully integral and developed form that the join is perfectly invisible, and there is no knowing how or at what time this occurred, if it really did. It is at least a possibility that old songs were already re-written into forms of harmony and counterpoint, as popular tunes were by the English 16th century virginalists, by the time their propagation passed to the gypsy bands. In neither area is there any trace of the struggle to fit diatonic harmonies to modal melodies which is evident in, for instance, 18th century arrangements of Scottish tunes by Haydn and others.

As mentioned, there are recordings of the old Bonchida band which show them playing tunes sung as solos in a neighbouring village, and there are other examples on the Ördöngösfüzes CD (Kallós Archivum) and the 'Anthology of Hungarian Folk Music' series of LPs. It seems obvious that the gypsy band gained its clientèle in the villages by taking such tunes and orchestrating them. But given all the back-and-forth, did these songs themselves originate in the villages, or reach them from elsewhere, in part or whole? If we view the villages in isolation we assume that triadic harmony was introduced to a monodic music at a recent date; if we look at the whole nation we cannot at any point before c.1500 presume a music without triadic harmony other than church chant. If the elegant couple-dances are recognised as deriving from the renaissance courts, could not at least something of their harmony have come with them? The important thing here is that the borders between groups are never as impermeable as nationalist and other political principles render them, and human communities are not graded on a vertical scale of descent into simplicity.

#D/ii. Dawn Song and Court Dancing

It is accepted among musical historians in this zone that some of the dances descended (without anyone being able to say exactly how) from eastern European court dancing of the 16th century, which is itself only marginally distinct from that of western Europe. This applies particularly to the slow and graceful, walking-pace promenades commonly employed to open a dance sequence. According to Ferenc Pesovár (in Kaposi and Pesovár 1985) these have tended to fall out of use among the Hungarians and be retained by the Romanians, and so are often known by the term *Romaneşte*, but also *purtata* ('promenade'), *de preumblat* ('walking'), *de-a-lungu* ('with long steps'), and when used by the Hungarians, *jártatós*. These dances are not danced in Kalotaszeg, and it has been suggested (again by Ferenc Pesovár) that the presence of the characteristic slow songs of the area – dawn songs, laments, bridal farewells and songs for escorting the soldiers – shows that such dances were formerly practised, on the assumption that their melodies have been retained by the gypsy bands and used for other purposes. If correct, this means that the dawn song music itself descends from slow court dances, in spite of the fact that the harmonic sophistication should place most of them within the 19th century 'new song' category. My thesis (above) on the possible transmission of these melodies with harmonies, or of the harmonies with other melodies, which could inhabit a continuum from the time of the princes to the end of Hungarian aristocratic patronage at the break-up of the Austro-Hungarian Empire, could explain this. Incidentally this Romanian retention is another example of preference given by this underdog population to sophisticated and elegant forms which the dominant population seem not to have been too concerned about, like the Romanian dance music of Bonchida (Appendix 4B, p.103–106).

The dawn song is in fact somewhat slower than the *romaneste* as usually danced now in Transylvania, and retains its balance as something between listening-music and dancing-music. But when Netti plays a Romanian opening promenade (under the name *purtata* on "Transylvanian Folk Music", ABT Records 1999) he does it at exactly the pace of a dawn song. And perhaps 'walking music' (andante) would be as good a label as any for this particular pace, precisely between dancing and not-dancing.

I have my doubts about the statement that the opening promenade fell out of use in a place like Kalotaszég, since it remained in place in the instrumental dance sequences, often as 'dawn song', and the time it takes for preludial lament music to be followed by preludial promenade music is a long time for the assembly to hang around waiting to start dancing. The promenade is the regular opening of the event in the modern *táncház* scene, and at present-day arranged village dances in Kalotaszég.

One of Paul Nixon's videos of the Giurgui Valley shows the assembled dancers (Romanians) hanging around not dancing through an entire opening *de-a-lungu* played at a state-sponsored festival. But the reason for this was that the dance was not sponsored by any one village (as at a Sunday dance) or family (as at a wedding), and so the strict hierarchic ordering of the processional dance could not be realised. For the opening promenade is not only the most dignified of the dance forms, it is the one most strongly tied to propriety. It is at this initial point of the social dance that the village community declares its social structure to itself: everyone can take part, but not in any order. The promenade is led by the most important person in the village and the sequence behind him remains in strict descent to the end (Nixon 1994 gives an instance of outrage at strangers joining the circle inappropriately). The music is appropriate to this walking-tall, as was the pavane (and later allemande, etc.) to which European courts enacted the same promenade as a ritual of precedence for centuries. The monarch led the promenade if present, otherwise his representative, and everyone else followed in strict order. If the solo dawn-song sung at dawn takes its music from this procedure it is to some extent a final investing of that structure as a whole on the individual, who comes to comprehend the entire circle from highest to meanest, and most often espouses the latter. In spite of all the sacrosanct rites that particular villagers attached to precedence in the promenade and the right to command their own songs during social events, I have come across no mention of priorities or privilege operative in the order of the singing of dawn songs. (In some accounts it is for men only, evidently householders, but this is contradicted elsewhere). It might indeed seem inappropriate for 'the most important man in the village' to claim the first right to sing something like, 'I am a fool and an orphan with no future.'

The pavane was the music for the opening promenade in Italian and English 16th century courts, and was conducted with a certain rather ostentatious swaying movement known as 'peacocking' (which I have not observed in Transylvania). The other candidate for direct ancestry is the galliard, which was a male display dance with jumping, including twisting jumping, partly improvised. Men are said to have been appointed to high court positions by Elizabeth I as a result of their proficiency at the galliard. A very similar male dance is often performed in Transylvania (sometimes with the physical support of the woman), usually under the name *legenyes* (lads' dance – Romanian *fecioreste*). The strictly solo male display dance might alternatively be related to 16th century professional 'grotesque dancing' in entertainments, which always depicted alien forces. The galliard dancer was sometimes obliged to moderate the acrobatics so as to avoid profuse sweating.

Incidentally, I have seen several performances of 'baroque dance' within the early-music scene in England, and find that by comparison the dancing in a remote Transylvanian village is liable to be not only a lot more vigorous, but also a lot more graceful.

D/III

'Like dance music of all periods, that of the Renaissance tended to move upwards in the social scale; folk dances entered the ballroom, so to speak, although they probably lost some of their rough edges in the process.' Tim Crawford, booklet notes to the Naxos CD *Early Venetian Lute Music*, 1999.

There is no reason to think of Transylvania or the whole of Eastern Europe as in any way different from anywhere else in the second millennium so as to form an exception to this rule. The constantly met assertion that certain Transylvanian dances descended from court dances need not contradict this, because there is always the possibility of a 'downward' descent subsequent to the original 'upward' migration. The waltz was a refined and flexible form of the ländler, a country dance from the Landel region of Austria, developed in 18th century central Europe as a rather risqué innovation in the ballroom because of the maintained embrace-like contact between man and woman. It spread everywhere, and was returned to the villages under its new name.

Likewise the east and north European walking dances (the elegant group or couple promenades which may be ancestral to the dawn songs) may have an ultimate ancestry in ritual walking dances, passed thence into the court without being lost in the villages, and returned to the countryside with changed features. And from the same source (which is quite hypothetical) a route leads through southern European courts to the Italian pavane. In the form of the polonaise the eastern arm of this descent reached over to the west in the 18th century.

But my particular thesis is that the Transylvanian 'peasant' milieu has a transparency which particularly reveals itself in these forms (and others: décor, domestic custom, social deference structures…) to be the *same kind* of place as the Versailles court or whatever other cultural workshop and within the same cultural zone, and that the simultaneous confirmation and denial of hierarchic structure in performance has become an integral feature of this culture's history.

#D/IV Dance Sequences

There is a resemblance between the ordering of the instrumental village dance sequences and that of the 'suites' (setts, partitas, etc.) of C16–C18 European classical music. A sequence such as: pre-dance prelude (or lament) – promenade (or dawn song) – slow dances – fast dances, is close to the basic sequence: Prelude, Allemande, Courante, Sarabande, Gigue. For of course both are dance sequences and both are sophisticated formulations of the standard form of a social participatory event of movement towards a climax, musically by accelerando. The sequence remains basically thus even when the terms change, for the allemande was earlier, as the almain, a quite fast piece placed later in the sequence, and the slow pavane stood in the initial position. In Indian classical music this sequence seems to have melted into one continuous extended accelerando.

The function of the prelude is seen clearest in middle-eastern music as an introduction of musical tone into the proceedings, a static improvisational establishment of the tonal centre, as if it were a bell sounded as a call to attention, and a signal to prepare for action. In Transylvania the prelude music became the lament, presumably because of their very similar procedures in musical terms: motionless melismatic weaving, the extended formalisation of the cry.

The instrumental dawn song played next in the dance sequence is essentially transitional. It is the move into action at the end of the beginning, the first slow dance, or the song before the dance, the tentative introduction of primary movement, which is not-yet or only-just dance, and is perfectly represented by the slow allemande in 17th century suites, and the pavane earlier.

The course of events in classical music is here complicated by the intervention of an apparent need to alternate, so the slow Allemande is followed by the moderately fast Courante and the very slow Sarabande, whereas in the village music the sequence passes into moderate dance movement and a smooth transition towards the fast wild dance, which the suite reaches in the form of the gigue.

It seems to me that the dance-sequence lies behind most musical forms divided into movements in the 17th and 18th centuries, whether instrumental (suites, overtures, symphonies…) or vocal (motets and cantatas, sacred and secular). The nature of the sequence would of course shift in these pieces according to textual demands, but the final gigue and the obligatory 'happy ending' of most 17th and 18th century literary structures could be leaves of the same tree. The form of the masque is basically a dance-sequence, and even opera itself succumbed in some ways to this structuring after the very different formal conditions set in Monteverdi's time with reference to Greek drama.

These sequences of course developed into symphony and sonata form, mainly by tying the various movements together thematically and developing most of them into more complex abstract forms, though a back-reference to foot-movement usually remained in the minuet-trio movements, as an interlude. There is still some sense of over-all accelerando, but the first movement (sometimes with a prelude) takes on a central normative force, complete in itself, to which the rest might be an addenda of songs and dances. These connections diminish as 19th century music increasingly separates itself from performative social occasions, or simply becomes increasingly interiorised as it moves towards a final crash.

Many claims are put forward for the invention of 'thematic unity' in the suites of dance-pieces, usually in the 17th century, whereby successive movements repeat the musical material of the first piece in different rhythms and formulations. But this was already common in 16th century pavane-galliard pairs, and must also have been normal practice in earlier semi-extemporised Italian dance music based on chord sequences. It is also a particular feature of the Transylvanian dance sequences, though not all of them, and not the entire sequence. Several of the dawn songs recorded within dance sequences are followed by a csárdás or other dance clearly using the same music in a different rhythm and pace.

There is no need for this to have derived from some classical practice. It may have, but it is also a natural product of the bands' need to create new and attractive instrumental pieces out of the sung repertoire, and to keep the music tied to particular places and persons. It should be perfectly easy for a good band leader to transform, say, a pavane into a galliard, or a gigue, on the spot, and I take the 16th century pavane-galliard pairs to be a reflection of such practice. In the video devoted to him Netti demonstrates his ability to transform the Hungarian national hymn into a csárdás, 'or a szapora, or anything you like', in order to play it under the noses of Ceauşescu's military police, safe in the knowledge that they would not recognise it. And there are instances of the same melodic line used for slow and fast songs in pre-band village singing (e.g. numbers 142 and 143 in Bartók and Kodály's *Transylvanian Folksongs*.)

But the particular formal satisfaction resulting when a whole set of pieces is made to cohere by inter-relating the musical substance of the individual dances, goes beyond the working requirements of a social music. It might have occurred in Transylvania though I haven't identified an instance. If it did it would represent a refinement of taste developed between musician and customers in the history of the music over a long period, such as a village recognising a whole suite of pieces as 'ours' by thematic content.

These dance sequences are invariably accelerandos. The real, sung, dawn song at the end of the entire event terminates a big series of these, and is the optimum finale of the largest structure possible in this repertoire. And its music, by its relationship to the slow couple dance, must also carry a sense of beginning. The Lament prelude cannot be performed in its original nature within the social event at all; it belongs in funerals and remains 'outside' the cycle. The dawn song is within or marks the very edge.

I have a suspicion that the slow sad or tragic ending to an extended musical sequence is a thing unknown outside European tradition, and rare within it. There is quite properly a pressure from the condition of entertainment to conclude gaily as a factor of the very separation of the performance from normality. Or the need for the creation of a completion requires that things not be left in an unsatisfactory, unresolved condition. This does not necessarily imply an optimism, and a concluding lament does not necessarily beg any further act of resolution. The tragic format is normally enriched by various factors in the last act serving to restore a nascent sense of hope, the return to a diurnal condition which we know must hold at least the seed of regeneration, and this is exactly the niche I see the dawn-song as occupying. It caps a whole series of happy-endings with a despair which is regenerative if for no other reason than that it is acknowledged to be authentic, to be tied to the real. I think it is miles away from 20th century cultural despair (Beckett, Larkin, Celan, heavy metal etc.); it grasps the actual structure of living by the edge and holds it intact, rather than exercising the bathetic hopelessness which can be made to seem true by sophistic manipulation of expectation and denial of formal completion.

#D/v Dancing and Not Dancing to Dance Music [ASIDE]

It is interesting to speculate on the relationship of the written suite of dance-pieces which developed into sonata form etc., to actual dancing, in court, hall or anywhere. It is usually assumed that there is a point of transition, at which the suite of dances was 'removed' from the dance-floor and became a concert item. The dance forms of musicians such as William Lawes or Marin Marais seem to be too complex and flexible for actual dancing, and yet dancing went on, in their time, to precisely those forms, as it had to the dance forms set out for private playing 50 years earlier in the *Fitzwilliam Virginal Book*. No written scores of what was played for dancing, if it was not these pieces, exist, and musicologists dealing with these zones are distinctly guarded on the subject. Did the same musicians (or Haydn for that matter) who were after all employed as performers more than as composers, supply both the concert pieces and the dance-music? Were they one and the same?

In fact, music for dancing in 16th–17th century society was provided by a separate profession of musicians who mainly extemporised on familiar and quite simple basses and chord sequences, adaptable to different dance forms. Most of these forms were known across Europe by their Italian names, such as Passamezzo (anglicised as 'Passing Measures') which could be a pavane or a galliard and possibly other forms. A dance piece which occurs once as a written item is of course on the dance floor repeated *ad infinitum* or as many times as the dancers demand, with ever increasing extemporised decoration, at the discretion of the leading musician and dancing master. What survives of European dance music from the 15th and 16th Centuries shows it bearing a nascent major-minor tonality and cadence structure (necessary for practical purposes) in contrast to the strictly modal scholastic art of church music and courtly song of the time, neither of which has any avowed pace at all. The whole development into modern (17th–18th century) music in both harmony and rhythm could be seen as the accommodation of the tonalities and repetitions of dance music to more sophisticated structures and thus as the intervention of the village into metropolitan practices.

But is a music for actual physical dancing necessarily cruder (simpler, more repetitive and inflexible) than a dance-based music for listening to? If we think only of halls full of people milling around rhythmically, it probably is. But a lot of the 'courtly' dancing of the 16th–17th centuries was solo dancing, or performed by one couple, in the course of a social event involving many people, and these were not professionals but the patrons themselves. As already mentioned, Louis XIV himself danced solo at the Versailles balls and was known as an expert dancer. It is quite easy to imagine this as a collaborative exercise between the dancer and the lead musician, and that in the slow dance especially, this might introduce a lot of elasticity and irregularity into the rhythmic structure.

In any case, all dance music is also for listening. Even in a Transylvanian village, where it is generally assumed that if you can walk you can do quite complicated dance steps, there are those who do not dance, as there are those who do not drink the 'ubiquitous' home-made spirits. These non-dancers would not, of course, be the only people to value the music *as music*, and to criticise its failures as such.

#E Accompanied Singing

There is some uncertainty as to the antiquity of the practice of singing to the string band. In some of the recordings collected before the 1980s the impression given is that never the twain shall meet. They seem to consist almost entirely of dance music for string band and unaccompanied solo songs, with a small amount of accompanied unison group singing. This may have been be due to circumstances of recording, for none of those I have heard was made at an actual social event, and there are some exceptions such as the CD of the Szék band (1969/72). The adoption of accompanied singing might have depended on how far the *primás* was able to extend the social repertoire of the band, and probably the playing of the melodies without singing would have preceded it as a way of preparing the singer. It is not impossible that it is an urban or nationalist construct, at some time fed back to the villages.

Declaimed- or shouting-singing (*strigătura*) is a completely different structure which must always have been performed with dance music. It is more a form of vocal dancing which involves extemporisation and does not hold the music to the structures of song, in fact it often syncopates its phrasing in rhymed couplets against the structure of the dance music, avoiding the periodic cadences for its starting and stopping, and playfully contradicting the instrumental phrases. It joins with dance in bringing to the music a formal elasticity and irregularity which is in fact a feature of the village music of the whole of the south-eastern side of Europe (Carpathians and Balkans), wherever a rigidification normally assumed to be urban has not been imposed. The marginal region of Oaș is (or was) particularly given to this practice and the collaborative synthesis there, worked in a repertoire of musical motifs rather than pieces, is closely analysed in the Bouët, Lortat-Jacob, Radulescu book.

#F Listening Pieces

Wherever full accounts are given of the old gypsy orchestras such as Liszt heard, which must have been something different from the modern urban gypsy band, the repertoire includes music for listening, interludes between dances, or 'table songs'. Liszt mentions that such pieces were listened to intensely and in silence, but does not mention singing to them. John Bihary, he says, used to play slow piece between dances which could be 'even funereal in character'. In Transylvanian villages little intermezzi were sometimes played, too brief to amount to compositions, to modulate from one dance or piece to another, which the Romanians called *floricele* – little flowers – but no substantial slow pieces were used in this way; they were always preludial or final. Slow pieces of a kind usually called "table music", for listening to while eating drinking or sitting at table, are widespread across the Asian side of Europe and the European side of Asia. They could be extended sequences of lyrical pieces played to the company before any dancing started, and they were freely used as dance preludes or interludes.

#G C19 Hungarian Nationalist Culture and the Csárdás

In Budapest, as a result of the developing disaffection from Vienna through the 19th century, the csárdás was taken into the town ballrooms as a nationalistic gesture, and danced there in a somewhat more refined way. Gypsy bands were used for this, and this may have been the point at which they first came into their own. Sometimes the csárdás were still interspersed with Viennese dances such as quadrilles and waltzes, and for these a second band was used, of 'Bohemian' (Czech) musicians. The ball Mrs Gerard witnessed at Koloszvár in the 1860s (Appendix 4B, p.97–103) was almost entirely devoted to csárdás, but in the ball scenes in Miklós Bánffy's novel, at Koloszvár and Budapest at about the same time, mostly western dances are mentioned.

The csárdás was in fact virtually invented at this time, and is sometimes claimed as the creation of one musician, Mark Rószavölgyi, circa 1800. It was probably a synthesis of Hungarian peasant dances and current town dances, and it spread quite rapidly into the villages of both countries. The 19th century nationalist movement in Hungary had a major cultural component which included adaptation of peasant dance and song, dancing classes, costume, collecting of artefacts, educational drives, cultural festivals, travelling theatres performing nationalist entertainments with song and dance… In a sense this continues still, with regard to the Hungarian claim to Transylvania, which is seen as the point of origin of Hungarian culture, though the political demand has for the most part mutated to an emotional attachment, as in the *táncház* movement.

#H Marginal Zones

Apart from Gyimes (see Appendix 1, p.73) the major edge-zone anomaly is Maramureș, already mentioned as a mountain (mostly big hill) fastness in the far north, peopled mainly by Romanians and with its own music: melodic/ornamental violin, with drone, or more commonly shifting-drone, on a strummed guitar, with a small military bass-drum and cymbal. How this particular trio got together is one of the mysteries. Maramureş music can be explained as that of a zone which never had a Hungarian aristocracy and so did not inherit the gypsy string band (though some of the fiddlers are gypsies and perhaps at one time all were). The Romanian rural aristocracy from which the principal families still claim descent was another landed and privileged 'military peasantry' established by the Hungarian royalty in the middle ages to defend the Ottoman or Slav frontier. But it seems that string bands did operate in Maramureş earlier in the 20th century. The band from Viseu de Jos on "Musiques de Mariage du Maramureş", (Ocora, France 1993 recorded 1973), now long defunct, has a second violin which sometimes plays in unison but more often takes the 'contra' role, playing accompanying notes and chords. There is also a strummed guitar in this band. The bands from Borsa and Berbesti on the same CD have a 'bass fiddle' under the violin and guitar, and in one case an accordion taking a contra-like role. Some modern Maramureşeni musicians such as Ioan Pop are concerned to re-introduce the contra and bass into the music and to diversify the harmonic vocabulary. The Maramureş lyrical repertoire is in most respects highly distinct, but has a number of tunes and songs shared with 'mainland' Transylvania. The guitar, which is a quite small thin-toned version with 4 strings, of distinct origin, is known as *zongora* which happens to be the Hungarian for pianoforte – how this came about is anybody's guess. Many Maramureş tunes have the character of transferred bagpipe-tunes, so we can suspect a process of stringed instrument take-over here too at one time. There is a constant suggestion that for all its individuality, and although the area is counted as outside Transylvania proper, Maramureş music has participated in Transylvanian music as a whole. Never having been patronised by Hungarian nationalist movements it has not been frozen in folkloric authenticity, and having been commandeered by Romanian Communist nationalism seems if anything to have projected it into an authentic modernity, given a lot of wastage and diversion prior to the 1989 liberation. See for instance additional note Y, p.160.

The Land of Oaş which adjoins Maramureş over the hills to the north-west also has the fiddle-guitar-drum trio as its principal music. In Oaş the violin is tuned higher than normal and the instrument reconstructed with shorter fingerboard and reinforced neck to take the increased tension. It is a very distinctive, shrill and elaborate fiddling with much *portamento*, and this combined with the particular Oaş version of shouting-singing, which they are much given to, in a very strong tone best described as 'screeching' produces a loud and insistent dynamic music-dance-screech-and-howl scenario which very few 'westerners', in my experience, find bearable. It is a highly distinctive music, and yet Oaş is by no means a distinct geographical area or mountain fastness, but simply the northernmost end of the great plain where it starts getting a little hilly. The Oaş sound has never been effectively moved into professionalism, and according to the experts is dying out fast, though films of Christmas and wedding events with music still being sent to YouTube suggest that it is nothing of the sort.

The strummed drone guitar or *zongora* might in these zones have replaced the *koboz* or *cobza*, a lute-shaped strummed instrument of clearly near-eastern affinity, still played in Romanian Moldova. The Ghimeş *gordon* similarly gives the impression of being a long strummed lute which somehow got surrealistically crossed with a 'cello, and early forms of the *zongora* have more of a lute-like belly. Such factors suggest a separate development in these edge-zones, influenced from Turkey, but other factors, such as the melodic material, tie the music to Europe.

#I/i Duration
(cf. p.33, second paragraph, and footnote 2, p.53)

One explanation of the progressively shorter duration of weddings and other festive events in recent years is that it is not caused by cultural marginalisation so much as by the physiological consequences of amplification. The increased volume is simply more tiring in itself, and people cannot sustain themselves through successive nights of it. The music of the sempiternal ball which Mrs Gerard witnessed in Klausenberg was of course purely acoustic, and the way all present conducted themselves, including the dancers, must have been such as to leave what to the electronic world is a slight sound constantly audible to everyone, not to mention immensely stimulating.

Another explanation is given by Paul Nixon (1994), who points out that from the 1950s to 1980s during 'New Order' nation-building (actually national debt-paying) restrictions, most musicians were forced to work in factories and could only play at week-ends, thus reducing the wedding to 48 hours at most, since any part of a wedding without music was unthinkable. Indeed playing for two days was a problem for the gypsy bands, with the need to get back to the factory, perhaps some distance away, in the early hours of Monday morning the moment they had finished playing. These restrictions were sometimes evaded by illicit bribes to factory officials, or by paying someone else to take over a shift. Netti in his interview on video mentions doing this.

But there is also clearly a general retreat from extended festivities as culture moves from 'peasant' (and court?) to urban. One of the things repeatedly mentioned with amazement by visitors to the American slave plantations in the 18th & 19th centuries was the night-long duration of the permitted slave dances or parties ('plays') including the habit of night funerals.

#I/ii Fortitude
(cf. p.33 para 2)

Endurance of energetic activity over long periods of time was not the only fortitude in evidence. Charles Bonner reports a dance in the main street of the Romanian village of Nasaud in the winter which lasted all night, in the open air, in the snow and ice; and the dancers were not wearing heavy clothing, nor was the dancing highly animated – it was mostly couple dancing, which can be not much more than a choreographed walking. (Bonner does not mention the part 60% proof spirits might have played.) Indeed winter was the favoured season for weddings, when the time was not required for agricultural work, and much of the dancing will have been in the bitterly open air of the yards of the farms. There is a photograph with the CD of music from Ieud, Maramureş (Új Pátria series) of people dancing between banks of snow.

#J 'Pure' Melancholy?
(cf. Appendix 4A)

Dowland is only one instance which comes immediately to mind. There is of course a vast repertoire and tradition of melancholy song across the courts (and other things) of Europe through the 15th to 17th centuries, not to mention predecessors, such as the Troubadours. It might be true that in the most general terms court and peasantry share an interest in the deeply sad song, whereas urban song whether bourgeois or proletarian, takes misfortune lightly.

To search through all these song texts would take a life-time. I have continued to look out for song texts in the so-called 'courtly' zones whose melancholy is projected in the manner of the 'pure' dawn song – i.e., without specifying a temporal causal situation and thus a possible remedy or limit. I remain convinced that the most abstract of these still implies a love-loss causality which can on occasion go entirely unmentioned, since it pervades the entire genre.

An example is Sir Thomas Wyatt's 'Alas fortune what alith the' (Muir & Thompson edition 1969 No. 112) which is addressed to fortune itself throughout in the terms normally used to address the woman, because 'Thow wylt not chaunge'. I don't see how this can, within its genre, be read as lamenting anything but love-loss, though there is nothing intrinsic to prevent it being a lament for monetary loss or career demotion – such things simply do not exist in the sphere of this poetry except decoratively.

Seeking further afield, in texts possibly contemporary with the dawn song, i.e. the 19th century, the situation does not seem to change. The 'courtly' love-loss ambience has evaporated, but there is still a demand for a cause, which is still quite likely to be love-loss. There is also a new feeling that the sad fate is a personal infliction, an innate psychic condition which *disconnects* its victim from the common lot of humanity, or finally a despair at the sheer fact of death itself which is entirely alien to the Transylvanian ethos. Isolated from the narrative, Wilhelm Müller's *Einsamkeit* (No. 12 of Schubert's *Winterreise*) offers a glimpse of harmony with the dawn song such as one gets on rare occasions throughout European written lyric. But the dawn-song singer is, of course, precisely not 'einsam' in that individualistic sense. When he or she sings 'I am an orphan left to wander the world without a home' it is, or should be, a recognised fictive condition of the commonality, quite separated from the possible, and not internalised but rather theatricalised. I would not deny, though, that there could be some lurking Viennese transaction in the history of this particular trope.

K/i Urban Contacts

Kalotaszeg was in fact one of the least isolated zones of 19th century Transylvania as it was on the main route from Budapest to Koloszvár (Cluj). It was open to the international tourist market in textiles and ceramics from the 1830s onwards, and in acceleration from the 1880s. 19th century art songs and new-style Hungarian songs were commoner here than elsewhere in Transylvania.

Netti (in an interview published in English on the web-site of Amerikai Magyar Folklór Centrum) says that his teacher, Fery Csipás, was 'the best-known musician in the whole area. He played in the hotel restaurant at Bánffyhunyad [Huedin]. He got the most recent sheet music from Budapest every month, and even played in a movie…' Huedin is on the main road that traverses the area between Oradia and Cluj, and is the biggest town between Cluj and the border. Netti must here be talking about the 1930s, and this confirms a sense that this music has fairly recently retreated into the villages. Similarly, some twenty years earlier, New Orleans band leaders, not yet called 'jazz' musicians, were getting sheet music from Chicago and New York on a monthly basis and studying their ensembles into the 'classic' achievement of New Orleans jazz, and beyond into the 1930s diaspora. The Transylvanian gypsy bands, rather suddenly losing their principal clientèle, probably lost with it the emphasis on intrusive progressive novelties, but dug into the villages, and changed henceforth only according to native demand. Most musicians couldn't move to the big city when times became hard, because the big city already had plenty of gypsy bands, to whom the village way of playing would have seemed alien.

K/ii More Urban Contacts, & 'Gypsy' Alternation

The 1870s traveller A.F. Crosse mentions attending what he called a 'summer theatre' in the town of Oravița, in far S-W Romania near the Danube. This took place in the garden of an inn where there were tables and chairs and a small stage for a 'gypsy band' (violin, cello and cimbalom). Apparently customers, who were nearly all German, drank and listened – there is no mention of dancing. Orovița was a small market town and I would not expect musicians working there at that time to be 'urban' musicians as distinct from musicians working in the villages, but the repertoire included 'airs from Wagner'. They may of course have had a repertoire reserved for the Germans, whatever else they did, but the point is the extent of their knowledge.

Crosse also stresses the strong emotional projection and overwhelming effect of the more normal repertoire of 'gypsy airs' which had contrasted slow-melancholy and fast-dance sections, much as described by Liszt and taken into his own 'Hungarian' music. This alternation within one movement of fast and slow, energetic and pathetic, is a feature of much derived 'gypsy' music such as Budapest restaurant music, but is present much earlier in Haydn's 'gypsy' movements and Schubert's 'Hungarian' pieces, and seems to have become a possible way of constructing a movement or part of one without specific 'gypsy' labelling (e.g. Beethoven's Quartet Op.18, no. 4, last movement, Schubert's Quartet in D minor, 'Death and the Maiden', first and last movements). This was no doubt part of the process of extending and intellectualising the forms of instrumental movements, away from the strict unity of earlier pieces.

There are extant pieces in Hungarian and Romanian village band repertoires which behave like this, of which by far the best known is the piece usually called 'The Shepherd Who Lost His Sheep', a kind of programme-music item, the only one in the repertoire, which was widely popular all over the Carpathians and especially Transylvania. Every gypsy band had it in its repertoire, and being a pastoral piece it was also, of course, known to, and probably derived from, flute players. The music represents a shepherd who has lost his sheep and several times sees in the distance some white or sheep-like things (white rock, bush in flower, cloud etc.) which he takes to be his cares, then realises his error, but finally regains them in the end. Hence the alternation in the music of sad, lamenting the loss, and joyful, celebrating the apparent recovery, which was usually done by alternating a lamenting rubato section and a fast dance tune, usually a special one not drawn from the dance repertoire. Usually the primás speaks the story while playing, but there are also sung and enacted versions. There are references to it from the 16th century. The other principal alternating music is that for the energetic young men's dance (*legényes* in Hungarian) which in some versions supplies slow music as respite from the high-energy leaping dancing; this music is also connected with recruitment. Nothing in any 'court' repertoire that I know of alternates like this except for some of the quasi-descriptive 'battle' pieces of the 16th century. The implication of alternating music, that life has its ups and downs, seems normally to have been received as an accepted fact which didn't necessitate serious consideration; even the battle pieces are a kind of joke as to how instrumental music can represent different kinds of physical action, deathly or not.

#L Written Sources

Hungarian research has revealed written sources of some antiquity for some of the tunes known in the villages, a connection first noted by Kodály. Of about 600 tunes from 16th and 17th century Hungarian sources, 160 were identified as surviving aurally in the 20th century in Hungarian and Transylvanian villages, and work on 18th century tunes remains in progress. The melodies, from both manuscript and printed sources, were predominantly church chant and hymnody, plus verse chronicles, but included theatre tunes, dances, marches, song-books, tablaturas etc. Many were already ancient or had travelled a good distance by the time they were written in Hungary. In all cases they had been more or less transformed by the village singers. The booklet with cassette by Szendrei presents seven tunes played straight as written, and versions of them recorded in the villages. One of them is a German Christmas carol which J.S. Bach also used. In some cases it remains uncertain whether the manuscript tunes were original compositions or annotations by educated persons of popular songs they had heard, or even early instances of collecting. As elsewhere in Europe there were of course dancing-masters and music-teachers in some of the smallest towns and possibly even in villages, educating the locals in correct musical practice for church and social use, though surely not to the ubiquitous extent this trade attained in England in the 18th century. The CD of the Jánosi Ensemble presents 77 tunes from 18th century Hungarian manuscript and printed dance collections in string-band performances.

As this research continues into 18th and 19th century sources, utilizing more and more of the immense archives of recorded village songs in Hungarian, the links proliferate and the impression is that a majority of folk songs were originally written compositions. In the Hungarian case urban origins include not only 19th century popular salon music in a folk style (the commonest source) but such things as military band music, and opera.

No one has ever witnessed a traditional song being created for the first time – it is pretty-well a condition of something being such a song that it had a previous existence. Metropolitan society is certainly not the sole origin of this earlier life, though it is a major one; there is also the church, and the village itself, or rather the entire rural, pastoral and agrarian society in which the song occurs, and its history. Whole genres (e.g. the lament) are without any traceable notated origins, and these tend to have common structures as if they are all derived from one hypothetical original single song or tone-row, by the proliferation and redistribution of formulaic figurations. Within these hypotheses the arc or curve of the epic line seems sometimes to stand behind just about everything, except where the falling line of the lament takes its place.

All these researches into written origins are of course directed backwards towards the west as if culture had only one gravitation. This was obviously a major route, but no one, to my knowledge, has attempted to seek connections between Turkish or Greek Orthodox tone rows and Transylvanian songs. Such research would be Romanian, and no one there has been willing to pay for it.

#M Diversity of Village Music
(cf. footnote 25, p.66)

In the 20th century a strange kind of specialisation took place in national and regional musics as projected beyond their frontiers, and sometimes within them. Thus you go to Georgia for male choral singing (later also female), to Transylvania for chordal string bands, to Epirus for clarinet bands, to Ireland for a monodic dance-music on fiddles, to Bulgaria for women's choirs and clarinet wedding-bands, to Andalusia for a stylised guitar-song dancing, and so forth. The so-called world-music scene has greatly emphasised this particularity, but it seems to predate it. I am sure that at one time the villages of all these areas had a far greater variety of musical formats available to them. Choral singing, for instance, must have taken place almost everywhere for there was nothing to stop it – it requires no expense or training in instruments and the harmonic and linear vocabularies surround everyone. And everyone has a voice. In Transylvania it survives only, as far as I know, in the village of Szácszsávás south of Tirgu Mureş, with traces of it in revived forms scattered here and there through Romania. In all cases it seems to be strongly connected with the church. It has not been issued on record (though Muzsikás have collaborated with the Szácszsávás men's choir in concerts). Similarly the survey in Carlos Suares' film *Flamenco* includes a session of choral table-singing which likewise seems never to have been put out onto the smallest market. A recent BBC broadcast (2002) from the Veracruz area of Mexico revealed an archaic male choral singing in what we thought was the sole preserve of strummed guitar and harp bands. There must be hundreds of such instances.

There have been other kinds of specialisation for export purposes too, such as the election of one regional mode to represent the nation, as with flamenco in Spain. The village and urban social music of many South and Central American countries appears to be one hundred percent medium-paced syncopated dance-music. The idea that Argentinian music can be anything but a tango probably occurs only to certain Argentinians.

#O/1 The Laments

A lot of what I say about dawn-songs could also be said about the harmonised and orchestrated laments, some of which are magnificent pieces which should be welcome in any court or academy of Europe. I think they may sometimes have been used as dawn-songs, but the true dawn-song is distinguished from the lament by its sense of motion. The Transylvanian lament may be as deeply and richly fulfilled as anything by Monteverdi, but the time-sense in it is static, without pulse, it represents a state of suspended motion which is a removal from diurnal time in the face of death. This difference is very evident in the instrumental sequences which start with a lament followed by a dawn song.

As the music moves into the dawn song a slow and steady pulse begins, and the effect is like someone getting up and starting work, or a ship moving out from harbour. It is always danceable, whether such was the practice or not. This motion is essential to the meaning of the dawn-song, by which it forms a bridge to the diurnal, its insistence on return, the call to movement or journey.

#O/II

Lament and dawn song are historically related by some folk-song research, the latter representing a degree of versification and regularisation of the improvised lament, carrying with it the lament's individuation. In the monumental *Catalogue of Hungarian Folksong Types* by Dobszay and Szendrei, (Vol. 1, Budapest 1992) the large Type 1 is the 'pentatonic recitative' and its derivatives, which begins with the lament proper but most examples of which are strophic. Sixty-five different sub-types are recorded. The commentary places this whole type as balanced between recitative and metric song, ancient in origin and related by certain archaic features to liturgical tone-rows prior to practices of the middle-ages. The textual tradition it bears is dominated by ballad and 'plaint' (which would include dawn-song), followed by 'wandering songs, soldiers' laments and beggars' songs'. All of these except the ballad, Szendrai says, are 'improvised, when one considers the verse as a *whole*.' He continues, 'Here the strophes relate the individual lot with the help of many stereotypes, but nonetheless in an individual manner, and they follow each other in a loose string which can be broken off at any point, or if the mood or occasion demands, continued almost indefinitely. (…) The closest relative to this singular, specific form of text is the improvised prose lament. (…) The plaint may be defined as a verse lament on the individual lot.'

Szendrai does not actually permit himself the supposition (which is what it would be, however seemingly obvious) that the 'plaint' song derives from the recitative lament, possibly by the intervention of the gypsy instrumentalist into funeral and mourning customs. He mentions that 'plaint' music was played during funerals by the solo violin, and it would be easy to suppose this to have been an adaptation and metrication of the regular lament tone rows, and that this would regularly pass back to non-funereal village custom, allied with the medium-slow music of the opening dance.

Sendrai's type 1(A) with 35 sub-types is in fact marked (but not defined) by the incipit motif of two rising tones with the third note repeated, which is one of the commonest dawn-song incipits (see latter part of additional note T).

#O/III

If we indulge comparisons we should note that both the lament and the dawn-song are closer to the lament as conceived by Monteverdi, as a unified accompanied melodic line, than to the later (and very swift) development of the genre into a series of melodramatic episodes, from which derived the later operatic lament, allied to the conventions of the 'mad scene'. The former signifies a mass of despairing emotions but unified and owned as well as dignified; the latter signifies category-breaking avant-gardist anti-decorum, and is far more conventional in its implied ideology.

P/1 Gypsy Musicians
(Connecting to footnote 1, p.53 and various other points and begging further clarification, for which see 'The Last Gypsy', pp.166–171.)

Virtually everything about the history of the gypsy musical profession and its 'take-over' of local and national music is contested. Gypsies did or did not have musician among the established trades (metal-work, basket-work, herbs and nuts, fortune-telling, begging etc.) which they brought with them when they arrived from the east in the 15th century. Gypsy bands did not, or did, exist in the villages before the mid-19th century. There were some famous gypsy musicians from the 16th century onwards in court and town music but they may have been exceptional. Gypsy bands were also introduced into Hungary by the Turks among their entourages, and any 'oriental' elements in their playing (such as the interval of the augmented second) may derive from this employment rather than a remote past in India. The music played for the villages does or does not relate to music gypsies sing or play for themselves in their own company.

The music of the village bands of Romania proper (mainly Wallachia) obviously has more of the 'gypsy' in it. One of these, Taraf de Haidouks, has been elected onto the international 'world music' scene, though it is not exceptional, while the rest remain in poverty. (The name means Band of Outlaws and was given them by record producers; their original name, still used locally, was Taraf de Clejani, the village name. The band was to some extent created from the musicians of a group of villages but this was common practice when a large band was required.) Haidouks are marketed everywhere as gypsy music. But the documentation of these bands speaks of an insistence on the part of the bands' village customers on retaining the correct, old, Romanian forms of the music (which originally included extended ballads, sung by the musicians) and constantly keeping an eye on the local band to make sure it did not gypsify the music. The transfer of Haidouks to an international CD and touring market has obviously eliminated this local pressure, and the young members of the band are increasingly pushing the music in the direction of restaurant-style 'gypsy' virtuosity, especially since Nicolae Neascu, the old leader, died in 2002. Their latest CD (2007) includes pieces by Bartók, Kabalevsky and Albert Ketèlbey played in the band's usual style and thus reclaimed to their 'gypsy origins'.

In all these cultures the gypsy musician represents an innovating force comparable to that of international marketing in general. The gypsy professional has no homeland and maintains no territorial tradition, he camps anywhere, and he has to earn a living from scratch. To do this he provides what is wanted and makes it as attractive as possible by adding the shine of novelty, taking advantage especially of the desire of younger customers for the music to be updated. He learns the local music exactly and performs it embellished in a way quite beyond the capacities of the bagpipe or the lute, and he brings to it what lies beyond it and above it in urban refinement. It is the gypsy who imports Viennese operetta figurations or Schubertesque harmonic piquancy to Transylvanian peasant dances, much as he might these days import refrigerators. The gypsy offers the latest innovation, but also offers to reinforce a sense of belonging in a way perfectly appropriate to the 'peasant' view, which has always maintained awareness of beyond. He also offers an expertise indigenous to his ethnicity, like the gypsy horse trader.

That some kind of 'gypsy' quality, including both emotional and technical effects, was imported into the music through its practitioners is very likely, though it might have been something cultivated professionally rather than something lying 'in the blood'. The Romantic image of the gypsy (wild, passionate, etc.) is a product of gypsy professionalism unrelated to the *moeurs* of the Rom themselves, notwithstanding an undoubted reputation for violence in some communities.

The dawn song probably represents a convergence of a great deal of outside material on an indigenous monodic singing. Such meetings are common, but for them to work creatively is rare and it is difficult to elicit from what is heard exactly how the new thing becomes a true creation. But it must be to do with a balance which is kinetic. A useful comparison is perhaps the development of Scottish traditional violin playing, which was created out of a classical context in the 18th century, continued as a folk music, and at some point gained a piano accompaniment, which the old fiddlers (a proud and somewhat dour tribe) insisted on as a matter of professional pride – it would be demeaning to be expected to play without a piano – but which yet sounded a superfluous and even irritant adjunct. But when the music reached Cape Breton Island in Nova Scotia the accompanist took off, and the keyboard players met the bravura virtuosity of the fiddler with its like, in their own terms. It was the solution of a long standing incompatibility without resorting to reduction. Transylvanian monodic song never required or gained anything from harmonisation and in some cases its modality was incompatible with the diatonic harmonies of the gypsy band. The new construct is founded on a clash, but the clash is converted to a creative tension. For all the trust we may place in the 'kinetic', we again have to say that this was achieved 'somehow'.

P/11

I had not thought the sociality and demoted condition of the Balkan gypsies relevant to these notes, since I was concerned only with the gypsies as working musicians, in which role most of my experience and reading led me to believe that they were valued and respected in the communities they served, and certainly they set themselves apart as a cut above the Rom, a term which they usually refuse to apply to themselves. Paul Nixon's thesis gives a very different picture, from a village of the Upper Mureş region in 1979 and 1990/93, of the gypsy musician treated as an inferior hireling who could be scorned and abused while playing by drunken male wedding-guests, and who could be worked continuously for days without refreshment or respite if the patrons so chose, or rather neglected to do otherwise. This clashes with the picture generally given by musicologists, travellers, collectors and urban musicians seeking to learn the authentic skills of the bands. Nor does it relate to my own experiences of bands at work in Kalotaszég, Mezöség, Maramureş (where most musicians are not gypsies anyway), Szászcsávás, and the central plain. But there were admittedly occasional remarks dropped, such as Béla Kodoba mentioning during Simon Broughton's video that if musicians got drunk while working at a wedding they would be beaten up and sent home unpaid. And obviously the endurance of the 48-hour stint was nowhere welcomed.

The gypsy musician's position must have changed a lot recently, with a number of musicians rising to a position of some respect in the village because of international attention, recording and touring, and the infiltration of *táncház* ethics into at least the Hungarian villages. But how deep this respect goes is uncertain. However much it is valued the gypsy's musicianly ability may well be viewed by their customers as a typical gypsy piece of virtuosic cleverness that gets them out of 'real work', if labour is the final test of human good in a peasant culture. Playing music is not labour any more than trading is. (See Stewart 1997 on the prevalence of this attitude to gypsies in a Hungarian urban context).

The village of Csávás has one of the must successful gypsy bands, now able to travel nationally and internationally, and to charge fees such that the villagers themselves can no longer afford to employ them. A few of the musicians have been able to buy houses in the village proper, thus escaping from the gypsy ghetto. They are also now the draw for all the visitors from Hungary and elsewhere for whom the villagers supply accommodation and must at least be valued for that. Yet the majority of the gypsy population remain in dire poverty.

The distinction between musician-gypsies and the rest of the gypsies is here very clear, though whether the former gain acceptance and respect from it is difficult to determine. From my own observations of the band at work in the village I know that the proprietors, when invited along to sing, are still prepared to treat them in a proprietorial manner, though by no means with brutality, even when not employing them. It was also clear that some proprietors are on very good terms with the musicians and indeed fond of them; one of them was even taking violin lessons from the *primás*. The condition of the non-musician gypsies of the village is quite different, but there are links of family and community between them, for many of the musicians still live in the gypsy village and have to tolerate its conditions, and there are many more musicians in the village than the five of the Szászcsávás Band.

The gypsy village at Csávás was created during the Communist period of enforced gypsy settlement. It consists of four earthen streets of poor houses on a site unsuitable for settlement because on a badly drained hillside, and in rainy weather the streets turn to liquid mud up to 15 cms deep. There was until recently one source of water for the 400 inhabitants and all domestic conditions are fairly dire. At least during the Ceaușescu period the gypsy men were employed on state farms and received a regular wage, which must have given them some status and a chance to pay for improvements to their housing. After the abolition of the state farms the gypsies were left stranded. They were not of course recognised as being entitled to land in the redistribution, and deprived of their traditional itinerant trades they now depend mainly on labouring work for the proprietors, for which they get no cash payment at all, only food. Having no money they cannot do anything to improve their domestic accommodation. This work is naturally not available through the winter, and how the gypsies manage then remains a mystery. People who were asked shrugged their shoulders and said, 'They have a hard time.'

This is typical of the condition of gypsies throughout the country and represents what the musician-gypsies manage to escape from, though in the 19th and early 20th centuries they must have escaped from it much more thoroughly and securely. The shrinkage of their clientèle obviously brought poverty, but most signs are that they remained aloof from their brethren. One of the most telling documentations of this is from outside Transylvania, in a CD "Roma and Gypsies from the Village of Gratia, Teleorman" (Ethnophonie), which presents musicians from a village in eastern Romania in two groups: *Romi* and *Țigani* (lautari). The former use only drum, voices and body sounds, and play for their own domestic purposes; the latter is a band with violins, cimbalom, accordion and bass and at one time was a successful concern in the region.

In a place like Csávás there is obviously respect for the musician gypsies. There is also local concern for the mass of the gypsies but a derogatory attitude survives strongly, especially as it is linked to the farming economy of the village. There was recently conflict concerning a move to improve, or initiate, the education of gypsy children (currently 20% are literate), to which many proprietors were opposed. They no doubt saw the dirt-cheap labour upon which their agricultural system depends being eroded. And it will be – as the condition of the gypsy population inevitably improves through their own and others' efforts the self-sustaining smallholding economy, under pressure now from the E.U. as well as international capitalism, has a precarious future. And when that ends and the music loses any local social function whatsoever, it is difficult to see how it could survive except as a degenerate spectacle.

Q English and Hungarian Folk-song Collectors
(re footnote 25, p.66)

In recent studies of English folk-music there is an influential sector of class-based leftism which has taken to severe criticism of the early folk-song collectors such as Cecil J. Sharp to the point of vilification, on numerous counts including robbery, but mainly for exercising aesthetic preferences. It is abhorred as elitism to reject all the music-hall songs, Victorian sentimental ballads, Tinpan Alley material, even country-and-western numbers, which most village singers had in their repertoire in the earlier 20th century. Sharp is also accused of producing a false definition (i.e. 'folk song') by refusing to relate what are called 'cultural products' to 'history' but instead valuing their beauty, with national and pastoral subtexts. Related accusations have been brought against A.L. Lloyd. The Hungarian collectors have not, to my knowledge, met with any of this kind of attack, though they were doing almost exactly the same thing, perhaps because in Hungary and all neighbouring countries Marxist polemics are viewed as reactionary rather than insurgent.

Sharp and his contemporaries were not carrying out socio-musical surveys – they were seeking out an older stratum of aurally-transmitted national music, and were doing so with a sense of urgency, before it disappeared. This hardly left them with the need or leisure to annotate or record pieces written a few years earlier by popular music professionals for the London stage. This selectivity is exactly that of Bartók, Kodály and their colleagues in central and eastern Europe, and with the same sense of urgency, and similarly within a working sense of national identity. Bartók in fact rejected from his surveys virtually the entire intrusion of the gypsy band into Carpathian village music, the subject of this essay, and did so on the ground that it contained musical substance of urban origin, or which could not be proven to be otherwise. Both teams were concerned to reach strata at which no 19th or 20th century urban factor operated, and the material could be assumed to have been passed from a pre-industrial condition, however modified in the process. They both sought through their informants to locate something not only beautiful but also exemplary, something which the urban world needed to remain aware of in the formation of its values.

But Bartók's work was scientific and historical, while the basis of the English collectors' work was for the most part aesthetic. Sharp himself was one of the first to understand and describe the basic nature of oral transmission but saw it as in some measure a process of deterioration or diversion. He treated his singers with respect, but regarded their own creative handling of the material as distortion of a pure original which he felt enabled to recover by elimination of inessentials, or to imply in the accumulation of 'variation'. Percy Grainger was the first to challenge this view on behalf of the artistry of the individual singer. Bartók believed in the peasant singer as a musician and wished to record every nuance of the performance, by a combination of sound recording and detailed transcription.

Most of the collectors in both zones were composers and represented what they collected in their own compositions or fed it to others for that purpose, or their work enabled a music coloured by its modes and rhythms. Here the difference is striking. English purism suffused the melodies in a sense of lost worlds which can be stifling. Through Sharp and company village dance-songs became purgatorial exercises in theatrical rusticity for generations of schoolgirl victims. Through Delius a straight and decisive fragment of a Lincolnshire song ('Brigg Fair') became the purple twilight of the English gods, a texture soaked in delusional regret, an expiring moan as the simplicities of a carefree natural existence sink into slide-rules. Stamford, Vaughan Williams, Butterworth... always there is this deep regret built into the late-Romantic harmonies inflicted on the tunes, often with considerable skill, but always in the mode of a retrospective lament, however bucolic. Even Percy Grainger, the most inventive of these musicians, built his folk-song pieces into more or less desperate laments. I know of no other nation which treated its village music so consistently in this way. Grieg's handling of Norwegian tunes was wistful but with none of this operatic despair. Bartók (and to a lesser extent Kodály and other Hungarian composers) fed the tunes into a different musical theatre, to which nostalgia was alien, a careful version of European modernism quite opposed in tone to the nostalgic pastoral: a driving-forwards music. The research and the melodies were also useful in developing his own music away from the aggressive academicism of Germanic modernism without lapsing from contemporaneity. The only exception in Britain to this contrast is perhaps Gustav Holst, who was not very interested in such exercises but did occasionally treat a folk-tune or two to his own rather eccentric and pedestrian version of modernity.

By the time Britten came to write his so-called folk-song arrangements, the concept of an English pastoral enclave, true or false, no longer came into it, and his peculiar skill in locating quite outlandish harmonic settings which then seem to have been implied in the original tunes, brought the songs into a rather halfheartedly modern environment, as new songs in a balanced idiom between nostalgia and adventure. By applying his rather dangerous facility to these classical song forms he also produced some of the best music of his career. But some sense of origin is still there, which inevitably wells up when truly archaic material is being deployed, and the tone is again regretful. How could it not be? – With a few exceptions in his early music, Bartók simply did not have trained tenors singing the basic contours of village songs against sophisticated accompaniment figures, because he knew that the combination of reduction and elaboration would carry an acute dichotomy through the music, making it into a thing paraded and traded but not actually believed in.

The Romanian 19th century composers, by the way, all of whom lived in the 20th century, subjected 'folk' material carefully selected for its non-Hungarian credentials to absolutely standard European symphony-orchestra treatments in that straitjacketed version of culture in dark grey which has always distinguished the concert halls of Bucharest. There was a tremendous amount of this production during the Communist periods, often to the anger and resentment of the village musicians, who saw not only melodies but also styles of ensemble which they had transmitted being appropriated by composers who got paid for them while they did not. The best were Enescu and Silvestrov, the latter realising some forty years after Bartók that village music related to urban innovation rather better than to urban failure.

The Hungarian *táncház* movement is, however, ridden with acute nostalgia of a particularly painful kind. It deeply regrets the termination of this music, dance, and all associated village culture, which it sees approaching and is powerless against except by salvaging what it can through fieldwork, archiving and imitation. One of its archival CD compilations is even called 'Lost Eden' (Elveszett Éden). It sees much more than a national birthright in Transylvania. It sees a creative power invested in the individual historically and socially without prejudice of institution, with direct bearing on senses of purpose and value anywhere, and desperately in need of realisation in the arena of modern communication (viz. especially various CD booklet notes by Lászlo Kelemen). (See additional note V below.)

Sharp and company certainly brought about no rapprochement of the English musical establishment and the village musician; they remained poles apart in near-mutual incomprehension. A village singer might appreciate an orchestral aggrandisement of his song, and even participate in it, but the concert-hall musician still thought of village musicians as mere sources of raw material, if he/she thought of them at all, or as beneath contempt. This patrician attitude in Britain goes back many centuries, and is still with us. Everything which has been learned about folk music through the 20th century can remain completely unknown in high-culture zones. It is for example extraordinary to find a 2002 British programme note (Royal Academy of Music) to Bartók's *Village Scenes* saying –

> Bartók does not adhere to the usual restrictive constraints of folksong. In the third song Bartók intersperses two verses of two different Slovakian folksongs. In the fourth, he uses two songs to create a ternary structure. Bartók also often transposes the verses, which is also a foreign concept to folksong.

– an ignorance which both Bartók and Sharp would have found shocking in 1910.

And so England does not have (with two provincial exceptions) university departments devoted to what was formerly called folklore or folk music, and the ones it does have are largely devoted to a rabid anti-aestheticism betraying a more-or-less complete lack of interest in music as such. Thus the great published collections of Sharp et al., including the Appalachian material, are classified by a major copyright library as 'secondary', not normally required for academic study, to be stored alongside cheap thrillers and issues of *The Beano*.

#R Proprietorship of Melodies among the Gentry of Transylvania and Norfolk

A quotation from Miklós Bánffy's *Transylvanian Trilogy* (Book One) on individual proprietorship of melodies (footnote 12, p.58) indicates a different function of the practice.

Book One Part III chapter 8. The scene takes place after 6 a.m. on the last night of the carnival ball at Kolozsvár. The women, young and old, have all gone home, leaving a group of men.

'They pulled up chairs around the now devastated supper table and called for more champagne. This was the moment when Laji Pongracz came into his own and he played with renewed fervour, wittily titillating his hearers by subtly juxtaposing the tunes of all those he knew to be involved in courtship or dispute. Laji never forgot anyone's special tune, nor who was or had been in love with which girl, and who no longer spoke to who. Now that he was not restrained by the presence of the ladies the tunes he played chronicled the loves and hates of more than a quarter of a century. With a roguish look in his eye he would gaze pointedly at the man to whose past the music referred. Sometimes he would stop close to someone, his violin barely audible, just breathing an old tune in their ears and sometimes with a wild flourish he would make everyone laugh as they recalled a forgotten scandal.'…

'…After another csárdás he broke into a Godefrey waltz of the '60s, the 'Gardes de la Reine', which old Dani Kendy had always asked for in the days when he could afford to reward the musicians himself. Pongracz played it specially for the bankrupt old aristocrat, knowing that it would remind him of the days when they called him *le comte Candi* in Paris and when he had been an ever-welcome guest at the Empress Eugènie's court at Biarritz.'

Pongracz was the real name of a dynasty of Gypsy musicians in Kolosvár, in fact the one Mrs Gerard spoke to there had the same name. The time of events in the novel must be around 1900, so that Mrs Gerard might have spoken to the very same musician. Note that his repertoire includes pieces enjoyed in courts or salons on the far side of Europe.

In a different arena, Walter Starkie (1935) explains the accumulation of the repertoire as itinerant gypsy musicians go from village to village and learn the melodies and dances that the peasants value in particular villages, or even individually, and can adjust them minutely to their state of mind at the time –

> By his intuitive, wizard's eye he knew at a glance what mood the peasant was in, and he would then tune his fiddle or his guitar to that mood. That is the reason why today the Gypsy approaches the table of the revellers and plays to the expression on his listeners' faces.

which sounds not unlike the skills of a Gypsy fortune-teller in assessing with speed the mental condition of the customer.

A comparable but different practice in which the non-professional singer has rights over songs is described by the old Norfolk singer Walter Pardon:

> My Uncle Bob sung "Jones's Ale"... That was his song and no one else would sing it, and "General Marlborough", and no one would sing "Bonny Bunch of Roses" only Tom, that was Tom's song. If you asked one of the others they'd say No. They'd never sing somebody else's song. They'd sing perhaps when they weren't there but not in their presence. ... [When I started I sang "Dark-Eyed Sailor" because nobody else wanted to sing that one...] They were specially for them and I think if anyone else had sung their song they'd have been offended by it. [and this was sometimes a reason for not passing songs on to others, e.g. in a pub singing omitting verses so that no one could learn the full song].

(My summarising transcription from Track 5 of the CD Walter Pardon, "A World without Horses", Topic TSCD514, recorded between 1974 and 1980. Pardon was a domestic rather than pub singer, but the context here is the pub singing of an earlier generation. It is perhaps worth reflecting on a relationship between this form of proprietorship and the frequently fragmentary preservation of narrative songs in the English tradition).

#S. Hungarian or Romanian Music

Netti in his video interview speaks of playing for Hungarians or Romanians as of playing in two languages. He explains his local popularity – 'You see, I can play in Hungarian, but I can play in Romanian too.' This may reflect a tendency (noted by Bouët for Oas) for the instrumentalists to think textually while playing, since most or all of the dance pieces they play derive from song or have available words, original or new. This might itself, given the different inflections of the two languages, produce slight stylistic distinctions.

Nationalists of both sides (joined recently by Rom nationalists) have of course claimed the music as their own, sometimes fiercely. The *táncház* movement itself rose from a Hungarian nationalism which sought to wrest this music away from any Romanian connection; earlier issued records, both field and revival, were usually labelled 'Hungarian music from Transylvania'. Similarly Romanian documentation ignored Hungarian-speaking musicians and never mentioned any possible Hungarian connection. This separatism has been eroded as the fact that Hungarian and Romanian bands were playing the same music increasingly stared everyone in the face, but there is still plenty of unease on the subject and indeed enmity.

It still seems likely to me that the music arose in the Hungarian sector, if only because Transylvanian Romanians in the mid-19th century did not have the infrastructure to support it. This hardly effects the present dispute as whatever its sources it was taken by the gypsy bands into every nook and cranny of the country and became the music of whoever commanded it, principally but not exclusively Hungarians and Romanians.

The songs which the bands took into the music would of course have had strong ethnic and indeed local identities, and two presumably distinct village song traditions might be expected to inform the band music in different ways or even to make two musics. They don't, though it is with some justification claimed that villages with particularly strong singing traditions (such as Szék and Szászcsávás) have produced the strongest band music. But here as in other fields the gypsies played the role of assimilators; they subdued the songs under harmony and orchestration and reduced their regional identities to emphases, or colorations. They brought the two ethnicities into one aesthetic entity. The differences that remain are either inflective or are formal factors occasioned by the demands of particular communities, so they include such things as the order of events in dance suites, rhythmic and ornamental distinctions, and other details.

But beyond this, I have had an increasing sense while working on this material, that Hungarians, Romanians and all others who reached the condition of proprietorship in Transylvania for centuries, have been inhabiting social structures which are not indigenous, however delicately toned to shades of meaning which can distinguish villages a few kilometres apart, but are European, and possibly, ultimately, more than European, as with aspects of architectural and social styles. Almost all these dance sequences, Hungarian or Romanian, began at one time with a slow and elegant promenade in which couples walk round in time to the music, hand on arm, in order of social priority. They then moved into couple dances which get faster through the sequence – as at Versailles, Salzburg, Esterházy, Westminster or anywhere you care to name. So here too there is a suggestion that the 'culture' we are concerned with is pan-European, but within an ethos which nourishes the local and the particular. The result is international and local, and national only by appropriation.

The dawn song happens to occur in a region which is deeply Hungarian and has been open for a long time to Hungarian mainland culture. And it seems increasingly likely that its music derives from a particular kind of dance which has passed between court and village within a limited area. This doesn't, to me, destroy connections, which any outsider can hear with ease, between these unique songs and their relatives all over time and space – slow dances, melancholy songs, the *doina*, the pavane, 'Flow my teares'... As with the social structures, the stronger the distinction, the firmer the connections. Isn't this the structures of true persons? And of how poverty becomes a grace?

And then, just when we think we have it more-or-less wrapped up, gypsy ethnicity itself re-enters the scene, in very different guise from World Music marketing categories – see 'The Lasy Gypsy'.pp.166–169.

T. How Many Dawn Songs Are there and How does Netti Remember them All?

On the cassette of his repertoire from Néptáncosok Szakmai Háza (volume one) there is a selection of 21 dawn-songs (though I can only hear 20), played without singers and not identified individually in any way. On the Ökrös Ensemble's CD *Blues at Dawn* there are likewise 20 dawn-songs, and Netti probably plays on 19 of them (there are two violins and in some cases the leadership may be delegated; one is sung solo). But of these 19 only two can be entirely identified with any of the songs on the cassette. Elsewhere among all the recordings I have heard there are about a dozen with Netti playing which do not correspond exactly to any of these so far enumerated, and about twenty without Netti. Netti, although centred on Méra, was not tied to any village and worked over the whole of Kalotaszeg, and thus there should not be any 'Kalotaszegi dawn-songs' which he doesn't know. So the score at present is that Netti probably knows about 60 dawn-songs.

But how many he knows, or there are, is difficult to say, because the distinction between one dawn-song and another can be a very tentative business. The first strain of one dawn-song may be the second strain of another. Two dawn-songs may begin perfectly distinctly, but have the same ending, or be the same for three strains and then end differently. Three or four dawn-songs may have exactly the same beginning give or take a note or two, but those one or two notes may be specifically registered and lead to different consequences, and so cannot be treated as insignificant variants of the same tune. A number of dawn songs seem to consist of two tunes, each with independent words, played one after the other, of which the second may be the first or only tune on another occasion. And some dawn songs are faster tunes slowed down, and many are not strictly dawn-songs at all.

One reason for the complexity concerning incipits is that usually the gypsy musicians did not know the words of the songs which they were taking on from the villages, and so might easily re-structure them, as by beginning in the middle. In accompanying singing this would make the second strain an instrumental prelude to the entry of the singer.

There is a common incipit motif to dawn songs (and laments) of four or five evenly paced tones rising in step from the tonic, the third repeated two or three times: e.g. CDEE(E), with the main beat on the first or third note. This motif usually occurs twice. I have noted, as yet, twelve of these. This means that when Netti begins by playing this opening motif, nobody knows which of twelve or more dawn-songs has begun. But really there is no doubt at all, because the musician does not choose, or announce, the song – the patron and singer does. Netti knows who it is for (or who is going to sing) and plays in accordance. I would say that in the *táncház* scene this twelve is reduced to two or possibly three tunes, distinguished by different accentuations of the opening notes.

Perhaps the most remarkable feature of these conditions is Netti's ability to memorise all these minute variants, and, for instance, to have at his disposal at any time a dozen or more different melodies all beginning with the same initial motif in the same rhythm and pace. These are the practical terms of his casual remark that he knows 'everybody's tune'. There are not, of course, as many tunes as there are people, but there are potentially as many versions, and they had to be strictly adhered to – this is what was expected of any *primás*, and the rest of the band were not much less responsible, as they had to recognise and fit their parts to all these variants on the instant.

[Sándor Fodor 'Neti' died in 2004 but I have retained most references to him in the present tense. I spell his nickname indiscriminately Neti or Netti, as he did.]

U. Composition

The normal advantage that 'classical' or 'art' music has over traditional or popular music, is that there is so much more going on, a liberality of content, and as a corollary of this, that the course of events is less predictable. Proliferation of simultaneous musical lines, changing of keys, rhythmic flexibility, more extended structures, stretching of and departure from tonal systems, etc., – though no one pretends that any piece of music is successful simply by means of this liberality rather than depending on skill in figuration.

Traditional or local music by contrast will usually have simplicity of structure, but complexity in the execution. There are many mitigations of this condition, such as extended dance suites using the same or similar musical figurations in different forms, which may or may not relate to the intervention of classical music procedures at some point in the music's history. The dawn song is traditional (to a degree) but content-rich, therefore unpredictable in detail and complex in form. It is for instance liable to irregularity of phrase- and line-length, prioritising the text over the music. So it is not, like most dance-music, restricted to a unitary or regular patterning throughout; it maintains its characteristic pace but is free to augment or diminish rhythmic values, and to introduce unpredicated figurations. None of this has to be related to the intervention of classical music, even if such probably took place. The dawn song gains this distinction by being composed out of different and contrasted traditional genres so that it can reach both the regularity of the slow dance and the free-moving irregularity of the lament.

The songs must, of course, have individual origins of some kind. They were 'composed'. All traditional songs were composed, by someone somewhere, with or without recourse to writing. It is part of the definition of a traditional song that its original point of composition is unknown, not that no such point existed. But the rest of the definition is that it did not stop being composed but went into a process of more or less continual recomposition by individual singers. Recent studies in Yorkshire have shown how radical such reinvention can be within small limits of place and time – the same song collected from two singers a mile or so apart, or a song learned from a recording, rendered into something markedly different in a matter of months.

The composition of traditional music in general does not differ radically from the composition of any other music. No 'composer' invents *ab ovo* the entire figuration of what he/she creates. An indefinable proportion of the material is received and carried forwards as the 'language', 'vocabulary' or 'repertoire' without which there would be no recognition. We may for instance find Buxtehude exemplary, but virtually the entire North German organ school of the late 17th century participated in a mode giving priority to richness of content. It could not be escaped, in a context made possible by a multiple set of contributions from older musicians, organ-builders, church authorities etc., and informed by the Lutheran ethic of congregational rights. You either wrote richly and unpredictably, or you didn't write. Composition, folk or classical, is a collective enterprise over an extended period of time, realised at a particular juncture by an individual.

V. Táncház

Hungarian *táncház* music can be said to have begun in 1970 when Béla Halmos and Ferenc Sebö founded the Sebö Ensemble, at first very much a standard European 'folk revival' group involved in singer-songwriting, but also dedicated to collecting in the villages, studying with village musicians, and the recreation of village social events in the towns, so that it has come to reject the term 'revival' in favour of 'continuation' and this is to some degree justified. There have since been over fifty groups, most of them focused on the Transylvanian string-band style and deeply involved in recreating the music as a social as well as a stage and recording music. So some of the most prestigious *táncház* groups continue to play for folk-dancing classes in the towns, and even weddings, and the music is nurtured in collaboration with singers and dancers, everyone facing the music and participating in its movement. This has produced a strong music, capable of more than replication, and in some cases (such as some dawn-songs) the music has been brought to a finer, more intense or concentrated, state than many village musicians have been able to of recent years.

The political aspect is rather ambiguous. Originally it was undoubtedly another nationalist movement connected to Hungarian claims on Transylvania and at first it insistently claimed all the Transylvanian music as Hungarian. This insistence has been tempered a great deal in the labelling on CDs more recently by a recognition of Romanian and sometimes Gypsy contribution, but the activities connected with *táncház,* especially summer youth camps in Transylvania, selection of village bands to learn from, and general ambience, remain insistently Hungarian. The view of Transylvania as the lost originary site of Hungarian culture, as Kosovo to Serbia or Macedonia to Greece, is probably still felt within *táncház* as an emotional attachment to a lost condition of wholeness, as in any other cultural pastoral movement, and more and more of a saddened dream condition. But *táncház* meeting places are still quite likely to have on the wall a map of the 'Greater Hungary' which includes Transylvania and all the areas annexed from Hungary after the war shown as an entity (and see first paragraph of Appendix One, p.73).

There are immediate shifts in emphasis in the transfer of the music to Budapest. The village becomes metaphorical, represented by a gathering of persons so inclined, with no other economic structure than paying for a ticket. There is no question, of course, of replicating in an opening promenade the tense symbolisation of social hierarchic priorities, so from the start it is a matter of going through some of the motions without all of the meaning. *Táncház* musicians will work in the villages with the local musicians, and indeed have been known to put themselves through the ordeal of the 48-hour-plus engagement, but such necessities are never called for back home – events are of predetermined length under normal conditions of public performance. Decision-making is transferred from the dancer or singer to the musicians, both in the choice of pieces and (to a lesser extent) the course of the piece, which will usually end when the band knows it is going to end. And as the more successful groups increasingly work for international stage appearances and the CD market, the repertoire increasingly becomes a set of routines, with distinctly staged features.

So too it is up to the bands to determine how the music might change in the future, and there is inevitably a diversity arising from the inclinations of the various musicians, and the views they have not only of their clienteles but also of the market. In the villages there is a youthful demand for change which brings in accordions and electric guitars and these have to be accommodated if you want to continue to earn a living; in the dance-house there is a demand not to change which forbids such innovations. *Táncház* groups tend in fact to divide into those who stick strictly to the village style and explore the vast archived repertoire, and those who innovate. The former have generally been more successful, since the resources of innovation were at first restricted to rather dilute forms of jazz and popular music. But there has gradually come to be less and less pretence that any *táncház* group reproduces exactly what is or was heard in the villages, and some of the best results have acknowledged that the music stands in its own space. 'This CD is not meant to be the exact replica of the original folk music, it is rather a once-in-a-lifetime opportunity for intimate chamber music playing, a celebration of a beautiful living musical tradition.' (*Szerelmem Nagysajó*, Fonó).

Among the finest of these is the singer Kati Svorák's collaborations with Ferenc Kiss in delicately toned electronic enhancement behind solo singing, especially in 'Eclipse' (Hungaraton Classic, 1999), which openly enacts an acute distancing from the village itself, viewed from afar as a departing site of fated dramas within ordinary lives, a melancholy theatre of accession to distance with in-built recompense, climaxing in sudden release into a dawn song.

The melancholy remains. It is the reliable connection between Budapest and the Transylvanian villages. Without it the music spins off into stage bucolics and nationalist fantasy. But the irony is that this melancholy is not specifically Hungarian but is a feature of peasant culture itself, strongly informed in *tánchás* sources by Romanian and Transylvanian formulations. The best realisation of it in an urban theatre is to bring to it the urban resources of precision and dissemination, to offer the 'beautiful living musical tradition' out into the world rather than retreat with it into resentful dreams of belonging and exclusion. So that if the music dies, as it undoubtedly will, its own modernity will pass on into whatever forms of continuity can maintain it. The remaining melancholy will never be closely urban, but through its reaches will attach and harmonise human perception of distance itself, the dream of the ever eluding promise.

W. FLAMENCO AND PIBROCH

Recent historically informed discussion of flamenco proposes that it came into being as an activity of the young scions of the Spanish aristocracy in the 19th century (*señoros*), employing singers from the lowest social class (*gitanos*) to entertain them in sessions of license (*juergas*) involving alcoholism and prostitution. Wild parties, in fact. And that the particular characteristics of flamenco derived from this meeting. The rich young with nothing to do abandoned the gentility (Italian music) which the middle classes had taken up, and maintained their aloofness or superiority by cultivating a mystique ('art') out of the bottom end of society. Song forms from Spanish folksong and elsewhere were processed through a particular style of *gitano* singing with or without guitar (perhaps originally just a rhythmic singing to percussive sounds), in which the patrons were the experts (*aficionados*), passing or failing novice singers, appointing the stars, paying for everything. It was nevertheless a collaboration, which produced an expression of passionate contradiction, melancholy (*duende*) and gaiety, in a closely defined musical vocabulary with a strong emphasis on improvisatory elaboration, dominated by the solo singer. A very similar formative process has been suggested for the Portuguese *fado*, by which a possibly Afro-Brazilian derived dance-song music enjoyed mainly in Lisbon brothels (*casas de fado*) was taken up by young aristocratic bohemians in the 1820s and developed under their aegis into a melancholy song.

Another symbiosis of riches and poverty was the Scottish *pibroch*, the old, solo, 'classical' formalised playing on bagpipe of ancestral tone-rows with variations. The originary creative point of this music is lost in ancient time, but enough documentation exists for us to understand it as a music supplied by a commoner or servant for the laird in terms agreed between them, including both extemporisation and extreme formality. The commonest occasion seems to have been during baronial dinners, when the piper paced up and down the corridor *outside* the dining hall, a situation perhaps necessitated by the volume of the bagpipe, which is basically an outdoor instrument. There was probably once a quite different instrument, more like the border pipes, for use in villages and temporary strongholds, which gave way to the grander version with its military connections, refined by partly mythical father-musicians who seem to have come from Cremona (their names vernacularised as 'Crimmond'). The result, anyway, was a very strictly maintained and sophisticated musical discipline which was purveyed to the aristocracy as the ikon of its entire status, but on an instrument with a particularly 'peasant' character principally, of course, in the drone, so that in a sense nobody escaped it. In its later development this music suffered by comparison with flamenco or Transylvanian bands from the fact that the laird, now no more than gentry, maintained a grip on it and prevented it from moving out into society at large. The lairds became governors of the music through competitions and printed prescriptive documentation which it evaded only in the 20th century. It survives now as a global specialisation, as all particulars may eventually have to. I believe the pibroch clubs of Australia are particularly respected.

X. Tremolo

The pulsating bowing technique employed by kontra players most of the time, called *düvö* in Hungarian, was last seen in Italian and German professional music of the 17th century. There it was usually called *tremolo*, and the first indication of it in a score was by Biago Marini in 1617, though there is evidence of its existence seventy years earlier in Italy. The earliest instructions and directions repeatedly define it as an imitation of the tremolo stop on an organ. Its use spread with Italianate musical writing into central and northern Europe, and Buxtehude was particularly fond of it.

It consists of the ornamental subdivision of a note, not by other notes (as in trill or turn) and not by breaking it up into repeated notes (*tremolando*) but by a pulsation in the movement of the bow forming two or more stresses in one bowing action. It is thus a fluctuation of intensity during a held note, and donates a sense of pulsating movement to a music without breaking the held tone, which is particularly effective as the *kontra* is normally playing three-part chords.

In the Baroque it was favoured for serious and sad passages as an effect which heightened the emotive power of the music, though it was also used programmatically and it became almost a set cliché to use it in the section of the Requiem

Mass *Et terrae motus...* (and the earth shook...) Probably the only piece using it which is remotely familiar these days is Buxtehude's *Klaglied*, 'Muss der Tod denn auch entbinden', which he wrote for his father's funeral. But this is only because most Italian music between Monteverdi and Corelli is never heard.

The difference is that *düvö* normally divides the note only into two, as against a normal four in the 17th century, and is employed continuously, giving way in very fast dance pieces to a syncopated *spiccato* technique which was also first notated in Italy in the early 17th century in the process of articulation of stringed instrument technique which was taking place at that time.

There is of course no reason why *tremolo* technique should not have been a common procedure of unannotated dance music long before the 17th century in Italy or anywhere, especially if we assume that the rather sudden outburst of 'advanced' string techniques around 1600–1620 was at least partly supplied from the aural tradition. We may even suppose it to have been used continuously and to have been the principal technique for assuring an engaging dance rhythm in the absence of percussion. Nor would it be outlandish to assume that the *frottole* musicians (Appendix 4A, especially the remark about stringed instruments, 1st paragraph of p.94) employed it on bowed instruments, not annotating or even mentioning it if it were considered normal.

In Transylvania the technique is mostly strongly used among Hungarian bands of the centre and south. Among Romanian bands further north it is used but with less emphasis, the contra tending to maintain a more sustained chord with a little surge in the middle, especially in slow pieces. How it got to Transylvania at all and whether that has anything to do with Italians employed in the princely courts of the 17th century is another unanswerable question. The kontra-player Csángálo says in the notes to a CD of Szászcsávás (no. 10 of the Új Pátria series) that he used not to employ it at all before playing in the current band, and indeed does not do so on this recording where he is playing with older musicians. So again there is a Baroque connection which may not be anything of the sort.

Y. Electra

In August 2006 I was at Ioan Pop's house in Maramureş when IZA played in the evening for a visiting group of enthusiasts from Holland and Belgium, for entertainment and dancing. On this occasion the band consisted of Popic with the amazing fiddler Mihai Covaci known as Diavolul (The Devil), two other fiddlers, kontra, bass, and drum. It was an overwhelming onslaught of intensity in dances and bright lyrical songs, but there were also soulful songs, sung loud and strong as everything is in Maramureş including lullabies. This seemed like IZA at its best, and seemed to show exactly what it did and what it meant as the maintenance and rejuvenation of a still valid social music deriving its strength from the histories in which it participated. It seemed, in the festive moment, that its sociality could be transferred.

Next evening in Popic's work room we were shown a DVD made in 2005 of a production of *Electra*, a Romanian version based on Sophocles and Euripedes adapted and directed by Mihai Manuțiu, with IZA as live on-stage music. In November 2007 we saw this production in *Théâtre 140* in Brussels with subtitles in French. On the video the theatre troupe was said to be The State Theatre of Oradea; in Brussels it was given as Théâtre National Radu Stanca de Sibiu. On the video there were six musicians: Popic, Diavolul, Gheorghe Florea and Ian Covaci: three fiddlers, one doubling on drum, with zongora, and Geta and Voichita, Popic's wife and sister-in-law, singing. In Brussels the instrumentalists were reduced to three: Popic, Florea, and Grigore Chiva on drum, with the same vocalists.

Manuțiu has been quoted as saying that his entire concept of this production depended from the start on the participation of IZA. Against a simplified and reduced text without choruses, the musicians and a group of non-speaking actors constantly punctuated the narrative with reactive and supportive music and action, normally in the guise of something like a band of outlaws supporting the subversions of Electra and Orestes, projecting the emotive senses of the text by music, choreographic action and quasi-symbolic dumb-shows. The musicians were a constant presence on the stage from beginning to end, dressed like the rest of the cast in town hats and long dark coats, lurking at the back of the stage, coming forward between speeches, at climactic moments surrounding one character, usually Electra herself as if playing and singing to her. The musicians effectively replaced the chorus, constantly commenting and referring the action in a language of music and gesture. Yet they played exactly what they normally play: Maramureș music, songs and dances. The songs were specially chosen but unchanged, still bearing their traditional texts intact. The smiles, laughter, appeal, when playing for weddings or tourists became a serious, earnest and forceful demeanour with hardly anything changed, for it had always held that potential. The wedding dance had always been a lively funeral lament, the plaintive love-song had always been a political denunciation. The two sisters sang with the loud strength that the songs always elicited; nobody ever sang softly in Maramureș until they were on TV bingo shows, and this wasn't one.

It seemed to me as if the music had found its true place at last, as if it had been waiting since 1940 for this realisation of its inhering depth. It wasn't just that the musicians rose to the occasion so admirably, it was mainly that the material they brought with them belonged there. Some items had a 'ritual' function (wedding and funeral) with may have helped, but it was the whole sphere of the music which was suddenly dramatic and even tragic. Most of the songs were lively or lilting, but a kind of grim perseverance became evident in this context, within this liveliness. The 'darker' side of the music was brought out mainly by the choice of lyrics, which nevertheless remained perfectly authentic items from the village repertoire, such as a lively song with lyrics beginning, 'Let the fire burn you, bitter world!' For that darkness is always there, if not in the lighter texts praising the flowers of Maramureș, then in the persistent driving ardour of the music in Popic's version. Aside from all its dramatic qualities, this production showed what could be done with this music when its supposedly originating sociality abandoned it, other than putting it on CDs or sitting in rows listing to it. On a CD it can only be half listened to while doing something else unless the listening act is reinforced by the listener's own fantasy; people on rows of seats can only wait for it to end unless a staged social adjunct such as dancing is provided. What else can you actually do with any music? Do we not pretend to ourselves at the urging of two centuries of proliferating professionalism that any music is deep or meaningful in and of itself? Music *can* claim the whole attention, as can IZA, even without words or programmes or formal structures, which you need to be told about, or historical or ideological connectives, which are easily unhookable, but it remains yet to be shown that it is fundamentally anything but entertainment, consolation, dream and decoration, all subsumed under the term *pastoral*. It has become customary to attach the music to a dance-show or some format of situational fantasy – to attach it to a Greek tragedy was to set it in its modern home as an agent of realism.

No need to speculate on the obvious, concerning the long 'peasant' histories trailing behind this music as they or similar trail behind Aeschylus. Continuity itself is the important factor, a route out of peasantry in both cases, or at least onto its border. Tragedies which I view as acts of lyrical expiation against Greece's development of a ruthlessly exploitative military society and the invention of urban misogyny (both honours shared with Imperial China of course). A music which asserts long-standing resistance to and subjection under, empires, nations and businesses. Revenge and the perpetuation of harm are not peasant subjects, but resistance and fate are.

And at the beginning of Sophocles' version Electra appears at dawn and sings lines such as 'My bitter tears shall never end', and 'My way is the way of the tearful bird' and '…I have no child, no lover / I carry my never-ending burden, / Washed in my tears' [translation of E.F. Watling]. These are familiar tropes in Transylvanian lamenting songs. Electra will never stop being sorrowful: she will either disappear when the act is done or continue to lament succeeding sorrows. She is masked, she wears the mask of anger and despair which she cannot take off, just as she can never marry, for her name means 'the unwedded', another 'peasant' disaster. Greek fatalism is heavy with guilt, but the chorus, the circular dance, the hora, brings a relentless music of unchanging burden up through Macedonia to Transylvania, or across central Asia with the Magyars, which resides insolubly in the most energetic dance or the sweetest love-song. The burden is worn not exactly lightly, but like a ceremonial robe.

What this might mean for the future of the music I don't know. After the curtain comes down it returns, of course, to where it lives and where its future must still lie. It would be good to see it participating in a fuller dramatic text, for this version of *Electra* was in many ways reduced. The poetry of the choruses was lost, although there was a lot of non-textual intervention between episodes, suggesting a projection of the dilemmas and crises into a mental sphere. Costume and decor were modern but simple and sombre, the chorus garb suggesting a homeless or insurgent context. But for all the suggestiveness of text and action, the plot refused to follow Euripedes' ambivalence at the end (which the music certainly could have supported) and insisted on a final triumphalism stronger than that in Sophocles' version. After the murders of Clytemnestra and Aegisthus and a harsh lament-like song sung over the bodies by IZA, the final action was entirely one of rejoicing, Orestes' defiant speech followed by wild dance. In the whole course up to this resolution there was little suggestion of fated act, but only of determination against powerful odds. Consequent guilt and punishment were not suggested. One couldn't help wondering if in a Romanian context the revolution of 1989 might have been invoked; they did after all kill the king and queen. I found this stripping-down strange and rather brutal, but cannot be sure what difference the song lyrics might have made here or throughout, for unfortunately they were not included in the French translation.

As for what next, it is amazing to keep going to these places and being surprised by drastic innovations which seem to maintain a value rather than deconstruct it. Next visit, bewildered by the results all round us of Romania's entry in to the E.U., we get to see a video of IZA on-stage with a modern dance group, actually *not*, exactly, playing Maramureş music any longer, but what I can only describe as musical passages and effects derived from it, from the instrumentation, and from Popic's personality. How much more of this there is or might be I don't know, or what exactly I make of it, and obviously it will never become the sole option. But there was no sense that anything had been abandoned.

Z Field and Mud

There are two classes of 'field recording' – those where the music is set up and performed specifically for the purposes of the recording, and those where the music occurs within a social context and the recording machine follows it there. These can produce very different results, and I've already mentioned this in connection with participatory extemporisation between *primás* and dancer (and sometimes singer) in the extended length of pieces. When playing for a microphone you don't repeat a 16-bar dance piece thirty times, because there's no reason to, and as far as everyone's concerned when you've done it once you've done it. But when playing for dancers you do it as many times as the dancers need it, with reactive ornaments and variations. But there are differences in the sonority too when the music is serving its purpose.

Most bands recorded during social occasions in the last thirty years or so (mostly weddings), involve an accordion, sometimes two, but the instrument is normally absent from staged and studio recordings. Of the eleven recordings of real social events I'm able to consult at the time of writing, eight involve the accordion (village bands of Ádámos, Felsösófalva, Inaktelke, Méra (2), Hodac, Vajdaszentivány and one unidentified). The Erdöszombattelke band normally features an accordion and always has, and it is loud and clear on their cassette, but on the CD of the same band, although the accordionist, Grigore Varga, is listed in the booklet as a band member, he is absent or barely audible throughout. Perhaps the producers asked him not to play or edited him down or asked him to stand in the next field. The 'classic' Szászcsávás band also regularly includes an accordionist, Pal Mezei, a member of the musician family to which at least two other band-members belong, but he is absent from all their CDs and their tours abroad. The accordion is almost completely absent from the *táncház* movement.

It is obviously thought that the Transylvanian village band is essentially a bowed string band, into which the accordion is a modern intervention, though the instrument must have been around in the area for at least a hundred years and the 'classic' band may be no older than sixty or so. In the bands it fills the role of the kontra as middle-spectrum chordal infill, and does this quite well because if its ability to swell the dynamics, but it does tend to dominate the sound spectrum with its greater volume. Rather than replacing the string kontra it is usually added to it, and can render the viola inaudible. There are times when kontra and accordion fail to agree on the choice of chords, as quite frequently with the Erdöszombattelke band, and this is with an accordionist who has been playing with the present band for at least twenty years. It's not just accordions. There are other 'intrusive' wind instruments visible, for instance, on many of the older photographs of bands in CD notes, especially at weddings (trumpet, saxophone, clarinet, tarogato, etc.).

Recordings of real social events generally reveal a different sonority than can be heard on other recordings. If the recording is made from the *body* of the assembly, which is where most people will hear it from, rather than a privileged position in front of the band, it becomes evident that the music reaches its audience through a mud of sociality. The fine details of the playing are blurred, the *primás* no longer dominates and may be reduced to a quite vague twittering sound above the central harmonies, and a band with two accordions can very easily become little more than a rhythm machine, even when, as in Inaktelke, there are two or more *primáses*. All of the eight recordings listed above manifest this mud to a greater or lesser extent (Ádámos minimally) as do other recordings of the bands from Magyarpalatka and Szék (where there is no accordion). See the recordings from Hodac tracks 6 and 7 for accordion and saxophone drowning out the *primás*. Nine of these recordings were made at weddings, and this occasion may itself tend to reduce the *finesse* of the music, by the financial ostentation which swells the ranks of the band, and the excessive demands made on the musicians' stamina.

The clear string band sound put out on most of the CDs is thus achieved by removing the music from the mud of sociality and accordions and cleaning it.

If the cleansed product is a new construct, it also really is the music itself ; it is what the musicians learned and rendered, it is the music uninterfered-with, and no Transylvanian *primás* would fail to recognise it as such.

Sociality makes the music possible and sociality tries to destroy it: by insisting on accordions or bass guitars or synthesisers, by smothering it in thumps and shouting, by making impossible demands of the musicians and treating them as underlings… the sociality of the Habsberg court or Versailles as much as that of a remote village in the hills. Sociality also promotes the music and enlivens it from the performance of set pieces to a participatory creative process.

Certain kinds of ethnomusicologists and folklorists frown fiercely upon cleaning the music. To them it belongs in its mud, as the exclusive property of its sociality, from which it is inalienable. If the 'community' chooses to deface the music that is their privilege. If the 'community' chooses to sing 'What a funny bottom she had' alongside 'The Elfin Knight' the two become equivalent. And if the sociality begins to fade from existence, the music will have to go with it and nobody may intervene in its destruction. This is only one manifestation of an immensely prevalent belief in the West about academic cultural representation: that the duty of research and study is to restrict as far as possible the dissemination of cultural material away from its original location, to insist that only 'they' (and 'I' as specialist) understand or recognise what is going on. Only we can hear the music, and for outsiders to attempt to is specious, even an act of appropriation.

So sociality demands accordions, then drum kits, then synthesisers, then massively amplified rhythm machines which destroy the socialising, and loud-speakers strapped to the tops of cars beating out samples from cassettes, which destroy the sense of the wedding procession. And sociality finally cancels the whole thing in favour of discos. Sociality destroys itself in the process.

But value has means of survival and renewal which can be unpredictable, and however much sociality impels the music towards destruction it may at the same time promote the continuation and renewal of the music, through someone's ears. That that someone has to qualify by being indigenous (itself a hybrid condition) is doubtful.

Appended note

History of an attempt to locate a dawn-song genre in Mezöszég from the Erdöszombattelke Band at Füzes in August 2006.

"Would you ask them if they have a special tune for the ending, as of a wedding or whatever, a tune which announces that it is time to go home, perhaps sung at dawn? In Kalotaszeg they have very special tunes for endings."
…
"I asked them that but they just looked blank. I guess around here they fall off their chairs and that's the end." (With thanks to Elke).

The Last Gypsy (the last note) [a]

(1) *De Meseli*

Just as I was about to put the envoi on this research and close the book, information started creeping in which suggested the possibility of moving the gypsy musician to a more central position.

The essay by Speranţa Radulescu accompanying the CD of Emil Mihai's band, 'Gypsy Music from Transylvania' (Ethnophonie) introduces a genre played for the gypsy communities, *Cantare de meseli* – table song – which is the first clear documentation I have seen of a 'dawn song' practice outside Kalotaszeg or Ghymes, and beyond Hungarian ethnicity.

Prefatory to this, she confirms that as with other groups what is properly meant by 'gypsy music' in the context of the string bands is music played for gypsy occasions, which is for the most part the same music as is played for other groups, but played in a particular manner which varies somewhat from region to region. The details of this style are: a bravura unpredictability in the playing, with more improvisation, a more sophisticated harmonic repertoire, 'harsher' dotted rhythms, unrestrained sentimentalism in slow pieces, and a preference for the minor mode.

There are however some pieces said to have been performed exclusively for gypsies. Radulescu specified three forms: (1) music for a specifically gypsy dance, in slow medium and fast versions. (2) a virtuoso male leaping or acrobatic dance. (3) the table songs, *de meseli*. The first two of these seem to blur easily into the Hungarian and Romanian repertoires but the third is partly resistant to this and may have a distinct relationship to the dawn song.

This genre occurs also in the 'Hungarian' repertoire but possibly deriving from Romanian-speaking gypsies. In the notes to one of the Szászcsávás CDs Csángóló, the kontra player, speaks of the time when during the floods of 1970 he and Dumnezu travelled to the Mureş region as labourers and met there some Romanian-speaking 'black gypsies' from whom they learned the pieces listed as *Cigány asztali hallgató* – Gypsy table songs. 'We don't play these here,' (i.e. in Csávás, for the Hungarian proprietors) he says, 'we just play them among ourselves.' This is itself an interesting confirmation that the gypsy band is not simply a purveyor of Hungarian (or Romanian) musical ethnicity.

All the Szászcsávás CDs have items labelled 'gypsy' but the slow songs known as gypsy lament or table-song show a distinct musical character, and most of them are sung to lyrics in Rom (strictly Vlashiko Rom, in which Romanian words are dominant), alongside 'gypsy' dance pieces which were clearly played for non-gypsy clients. Obviously the musicians would not, at a village event for

---

[a] Notes to this section my be found on p.177

their normal clients, have started singing in Rom, and it is probably the new situation the band finds itself in, playing for foreign audiences and for CDs, which allows them to bring out this repertoire. So the possibility arises of a particular, private or even secret repertoire played for the gypsies themselves, both as clients and domestically, which in varying degrees might merge with other repertoire, especially the dance music (Csángóló says that most of the csárdás they play are 'half gypsy' in style) but some of the songs clearly remain entirely theirs. Most of the Transylvanian bands seem to have these slow gypsy songs scattered through their repertoire, especially gypsy laments, wake songs, mourning songs, and there is one labelled 'Cigány hajnali', all played instrumentally. A non-gypsy band[1] such as Soporul de Câmpie seems not to have them. Bartók is often quoted in his assertion that the domestic songs of the gypsies were entirely distinct from the music the bands played; but since he would only have heard the bands playing for Hungarian or Romanian customers, and was not interested enough to explore their repertoires, this is what he could be expected to have heard.

The whole subject of gypsy bands playing for gypsy clientele remains undescribed. In the kind of Rom society which Michael Steward (1997) depicts (for a Vlach[2] Gyspsy community in northern Hungary) such trade would not seem to be possible, given the acute poverty of the Rom and a sharp divide between two gypsy societies, that is, true Rom and *Romungo*. The latter are Hungarian-speaking gypsies who sell their work or labour to non-Rom and abandon the Rom brotherhood, and they are principally musicians. (It is of course especially these latter who can be most conspicuously 'gypsy' in manner when the market demands it). Each group has contempt for the other. But even here it is mentioned that the Rom did occasionally employ the musicians at certain festivities as a factor of the conspicuous consumption indulged by the male Rom on special occasions, when everything they had earned for months was liable to be flung away on booze etc. In Transylvania the poverty-gap between Rom and musicians seems often to be less marked except in the case of the bands with trans-national reputations, and certainly most musicians have not abandoned the Rom language. At Csávás one villager said that the band in its new affluence helps out the other gypsies during the winter, implying a solidarity, but another denied this. In any event, when Csángálo refers to playing 'among ourselves' this must surely refer to more than the society of the two musician families in the village, since a whole repertoire seems to have been reserved for it.

From the mostly Romanian-speaking musicians of the north-central plain whom she talked to, Speranţa Radulescu learned that the gypsy table-songs, 'are usually performed towards the end of the parties, when the Gypsies, physically and emotionally exhausted, are about to burst into tears. Nevertheless some of them are still able to make slight gestures of a calmer dance to the rhythm of the music.' They are apparently normally sung by the company in unison, and they all have titles in Rom which are their sung incipits. These may be original or translated from Hungarian or Romanian. (They were supplied by informants from various villages and in some cases may be one of many possible textings for a given tune, or personalised versions.)

To this day Romanian musicologists still seem to begrudge the existence of Hungarian musical village culture in Transylvania. They admit that it is there, but do not treat it as a significant formative factor; the music remains first and foremost 'Romanian'. Thus in describing the gypsy table songs performed by Emil Mihai's band, Radulescu emphasises that this is a 'gypsy' occasion quite distinct from Romanian practices, but passes by in silence its resemblance to the Kalotaszegi dawn song. Emil Mihai's band operates socially in the region of Gherla, north of Cluj (very near Bonţida) in the central Transylvanian plain, but it is implied that these forms are known to bands who play for gypsy occasions in most of north and central Transylvania. The dawn-song-like occasion of the *de meseli* songs should therefore be widely known, as the dawn-song itself is in Kalotaszeg, which is roughly on the edge of the territory indicated by Radulescu. But the Hungarian commentators who have done so much research in these zones do not speak of it is a gypsy phenomenon at all, and the Romanian commentators do not speak of it as anything but a gypsy phenomenon. Typically, each nationality excludes the other from the discourse.

Emil Mihai's band plays ten of these tunes on the CD. Five of them are distinctly lament-like, or perhaps more pertinently *doina*-like – meandering melismas over held chords without a sense of pulse. The remaining five are played at exactly dawn-song pace and sound like dawn songs in phraseology, without my being able to identify them as particular dawn-song tunes. One of these, track 4b, is sung (solo) as a 'gypsy lament' on a CD by Ökrös Ensemble, but not to the words indicated by the incipit here. In the track list Radulescu identifies tunes of known Hungarian or Romanian derivation, but none of the *de meseli* songs is noted in this way.

Since these table songs are all performed instrumentally it is not evident whether the words that would be sung relate to dawn-song words. If they regularly provoke tears they should do, but the incipits given are in most cases not encouraging ('Le romes cialeal e erme...': The gypsy loves cabbage...). There is only one incipit which evokes the dawn song – 'Gule mamo, kai kergean man...': Sweet Mother, when you gave birth to me... On the other hand the gypsy laments, mourning songs and *doine* sung on the Szászcsávás and other recordings are full to the brim of the hyperbolic melancholy of the dawn-song.

Dzam mange, dzam mange
Kaj na prîndzanel man

Khajdzeno pe lume,
Numa jo strejinja
Ceri cerhenjanca,
Me le strejinjanca

I'm going, I'm going
To where no one knows me,
No one on earth,
Only the strangers.
The sky has its stars
But I'll be among strangers.

(Szászcsávás, Új Pátria series 10, track 3. Note the similarity to 'departure of the bride' lyrics.)

Na mik, Devla, te merav,
Dzi kaj me ne cheljujav, jaj, da Devla,
Devla, kaj te dzav, kaj te phirav,
Ande lume te maj dzivav, da romale,
Devla, sar merav, da romale.

Don't leave me, God, to die,
Until I have lived out my life, O God,
God, where shall I go, which way shall I go
So that I can still live on earth, gypsies,
God, how can I die, gypsies.

(I saw Dumnetzu, the band's leader, sing this song with the band in August 2005, and he sang smiling, with an affection clearly directed towards the song itself as a manifestation of solidarity, with a distanced acknowledgement of fate comparable to that of the dawn song singer. When the song ended Csángáló affectionately touched Dumnetzu's shoulder in a gesture of congratulation and recognition.)

It does appear then that the gypsies of Mezöség, if not elsewhere, had a 'dawn-song' practice using the table songs, whether native to them or derived from Hungarian practice, and gypsy bands further south also had the musical and textual materials of the dawn song in their hands even if the practice itself is not recorded there. The Romanians might also have had such a custom; all I have as yet is a few hints from Maramureş, and, perhaps, Jewish, Saxon, and, possibly, beyond Transylvania in the Balkans and Carpathians. And who knows, all over Europe at some time or other. Always something must have marked the end of the occasion. What was it in Sussex circa 1200? What was its *tone*?

(2) Meseiecri Zili

The band from Szászfenes (Florești) in Kalotaszeg, recorded in 1998 (Új Pátria series, 13) , is probably the most archaic still to be heard (on CD and possibly off it). The four musicians all belong to the same family, surnamed Muza, and were born between 1922 and 1936. The band consists of two violins, viola and 'cello, which is the older format, in which the two lower instruments blend together to speak the harmony – the string bass is always more-or-less isolated in the more modern string band. The band is distinctive in other ways too: in a 'thrusting' playing with stressed cadences mindful of Mezöség, also in using only major chords to harmonise most melodies whether major or minor, and in a heterophonic relationship between the two violins. It is also, as previously mentioned, the place where the two singers were singing 'their own songs drawn from their own fates', in fact the only recorded village band in this whole big field to confirm this hypothesis. Szászfenes is a semi-urban village just west of Cluj, and they are rarely called upon to play; 1998 may have been the last time they ever did.

Although Hungarian-speaking they have played mostly for Romanians and Gypsies, and their repertoire abounds in Gypsy titles, and among these is the Rom word *zili* which simply means song (elsewhere *djili*) but here seems to designate only slow songs and is used generically for two forms: *romani zili* which is the lament, and *meseiecri zili*, table song. These terms correspond to the Hungarian *halottkísero*, 'funeral tune' and *cigány asztali ének*, 'Gypsy table song'. (The former seems to be an instrumental version of lament, which is called *keserves* when it is sung, but it is less *rubato*, somewhere between lament and dawn song.) One of the *romani zili*, 'Putre Devla tri granica...' is described as associated with the deportation of the Gypsies, and sounds like a slow dawn song or metricated lament. We are clearly here in the zones of loss and melancholy which elsewhere in Kalotaszeg are gathered round the dawn-song concept.

The linking of dawn song and *zili* is confirmed in the other place the word appears, the repertoire of the band from Nagysármás. This excellent band is less archaic in style than Szásfenes, and although in Mezöség has in some respects the features of Kalotaszeg playing. It is also sufficiently to the east of Mezöség to be influenced by the style of Marrosszég, and even has some traits (violins playing in parallel thirds) of city 'gypsy' music. Its customers are now entirely Romanian and Gypsy, though the music has many Hungarian melodies and titles. The pieces labelled *zili*, here not glossed in either Hungarian or Romanian, not only correspond to those played by Szászfenes and the *de meseli* songs, but here they twice occur as the second item in a dance set, the first being a slower and free-er lament-like piece (labelled as *Cigány keserves* and *halottkísérö*: gypsy lament and funeral song). As in so many Kalotaszeg sets the adagio music moves into a slow rocking four-time (andante) as when a dawn song begins. At least two of the four *zili* tunes seem to me to be melodies related to those of dawn songs in Kalotaszeg. Furthermore two of them have personal names attached: 'Gáspár Ármin zilije' and 'Varga Emanuel zilije' (*zilije* is the 'possessed' form of *zili*). Ármin Gáspár is the bass player of the band and it is he who sings his *zili*, in Rom. The singer of Emanuel Varga's *zili*, also in Rom, is not identified.

Romani means, of course, 'gypsy' so that 'gypsy song' here means 'lament'. A clue to this usage lies in the observation that the melancholy songs which bands such as Szászcsávás are increasingly bring out of their hidden repertoire, such as the one quoted above, frequently involve an appeal to two entities as if for help – *Devla*, God, and *romale,* gypsies.

Gypsy assimilation of principally Hungarian forms and practices is likely to remain a common assumption, if they were the last to gain the ability to employ the bands and the Hungarians were the first. But since the bands were themselves gypsy the transmission could have been more complicated, involving for instance the bands' not only taking their repertoires home (to their families or to the gypsy quarters), but also deploying at home their skills in arranging domestic songs. But who knows whether the tone and musical specifics of the dawn song came into being before or after any such hypothetical process? I.e., whether at its heart lies a Hungarian or a Gypsy impulse, or the meeting of the two, and/or their crossing with Romanian mysticism, or something transcending all three? It should be born in mind that in many respects the social framework of all these peoples except the gypsies was a common central European phenomenon, probably centring in Transylvania on the Saxons as the first to establish the pattern of the landed smallholding and its extension into the village with all attached customs and developed 'peasant' culture – a 'western' phenomenon, as is the music (with 'oriental' traits available in the far histories of all ethnicities except the Saxon). But from what can been seen of Saxon culture the kind of musical ecstasis and catharsis represented by the dawn song was absent (as it was not absent, for instance, from the Jewish communities). The ex-Germans, Protestants, maintained a life-line from the west which fed them art-music and ländler, with their 'folk music' squeezed under the weight of scholarly music and emerging as four-square bucolics. The rest got their who-knows-what Italian courtly / shamanistic / backyard swoons from some complicated network of transmission always involving the gypsy. It seems to have been their way of maintaining their separation, not from each other so much as from something from the west threatening to reduce everything to a rational lump in which Everyman ceases to exist.

(3) Mulatsago

There are many references to table songs and even dawn-song-like personalised slow songs in Gypsy culture (and most others), but no reference outside Transylvania to a dawn song practice. Michael Stewart (1997) gives an account of the 'celebrations' (*mulatsago*) of a Vlach gypsy ghetto outside a town in northern Hungary in the 1950s which shows a particularly intense manifestation of the slow melancholy song in an almost puritanical context bringing it into a paradoxical relationship with the community it confirms. The *mulatsago* are weekly (pay-day) or occasional gatherings reserved for gypsy men, dedicated to food, alcohol, and a special kind of formal and correct speech-making ('true speech'), the whole event interpreted as the expression of a brotherhood rather than a community, which maintains and confirms gypsy separation and the gypsy way of life in contradistinction to the necessities shared with non-gypsies, such as wives, families and reproduction. The only songs admissible are slow and serious, and semi-improvised within formal constraints as a declaration of the singer's fate or condition, or a particular occasion such as the departure of a son, whether to the army or out into the non-Rom world.[3]

These are songs of 'the stereotypical, ideologically stressed moments of Gypsy life': including orphanhood, imprisonment, the parting of the son from the mother, conflict with the outside world referred to the mother's protection, as well as of horse-dealing (the principal trade for Vlach males) and of the celebration itself as a recompense. There are no songs of unrequited desire, but there are some love songs and laments of a wife's infidelity (usually fictive). They are dominantly sorrowful in mood in a way which is not set apart from the mood of the moment – they can arise from, or end in, tears. But the desired mood is one of tranquillity, and the emotional tone is generally not one of dramatic loss, but of 'loneliness in the world'.

> For the son is departing
>
>   Ke zaltar o sávo
>
> The son of the mother
>
>   E mamako rakho
>
> Don't cry, Mother, don't cry
>
>   Na rov, mama, na rov
>
> Don't cry bitterly
>
>   Na rov, *keservesen*
>
> You're crying out, Mother
>
>   Avri roves, Mama,
>
> Your two dark eyes
>
>   Tje duj kale jakha
>
> (for) I'm going away, Mama

And already I'm crying	Ke savtar aba mama,
	Maj me aba rovav
I'll come back later	
	Maj avasa de jaj
From the big world	
	Ande *luma* bari

The music is described as mainly descending, in four lines, *parlando rubato*, with half-sung interjections and a tendency to swallow the last note of a verse or leave it unresolved (which is a not uncommon habit among Hungarian singers). But the concept is not entirely musical. The main occasion of the gathering is the making of 'true speech', a formal speech-making, sometimes close to story-telling, which confirms fraternal solidarity in the expression of personal circumstance and sentiment, and the singing participates integrally. The concept 'true speech' *includes* the songs.

Most men had a personal song which they would sing repeatedly and re-personalise on each occasion both musically and textually, sometimes with a degree of elaboration or virtuosity, but no song was so freely improvised as to depart from a basis of formulaic elements in text and music which referred the individual back to the group, especially as the company joined in the song towards its end, and indeed any excessive originality or deviation was frowned on. Experience is stripped of motive and context in the singing and offered as a naked situational zone which the group can take unto itself in recognition and endorsement.

Stewart sees these songs as essentially transcending the opposition between the individual and the group and thus consolidating a condition of fraternity which is the Roms' answer not only to their societal debasement but to the necessities of survival and reproduction. But song may also trespass beyond its occasion both in public and in private, it may re-emerge, whole or fragmented, in other sections of the lives lived around it, and the fences put up by the male Rom around their ceremonial foci may have gaps in them. A song may sometimes escape much further, into an ethnomusicological article or a CD where it may survive in a new concept of validation in which the worked contradiction may be all the more meaningful set into a common ground but authenticated by the individual life responsible for it. Not only the song's after-life but it's pre-birth also may be represented as a diversification and spread emigration of its substance. The successions of singers who have formed and re-formed items of its lexicon, spreading backwards beyond Rom or gypsy or Hungarian or even Carpathian… A Vrach Rom lament forms itself to a greater or lesser extent out of Hungarian figurations, or a Hungarian dawn songs forms itself likewise out of Rom, and Romanian, figurations. These elsewheres can only be avoided, in lyric as in poetry in general, by deliberate, usually aggressive, acts of dissociation which threaten to undermine the entire structure to the point where the work cannot continue to exist.

The song quoted above is entirely in Rom but for one Hungarian word (*keserves* – lament) and one Romanian (*luma* = *lume*, world). Kertész-Wilkinson (1997) quotes a slow song in Rom from a wake, generally happy and proud in tone concerning the male gypsy life, with almost no original intervention. Towards the end the mood changes to a more melancholy one, at which the Hungarian language starts appearing in a vocabulary which belongs to Hungarian melancholy song rather than anything else Hungarian, and the lyric seems to wobble between the two tongues, moving sense back to Rom once established then abandoning itself to Hungarian for the final lament (Hungarian words in italics):

Me te mero, *édesanyám*
    When I die, mother
Apol *szépen temessetek*
    Bury me beautifully
Me te mero, *édesanyám*
    When I die, mother
De sukares de praxon ma.
    Bury me beautifully.

A feifám se legyen fából
    Let my headstone be made of nothing
Legyen nyíló orgonából [bis]
    Made of nothing but lilac blossom
Ne as anyám könnyeiből
    Not from my mother's tears.

She then quotes what is nominally the same song (called *Foro* = Fair) from another wake in which very little of the familiar song survives and the tone is entirely lamentational. It is all in Hungarian but for one Rom word. The sense of the Hungarian/Transylvanian melancholy song is very strong, not so much in the formulae, though they are there, as in the whole cast of the text –

I wander around and cannot find a place
    Jálnok nem lelem a helyem
Where I could lay my head down?
    Hová tegyem a fejemet?
I put my head on the soil,
    Födre hajtom a fejemet
Look, how much I suffer

> Nézzed,[4] *hogy szenvedek érted*

I live, I live, but what for
    Élek, élek, *minek élek*
When I never have a single happy day.
    Ha eg víg napot nem élek
O God it is so bad for me
    Jaj, istenem, jaj már nékem
My life is full of mourning
    Gyászba borult as életem

The Vlach gypsies are fluently bilingual (sometimes trilingual) and other songs, especially those sung on less public occasions, show a racy immediacy in the Hungarian lyrics as against the quite ponderous and dignified appeal to distance in this one. It is the public siting of the song which extends its connectives, and the more it is 'for us here' the more it stretches back through our travels.

Which came first is not important. Orphanhood is not a likely personal experience either for Kalotaszeg villagers or for a Vlach Rom ghetto, because, even if it were to occur biologically, in both cases there is or was an operative local family-based sociality which would work to heal and substitute. But the image of it stands out in their slow songs. Wandering the world without home or parents or any help would be a near-impossible exceptionality, especially for the Rom where outside the immediate community there is (in principal) an international Rom solidarity (if you see a car broken down by the road and its occupants are 'stranger Rom', you stop to help). It has been seen as an image of the separation and abasement of the entire Rom population, sung with a smile as confirming the protective unity, while lamenting its endangering status. This can't be said of old-style Transylvanian peasants, who lived at the very heart of their society until interfered with from outside. What are we left with in the end but 'existential sorrow'? But the poetical moral of this is that you do not attain a transfer of that scale without the personal forces of immediacy and accession that empower the artifact, a passionate duality revealing the actual force of the particulars, and so you do more than intend it.

(4)

I've passed through Szászfenes several times. You would hardly notice it because it's almost a suburb of Cluj, which as you approach from the west looms on a hillside beyond the village bearing an enormous cemetery. It is a place with few signs of age but plenty of poverty and neglect. The houses look like old breeze-block constructions; there are always road works through it as the Romanians attempt to modernise the main road from Cluj into Hungary; and there is a big army barracks pressed against the side of it.

And from this place the last shred of evidence, caught before they all hung their fiddles on the wall for ever and turned back to digging holes in the road, which brings the gypsies back to the heart of the dawn-song music? In symbiosis with 'Hungarian melancholy' and other things perhaps, perhaps not, the song of those who stay on the outside. When the dawn-song singers sang themselves into loss was it, unbeknown to them, the condition of the gypsy they were actually enacting? The condition of those who made the quasi-aristocratic 'peasant' society possible by supplying cheap outsider labour and having to suffer dire poverty through the barren winters? The condition of 'wandering the world without home'. *Unbeknown* – does this music cohere the whole of this society in a way only visible to outsiders? Hearing the gypsy woman 'Ikola' singing 'Csigány hallgató' (gypsy lament) with the Szászcsávás band is all you need, whatever time of day it was. For all the complicated trading of ethnic labels that goes on, I know that these sad tunes belong to these peoples as a whole and anyone caught in the glow of it, where they construct the theatre of what is, directly, everyone's fate.

(5)

As the footnote to the last footnote to the last footnote… When everything was surely wrapped up again and it was time to prepare this text for publication, a further manifestation occurred which spoke of a possible future to this music. Since about 2007 interest in it seemed suddenly to hit a very low point. Undoubtedly there would still have been some but the issuing of CDs of the music virtually stopped in both countries and very little more was heard of it. Of those I knew, only Ioan Pop's Maramureş music seemed (judging from his Facebook manifestations) to be thriving. Then two left-overs from Neti's last band in Mera, the kontra player Rudolf Toni and the bassist Victor Berk, were found touring internationally (including London) as a trio, with either István Varga (of Huedin) or Tcha Limberger on fiddle, the latter trio also on a British small-label CD as "Tcha Limberger's Kalotaszeg Trio". These performances represented a new sophistication on the part of the accompanying musicians. Kontra and bass were now participating fully in a trio music which was very much the old Kalotaszeg village band music but had taken a step forward. No more steady repetition of the same chord and bass note for whole measures. They were moving harmonically and rhythmically with the violin, with transitional chromatic harmonies, independent interventions through pauses and codas… In fact this is what they were doing in Neti's band, as did Rudolf Toni's father earlier, perhaps not quite so developed but it was a distinguishing feature of the band. It nevertheless still sounded like an advance, that the music had found an avenue into the world. The Limberger CD takes a special interest in dawn songs with seven of them played, several very well sung by Limberger. This is now, I think, the CD I would turn to to show what this music can be in the hands of the most talented musicians, and also as one of the two best exemplars of the beauty of the Kalotaszegi dawn song. And the leader is not even Transylvanian, but a Flemish gypsy.

Notes

[1] The family of the Soporul de Câmpie band declared to me in 1998 that they were not (or not all) gypsies. Certainly the band-leader's wife was not, but of Hungarian descent. But they are usually classified as a 'gypsy band' like all the rest. In the U.S.A. they seemed to be marketing themselves as 'Rom'.

[2] The Vlach gypsies fled Transylvania at the time of the princes, and their name indicates this origin. They should not be confused with the ethnic categorisation 'Vlach' = Wallachian, Wollack etc., a blanket term for descendants of Latinised peoples of East and Central Europe.

[3] Studies of other Hungarian Vlach communities, notably Kertész-Wilkinson's (1997) give the wider picture of Vlach singing outside the brotherhood rituals, including mixed *mulatsagos*, weddings, funerals and wakes, in which women may take a central role, with dancing. These abound in rules which not infrequently represent a relaxed and exceptionalised version of the male supremacy Stewart depicts. Her aesthetic approach insists that the music itself transcends the textual messages of the songs and dilutes the cultural constraints they imply.

[4] *Nézzed* is the one Rom word in the song, an expletive eliciting immediate attention – 'Listen here!'

List of Writings

(Rather than an academic bibliography of all source material, this is a listing of items I found particularly useful or interesting. Some others are given in footnotes.)

A) Transylvanian / Carpathian Subject-Matter and General Topics

Tiberiu Alexandriu, *Romanian Folk Music*. Bucharest 1980.

Miklós Bánffy, A *Transylvanian Trilogy* translated by Patrick Thursfield and Kathy Bánffy-Jelen. Three volumes. 1999. [novel]

Béla Bartók, *Rumanian Folk Music*. 5 volumes, 1967–75.

Béla Bartók, *Essays*, edited by Benjamin Suchoff. 1976.

Béla Bartók, *The Hungarian Folk Song*. New York 1981.

Béla Bartók, *Studies in Ethnomusicology*, edited by Benjamin Suchoff. 1997

Béla Bartók and Zoltán Kodály (editors), *Transylvanian Hungarians: Folksongs*. Budapest (1923).

Margaret H. Beissinger, *The Art of the Lautar:* the epic tradition of Romania. 1991.

J.Bernabé, *Le symbolisme de la mort: croyance et rites roumains*. Ghent 1980 [not consulted].

Charles Boner, *Transylvania*. 1865.

Jacques Bouët, Bernard Lortat-Jacob, Speranța Radulescu, *À tue-tête: Chant et violon au pays de l'Oach, Roumanie*. Nanterre: Société d'ethnologie 2002 (with DVD).

Constantin Brâiloiu, *Problems of Ethnomusicology*. 1984.

Constantin Brâiloiu, *La plainte funèbre du village de Draguș*. n.p. n.d.

Lucy Castle, "Last of the Transylvanian Fiddlers". *Songlines* 9, 2001.

Andrew F. Crosse, *Round about the Carpathians*. Edinburgh 1878.

Jean Cuisenier, *Le feu vivant: La parenté et ses rituels dans les Carpates*. Paris 1994.

Nancy van Deusen, 'Crossing Boundaries between Nature and Artifact: Folk Music Reconsidered'. *Studia Musicologica Academiae Scientiarum Hungaricae* 41/1-3, Budapest 2000.

Emily Gerard, *The Land Beyond the Forest* (two volumes). 1888. Reprinted 2010.

István Halmos, 'Towards a Pure Instrumental Form.' *Studia Musicologica Academiae Scientiarum Hungaricae* 19/2-4, 1977.

E Kaposi and E. Pesovár (editors), *The Art of Dance in Hungary*. Budapest 1985.

Béla Kása, *Transylvanian Musicians* [photographs]. American Hungarian Folklore Centrum, New York and Budapest 1997.

Irén Kertész-Wilkinson, Song Performance: a Model for Social Interaction among Vlach Gypsies in South-Eastern Hungary. *Romani culture and Gypsy identity*, edited by Thomas Acton and Gary Mundy, 1997.

Gail Kligman, *The Wedding of the Dead*. 1988.

Yehuda Koren and Eilat Negev, *In Our Hearts We Were Giants*. The remarkable story of The Lilliput Troupe – a dwarf family's survival of the holocaust. New York 2004. (Anonymous translation of the German edition, 2003.)

Károly Kós, *Transylvania*. Translated by Lorna K. Dunbar. Budapest 1989.

K. Kovalcsik, Aspects of Language Ideology in a Transylvanian Vlach Gypsy Community. *Acta Linguistica Hungarica*, 46/3-4, 1999.

Wayne B. Kraft, Improvisation in Hungarian Ethnic Dancing: an analogue to oral verse composition. *Oral Tradition* 4/5 1989.

Franz Liszt, *The Gypsy in Music*. Englished by Edwin Evans (from *Des Bohémiens et de leur musique en Hongrie*) 1926.

Bernard Lortat-Jacob, *Musique en fête: Maroc, Sardaigne, Roumanie*. Nanterre 1994.

Bernard Lortat-Jacob (editor), *L'Improvisation dans les musiques de tradition orale*, Paris 1987.

Ladislas Makkai, *Histoire de Transylvanie*. Paris 1946.

D. Masson, *Les femmes de Breb*. Études et documents balkaniques 4, Paris 1982.

Liz Mellish and Nick Green, *Romania: Dans popular, muzica, obicei, istorie, portul popular*. Published by the authors, Watford 1999.

Paul Nixon, *Sociality – Music – Dance: Human Figurations in a Transylvanian Valley*. Studies from the Music Department of Göteberg University No. 34, 1994.

Paul Nixon, 'Romania' and 'Doina/e' in *Grove's Dictionary of Music and Musicians*. 2nd edition 2001.

Speranţa Rădulescu, *Taifasuri despre Muzica Ţigănească / Chats about Gypsy Music*. Bucuresti 2004.

Speranţa Rădulescu, Traditional Music and Ethnomusicology Under Political Pressure: the Romanian Case. *Anthropology Today* 13/6 n 1997.

Peter Riley, *The Dance at Mociu*. Shearsman Books 2003. Second, extended edition 2014.

Bálint Sárosi, 'Gypsy Musicians and Hungarian Peasant Music'. *1970 Yearbook of the International Folk Music Council*. University of Illinois Press 1971.

Teodor Shanin, *Defining Peasants: Essays Concerning Rural Societies, Expolary Economies, and Learning from Them in the Contemporary World.* Oxford 1990.

Henry H Stahl, *Traditional Romanian Village Communities.* 1980.

Walter Starkey, *Raggle Taggle.* 1933.

Walter Starkey, 'Gypsy Folk Lore and Music'. *Journal of the English Folk Dance and Song Society* volume II, 1935.

Michael Stewart, *The Time of the Gypsies.* 1997.

Michael Stewart, The Puzzle of Roma Persistence: Group Identity Without a Nation. In *Romany Culture and Gypsy Identity* edited by Thomas Acton and Gary Mundy. 1997.

Janka Szendrei, *XVI-XVII századi dallamaink a népi emlékezetben / 16th- and 17th-century Tunes in the Folk Memory* [with cassette]. Hungarian Academy of Sciences, Institute of Musicology, 1993.

Katherine Verdery, *Transylvanian Villagers.* 1983.

Gregor von Rezzori, *The Snows of Yesteryear,* 1990 Translated (from *Blumen im Schnee,* 1989) by H.F. Broch de Rothermann.

European Meetings in Ethnomusicology, edited by Marin Marian-Balasa. Volume 9, Bucuresti 2002 ('Transylvania: Music, Ethnicities and Discord').

B) Comparative and Marginal Topics

Gennady Aygi, *Salute – To Singing. One Hundred Variations on Themes from Folk-songs of the Volga Region.* Translated by Peter France. Brookline, MA, 2002.

Anne Birrell, *New Songs from a Jade Terrace: an Anthology of Early Chinese Love Poetry ...* 1982.

Anne Birrell, *Popular Songs and Ballads of Han China.* 1988.

John Blacking, *How musical is man?* 1976.

John Blacking, *'A Commonsense view of all music' : Reflections on Percy Grainger's Contribution to Ethnomusicology and Music.* 1987.

John Burnett, (Ed.) *Useful Toil: Autobiographies of Working People from the 1820s to the 1920s.* 1974.

Ronald Blythe, *Akenfield: Portrait of an English Village.* 1969.

Jan Harold Brunvand, *Casa Frumoasa: the House Beautiful in Rural Romania.* East European Monographs no. DCXXX, Boulder, CO 2003.

David J. Bush, *Dance Music for the Ballets de Cour, 1575–1651.* Dance and Music series, No. 7, New York 1993.

George Deacon, *John Clare and the Folk Tradition*. 1983.

Linda Dégh, *Folktales and Society: Storytelling in a Hungarian Peasant Community*. trans. E.M. Schossberger. Indiana UP 1989.

Jean-Pierre Diény, *Aux origines de la poésie classique en Chine*. Leiden 1968.

William Donaldson, *The Highland Pipe and Scottish society 1750–1950 : Transmission, Change and the Concept of Tradition*. 2000.

Roger Elbourne, *Music and Tradition in Early Industrial Lancashire* 1780–1840. 1980.

E. Fel and T. Hofer, *Proper Peasants*. Chicago, IL 1969.

A.G. Gilchrist, 'Good-night and Parting Songs.' *Journal of the Folk Song Society* no. 28, 1924.

Wendy Hilton, *Dance of the Court and Theatre: the French Noble Style 1690–1725*. New York 1981.

David Johnson, *Music and Society in Lowland Scotland in the Eighteenth Century*. 1972.

Gábor Klaniczay, 'The Decline of Witches and the Rise of Vampires under the Eighteenth-Century Habsburg Monarchy', in his *The Uses of Supernatural Power*, translated by Susan Singerman. 1990.

Henry A. Kmen, *Music in New Orleans: The Formative Years 1791–1844*. Baton Rouge, LA: Louisiana State University Press 1966.

Emmanuel Le Roy Ladurie, *Montaillou*. Translated by Barbara Bray, 1978.

Bernard Lortat-Jacob, 'Music as a Collective Enterprise' in *The World of Music – Journal of the International Institute for Comparative Music Studies and Documentation* (Berlin) XXX/3, 1979.

Alan MacFarlane, *The Origins of English Individualism*. Oxford 1978.

Geert Mak, *Jorwerd: The Death of the Village in Late Twentieth-Century Europe*. Translated by Anne Kelland. 2000.

Timothy Mitchell, *Flamenco Deep Song*. New Haven, CT: Yale University Press 1994.

Paul Oliver, *Blues Fell this Morning*. 1960.

Paul Oliver, *Songsters & Saints: Vocal Traditions on Race Records*. 1984.

William F. Prizer, *Courtly Pastimes: the Frottole of Marchetto Cara*. Ann Arbor, MI 1980.

Graham Robb, *The Discovery of France*. 2007.

Harry A. Senn, *Were-wolf and Vampire in Romania*. East European Monographs, Boulder, CO, 1982.

Sorcha [Amhraín Shorcha Ní Guairim], booklet to her CD *Traditional Songs from Connemara*. Gael Linn CEFCD 182, 2001.

Allison Thompson (compiler) *Dancing Through Time: Western Social Dance in Literature 1400–1918:* Selections. 1998.

Paul Vernon, *A History of Portuguese Fado*. Aldershot 1998.

Eugen Weber, *Peasants into Frenchmen: the Modernization of Rural France 1870–1914*. 1927.

LIST OF RECORDINGS

A former list of recordings of Transylvanian village bands thought to be near complete has had to be abandoned as the number of CDs issued has greatly increased since, and the number of village bands known to exist has increased with them, especially on the Romanian side of things. This is now a list of recordings recommended for authenticity and relevance, some of which might still be available in five years' time.

SERIES & SPECIALISED LABELS

Új Pátria. A series of 18 CDs issued by Fonó, Budapest, principally of Transylvanian village bands. The musicians were invited to Fonó headquarters during 1998-9, where their complete repertoires were recorded for archiving, and a selection issued as a commercial CD. Those which were not village bands were mostly groups of singers and flautists. The best-known bands with commercially published CDs – Magyarpalatka, 'Neti', Vajdaszentivány… – are not included, and Szászcsávás only with an "older stratum" band. Recently another fifty CDs have been added, but these are not available separately except, apparently, in one shop in Budapest. This extended programme embraces musicians from other countries, especially Slovakia, but is focussed on ethnic Hungarians. Two or three complete tracks from each CD used to be accessible on the Fonó website, but it seems to have migrated.

Consilior Judeţean Cluj. This cultural institution has issued some 40 CDs of "traditional" music from the administrative district of Cluj (which is extensive), the majority being *muzică populara* of one kind or another, but including at present a dozen village bands in the old style, many of them previously unrecorded and 'hidden' behind the dominance of Hungarian research. Among these are two different bands from Soporul de Câmpie, neither of them 'Şandorica''s, both of which also accompany the singer Vasile Soporan. There are also two bands well known to the Hungarians but recorded under their Romanian names – Sic and Palatca. There is no commercial distribution, but all CDs can be heard complete on the website http://traditiiclujene.ro/index.php. There is an ordering tab on the site which seems to have no effect and the CDs are mainly given to other institutions and interested persons, including, in our experience, people who knock on the door of the office in Cluj.

Kallós Archivum. Recordings made by Transylvanian ethnomusicologist Zoltán Kállos, issued in the early 1990s in a series of cassettes. Several have been re-edited and issued by Fonó as CDs: Bonchida-Válaszút, Feketetelak, Magyarlóna, Mezökeszü, Visa, Ördöngösfüzes (1999-2002). There is also a CD of the Magyarpalatka band and (separately) three singers from Kallós Archivum.

CDs from **Fekete Antal**'s field recordings of instrumental ensembles in action on social occasions, usually weddings, in the late 1970s to early 1980s are being issued by Folk Europa (Budapest) as a series. So far: Magyarpalatka Band (two), Szóvidék, Gernyszeg, Magyarpéterlaka, Vjdazentivány and Ádámos bands, and a gathering of Kalotaszegi musicians for a wedding at Méra.

Ethnophonie based at the Romanian Village Museum, Bucharest, and edited by the ethnomusicologist Speranța Rădulescu, has issued the only commercially available Romanian collection of CDs in this field, including many "Taraf" or "Lăutărească" bands still operative in eastern and southern Romania, and music from Maramures (two of Ion Pop's "Iza"group), Codru, Emil Mihai's band from Gherla and the singer Vasile Soporan with the Soporul de Câmpie Band.

Netwerke Hongaarse Volkmuziek (Holland). CDs issued around 2000, studio recordings of the bands from Erdöszombattelke, Méra (two), Magyarpalatka and Vajdasszentivány.

Néptáncosok Szakmai Háza (Budapest) issued a series of undated cassettes by both village and táncház musicians for purposes of study and instrumental practice in connection with printed transcriptions. I've seen no listing of these.

Musician-issued CDs. Bands (or their aficionados) have started issuing CDs since they found themselves in demand beyond the villages. These are home-made CDRs and can be of very dubious quality or durability, but seem to be improving. They can normally only be got directly from the band. **Mociu Band** has issued one, **Magyarpalatka** about six. Four professionally produced and distributed CDs of the **Szászcsávás** Band have been issued independently of labels but not by the band itself. There are two CDs without label name of the **Vajaszentivány** band accompanying singing. At least two CDs of the singer **Grigore Leșe** from Lapuș are also independently issued for the local market. My copies rotted after five years.

INDIVIDUAL BANDS & MUSICIANS (TRANSYLVANIA)

Here I only indicate which musicians have had CDs issued and on which label, excluding those mentioned above. These are all "authentic" village-based musicians, insofar as such a distinction is possible, with emphasis on those I have paid special attention to for Dawn Songs. *Some (especially "Neti") are sometimes accompanied* by 'tánchaz' (urban revival) musicians, usually from Budapest. Village names are given in the language used on the labeling of the recordings.

Bonchida (Mezöség). There were several cassettes of the old Hungarian band from Kallós Archivum, and one CD from Fonó (Budapest). The distinctive music from here is imitated on CDs by Téka, Ökrös and Méta táncház groups.

Búza (Mezöség) and region. The "developed" band from here, known as Eszterláncs, led by Alexandru Ripa and with two or three singers, has four CDs, from Fonó and independently.

The violinist Emil Mihai was originally from Búza. His trio has two CDs from Ethnophonie (Bucharest).

Bogartelke (Kalotaszeg). János Czilika's band, recorded 1993. Double CD from Hagyományok Háza (Budapest).

Csipi Band (István Varga, Rudolf Toni, Victor Berki): Kalotaszegi Nepzene. CD issued by the band for sale at performances, undated.

Hodac (Mezöség). Recordings accompanying Paul Nixon's book "Sociality Music Dance".

Tcha Limberger's Kalotaszegi Trio: A hajnali csillage ragyok. LeJazzetal 2009

Magyarbece (Nagyenyed / Aiud). Ferenc Kulcsár's band, recorded 1993. Hagyományok Háza (Budapest). Also the violinist and flautist Ferenc Szánto accompanied by Téka (Téka/Fonó).

Magyarszovát (Mezöség). Márton Maneszes' band with singers, recorded 1997. Double CD from Fonó.

Mociu (Mezöség) as "Stîngaciu" [left-handed] Band. Lost Trails (U.S.A.).

Magyarpalatka (Mezöség) The band in two generations, under Martón then Florin Kodoba. Hungaraton and Fonó.

Méra (Kalotaszeg). Sándor Fodor ("Netti"or "Neti") solo, with his own band or with Budapest musicians: 4 CDs, from Hungaroton, Fonó and ABT Records (all Budapest).

Soporul de Cîmpie. (Mezöség). Band under Şandorică Ciurcui. Buda (France), 1992. Several cassettes for the local market.

Szászcsávás (Kis-Küküllö). In addition to the four independently-issued CDs, there is one from Figuras (Switzerland) 1998.

Szék (Mezöség). Ádám István's band and singers, recorded 1969–1973. Fonó.

Türe (Kalotaszeg) László Lengyel Türei (singer with local instrumentalists). Harmónia Produkció 2000.

Maramureş & Other Outlying Regions

Grupul IZA: Craciun în Maramureş / Christmas in Maramureş. Ethnophone (Bucureşti) Reissued by Buda (France) as Noël en Maramureş.

Ioan Pop şi Grupul Iza: Fête paysanne de Maramureş. Bienniale de la dance de Lyon, 2004.

Ioan Pop şi Gruppul Iza: Romanian, Ukrainian and Jewish Music from Maramureş. Ethnophonie 2002.

Fiddle Music from Maramureş: Vol. 1, The Mara Valley. Steel Carpet Records (Derby) 1998.

Musique de mariage du Maramureş, recorded 1973. Ocora (France).

Ioan Pop şi Gheorghe Opriş. Sonex Records (Zalau).

Fraţii Petreus: "Asa beau oamenii buni". Electrecord (Bucharest).

The Sicuţa Brothers, Botiza, Maramureş. Lost Trails (USA) 2001.

Oaş: Ensemble Tara Oaşului et les Frères Pitigoi. Arion (France) 1997.

Chioar and Codru. CDs of bands led by Călin Raţ and Dan Daniel, and one by Gheorghe Negrea of old–time dance music, from Ethnophonie. Daniel has several cassettes for the local market in a more jazzed-up manner of playing.

Gyimes. János Zerkula's Laments (keservesei) are in the Új Pátria series from Fonó. Other recordings of him and Mihály Halmágyi on Hungaraton and Fonó.

(Anthologies)

Roumanie: Musique pour Cordes de Transylvanie. Chant du Monde (France) 1992.

The Edge of the Forest: Romanian Music from Transylvania. Music of the World (USA).

Elveszett Éden / Lost Eden. Folkmusic recordings from historical Hungary, Moldavia and Bukovina… (archival recordings) Etnofon, Budapest 1996.

Authentic Romania. Sonoton (Germany). 1999.

Hungarian 'Táncház' or Revival Bands

The principal bands: Czík, Muzsikás, Téka, Ókrös, Tükrös and the singers Kati Szvorák, Márta Sebestyén, András Berecs etc. have CDs from the major Budapest labels and sometimes independently produced. The following are items of special regard for this thesis.

Az örök Kalotaszeg / Eternal Kalotaszeg. ABT records 2005.

Jánosi Ensemble: 77 Magyar Tánc, 1730–1810. Hungaroton 1997.

Ökrös, Kalotaszegi mulató énekek / Blues at Dawn. ABT Records 1996.

Kati Svorák, Napfogyatkozás / Eclipse. Hungaroton HCD18239, 1999.

VIDEO & FILM

The Miraculous Circumstance (Bartók and folk music) by A.L. Lloyd. 1980.

Beyond the Forest, directed by Esther Ronai. BBC Productions 1991.

Neti Sanyi (Fodor Sámuel "Neti"): Muzsikusportrét. A film by Béla Halmos and György Szomjas. Goëssfilm, Budapest, 2000.

Around 2007 all this issuing of recordings of Transylvanian village music suddenly stopped in both countries. This coincided with Romania's entry into the EU which may have been relevant, but why this should put a halt to activities in Budapest I can't imagine. An ever increasing amount of material can be viewed on YouTube, including both archival and contemporary performances and some particularly valuable footage of the bands in action accompanying dancers, in both public and domestic settings. I haven't located there or anywhere a film of a traditional dawn songs event.

3

On First Hearing Derek Bailey

You would have to refer back to the sound of the clavichord, in a European context, for a plucked string of such expressivity and rigour; to something like *The Fitzwilliam Virginal Book* for such sustained imagery, for such energy held in substance, actually facilitated and tensed by atonality to the point of cluster-chords, and such things as deadened reverberation.

The guitar is realised in the full range of its possibilities, every kind of vibration of which the strings and the wooden hollow are capable, by every manner of plucking and otherwise manipulating the length of gut or wire. A range extending from melodic/contrapuntal to percussive is potentially present *at each moment* of the music, and it is that simultaneity which removes the music from the familiar. You cannot speak of rhythm as distinct from pitch or timbre, you cannot speak of "harmony" except as the overlapping of independent moves and the reverberations set up among them. So it is a work of integration, but not of bringing things together so much as of operating with produced sound before it is divisible into such categories as pitch and rhythm. Operating with guitar sound as a unitary body ripe for exploration.

Webern has been studied, but set against jazz so that you can't talk of refinement any more than of its opposite. A music which belongs neither in the Albert Hall nor in the cellar bar (though the latter is where it has had to eke itself out more often than not). The brow is neither high nor low and certainly not in the middle: a brow-less music. An abstract music if you like, while it denies itself the comforts of perpetuating any musical style. And yet it seems to have digested so much of the history of the plucked string: from instant to instant I hear mandolins and balalaikas strumming in the distance, George Formby's banjo, Leadbelly's 12-string, Charlie Christian's electric, koto, lute, classical guitar and many other things, some outside the domain of the plucked string... They seem to be on the edge of the audible, widening the resource.

You can hear the Webern, the pointillism, which is little more than the instrument's natural shortness of sonic resource transcended: filling the emptiness with substance. No astronautical theatricals, no relaxation into mere vibrations, but a technique which speaks of solid work to maintain the currency. And you can hear the oriental lute (etc.) which is the instrument's prehistory, King Orfeo's harp. But can you hear the jazz? What became of the jazz? "A record of delightful chamber music which has nothing to do with jazz" one reviewer said of ECM 1013, though it took a jazz critic to find delight in it, or to notice its existence. To locate the jazz listen by contrast to some of the exponents of improvised vacuity such as Cornelius Cardew with AMM, or the Cage/Zen nothing-merchants, relying on "chance" as if the world will provide our dinners for us if we just let it... then turn back to *Incus* 1.

There is an assumption of responsibility for the sounds produced. That is to say there is a logic in the way any musical event proceeds to the next, which might sometimes be a matter of foiling expectation or sometimes a matter of maintaining a shifting continuum, or sometimes neither of those. A particularly fetching technique is that of, as it were, nursing the note. By which I mean on the occasions when a pure "note" is struck (and several other things may be struck instead) it is not necessarily abandoned to its natural fade-out nor replaced with another before it gets tired, but by fingerboard and electric foot-pedal techniques the struck note can be cajoled into a second or third upsurge of energy, or may be allowed almost to die out and just at that final moment, the edge of departure, permitted a faint throb or slid suddenly to a new pitch. Handled the way Derek does it, as perhaps by the best sitar players, it is like a vision of the possibilities of old age, the possible metamorphoses and diversions of lapsing energy. There are other ways: instant muffling and replacement when the context demands it. Determination, perseverance, are always the pressures behind continuance. A kind of "swing" perhaps. The ending of a piece is always an upswing into silence, half-unexpected, a decision plus an accession.

Why total improvisation? The question has been redundant for a long time. You could say, because post-serialist contemporary music has reached a condition where it might as well be, where really nothing is gained by writing it, or repeating it. But the regaining of the performative moment in music is probably more important, the restoration of the moment of delivery as the music's proper site. Even a small tone-row or a minimal jazz theme would wreck that tension of immediate creation where the artist is in front of you with no instructions of any kind, and is going to produce the whole thing, the piece of music, now. The art of listening to recorded improvised music is in re-imagining this moment.

So a true performance, an occasion. Not to be confused with the amplified swagger, adolescent heroics, of the permitted "rock" break, any more than the naïve totalitarianism of communal participation. Technical ability is paramount – there is an absolute division between performer and spectator. The spectator's role is realised as complementary to the performer's at the same time and place, the demand of close attention without which it is lost. So "hard" of course, to listen to, this offered joy…

And not necessarily solo, but any number in the group (I find it becomes increasingly difficult after five or six – it *is* a chamber music) in which nobody accompanies anybody, all partners are equal and the basis of the exercise is mutual trust (not to mention mutual aid when necessary). There is in such sessions a constant interplay of dominance and agreement, coagulations and dispersals of solidarity, quick matings and extended liaisons, flights and groundings, individual insistences and echoic accessions. No single discovery remains the property of its initiator, and there can be a quite mysterious concord fructifying in sequence among a set of people all appearing to be doing distinct things. Don Cherry referred to it as a "brightness". As when five musicians playing together at full speed suddenly stop without having signalled to each other.

It is a music best languaged with basic terms of the physics of it, rather than the development of codes. "Discontinuous decay of sound energy in an enclosure" > perpetual loss of language in speech > discontinuous recovery of language in writing > channelling energy to points of maximum reverberation at which a "thing" occurs > production of distributable objects > food-supply. In western music sheer *sonority* as opposed to coded forms of sequentiality, has not had such importance since the early 16th century (*pace* Berlioz).

"I have two interests, the instrument and improvisation, and the aim is to make them as complementary as possible." Is this like saying: "I have two interests, language and life, and the aim is..." Becoming complementary (being newly *seen/heard* as the complementarity they are from the start) the work and the instrument find their purpose in existence, as definition, advancement, attunement... Life led through the instrument becomes visible as sculpture. A kind of metamorphosis, but surely not the comforting recompense which ensnares randomness in an artificial measure. The music has to stand alone, unsupported by a social justification. In this music more than any other the inchoate venture of the beginning is preserved through the process. The "life" passed into the instrument never loses its fluidity, its unmanageable variousness, unpredictability, or, in a way, its futility.

And for why? For the sake of music and music's one purpose: to persuade, hurt and conduct humanity into acknowledging what it is.

Recordings referred to:

ECM 1013 = Dave Holland and Derek Bailey: *Improvisations for 'Cello and Guitar*. LP record, 1971.

Incus 1 = Derek Bailey, Han Bennink and Evan Parker: *The Topography of the Lungs*. LP record, 1970. Reissued as a CD in 2006 by Psi Records.

Derek Bailey's playing in the early 1970s is represented on *Solo Guitar Volume One*, Incus Records CD10 (recorded 1971) and *Lot 74*, Incus CD 57 (recorded 1974).

www.ingramcontent.com/pod-product-compliance
Lightning Source LLC
Chambersburg PA
CBHW022010160426
43197CB00007B/359